HILLWALKING IN WALES

VOLUME 2: FFESTINIOG – TARRENS

About the Author

Peter Hermon was brought up in Nottingham and was a frequent trekker on Kinder Scout in his school days. He remembers youth hostelling over the Hard Knott and Wrynose passes in the Lake District when they were still rough farm tracks.

For most of his working life he was an executive with BOAC and British Airways but, despite travelling the world – and a particular affection for the Grand Canyon – the lure of the British hills never paled and he has scaled the peaks of Lakeland, Wales and the Pennines many times.

HILLWALKING IN WALES

Volume 2: Ffestiniog – Tarrens

by
Peter Hermon

2 POLICE SQUARE, MILNTHORPE, CUMBRIA LA7 7PY
www.cicerone.co.uk

Second edition 2006
ISBN-10: 1 85284 467 1
ISBN-13: 978 185284 468 4

A catalogue record for this book is available from the British Library.

To David –
my first companion on the hills

The hills are beautiful. They are beautiful in line and form and colour; they are beautiful in purity, in their simplicity and in their freedom; they bring repose, contentment and good health.

F.S. Smythe
1930s Everest pioneer

Acknowledgements

I would like to thank Pam Boswell for preparing some early drafts before I had learned to use a word processor; Juliet Ryde for checking the whole draft; and Don Sargeant for drawing the original maps. Most of the photographs are my own, but I am also indebted to the following for permission to use some of their pictures: Steve Lewis (www.land-scapesofwales.co.uk), Kevin Richardson and Marion Teal.

Advice to Readers

Readers are advised that while every effort is taken by the author to ensure the accuracy of this guidebook, changes can occur which may affect the contents. It is advisable to check locally on transport, accommodation, shops etc, but even rights of way can be altered. The publisher would welcome notes of any such changes.

Front cover: Approaching Crib y Ddysgl on the Snowdon horseshoe (SN H1)

CONTENTS

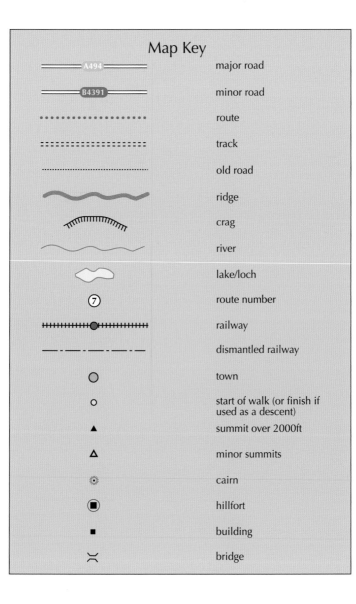

Map Key

═══ A494 ═══	major road
─── B4391 ───	minor road
• • • • • • • • • •	route
▪ ▪ ▪ ▪ ▪ ▪ ▪ ▪ ▪ ▪	track
··················	old road
～～～～～	ridge
⌢⌢⌢⌢⌢	crag
～～～～～	river
▱	lake/loch
⑦	route number
┼┼┼●┼┼┼	railway
─ · ─ · ─ · ─	dismantled railway
⊙	town
○	start of walk (or finish if used as a descent)
▲	summit over 2000ft
△	minor summits
☀	cairn
⊙	hillfort
■	building
)(	bridge

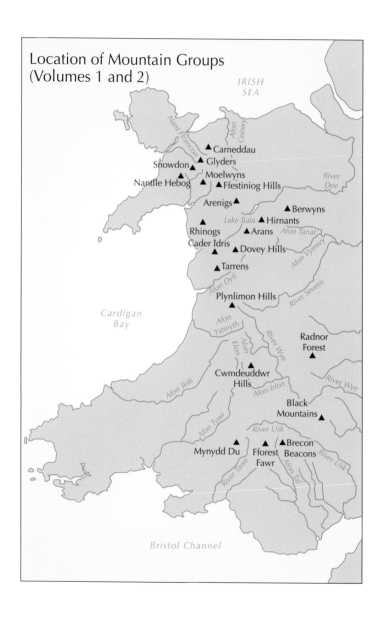

Location of Mountain Groups (Volumes 1 and 2)

IRISH SEA

Nant Ffrancon

Afon Conwy

▲ Carneddau
▲ Glyders
Snowdon ▲
Nantlle Hebog ▲ ▲ Moelwyns
▲ Ffestiniog Hills

River Dee

Arenigs ▲

Lake Bala

▲ Berwyns
▲ Hirnants

Afon Tanat

Rhinogs ▲ ▲ Arans
Cader Idris ▲ ▲ Dovey Hills

Afon Vyrnwy

▲ Tarrens

Afon Dyfi

River Severn

Plynlimon Hills ▲

Cardigan Bay

Afon Ystwyth

Afon Elan

Afon Elan

River Wye

Radnor Forest ▲

River Wye

Afon Teifi

Cwmdeuddwr Hills ▲

Afon Irfon

Black Mountains ▲

Afon Tywi

River Usk

Mynydd Du ▲ ▲ Fforest Fawr ▲ Brecon Beacons

River Usk

Afon Tawe

Afon Taf

Bristol Channel

Near the top of the Watkin Path (photo Marion Teal) (SN 10)

HOW TO USE THIS GUIDE

A full introduction to *Hillwalking in Wales* appears at the beginning of Vol 1, but a summary of the way the chapters are arranged will be useful. Each chapter is arranged as follows:

- List of peaks and lakes in each mountain group
- Diagrammatic map
- General overview
- Main ways up each of the peaks
- High-level walks
- Lower-level walks/easier days

All routes are numbered. Each number begins with a two-letter prefix to identify the mountain group concerned (eg RG stands for the Rhinogs). The main routes are then numbered sequentially (eg RG1, RG2, etc). Localised variations within routes are distinguished by numeric suffixes (eg RG2,1). High-level and lower-level/easy day walks are given H and L designators respectively after the mountain group code (eg in the case of the Rhinogs high-level walks are numbered RG H1, RG H2 etc).

The maps are diagrammatic only and should not be regarded as a substitute for the proper OS map. Their purpose is to show the relationships between the various routes in the simplest and most uncluttered way. Details of towns, roads, streams and so on are therefore only shown where needed to give a general sense of location, and are not necessarily consistent

between one map and another. To avoid congestion only the main ways up each peak are shown. The other walks are not marked, nor are the local variations indicated by numeric suffixes to their route numbers.

Each peak is considered in turn (the order in which they are treated has been chosen to minimise cross-referencing and is neither alphabetic nor according to height). Brief introductory notes on the peak itself come first, followed by descriptions of the routes on that peak. It is advisable to gain at least a general impression of each group as a whole before concentrating on any particular peak or route.

Taken together the walks include visits to all the lakes. Except in a few cases, where it would mean a rather artificial expedition of little interest to the majority of ramblers, this means routes to the very shoreline; otherwise it is to a nearby vantage point from where the really dedicated can make their own way. A glance at my diagrammatic maps will usually show which sections of the text to read to obtain the routes to a given lake. However, please bear in mind that these maps do not include the high-level, lower-level and easier day walks, nor the suffixed variations. (Alternatively the index gives the page numbers where directions for each peak may be found.)

Finally, there is always a difficulty over the spelling of Welsh place names – even the Ordnance Survey is not fully

Approaching Mynydd Tal-y-mignedd on the Nantlle ridge (NH 4)

consistent! I have therefore adopted spellings from the latest available OS maps at the time of writing and standardised on those. However, complete success in this would probably be too much to hope for, and I therefore apologise for any residual errors or inconsistencies.

THE FFESTINIOG HILLS

OS maps
1:25,000 – Sheets 16/18, 1:50,000 – Sheets 115/124

Peaks (by height)	Height (ft)	Map Ref	Page
Manod Mawr	2168	724446	14
Nameless	2159	727458	16
Moel Penamnen	2044	716483	17

Mountain Lakes (alphabetically)			
Barlwyd (2)	1476	712486	
Bowydd	1575	725468	
Du-bach	1476	719461	
Glas	1378	719455	
Nameless	1936	727451	
Newydd	1575	723472	
Pysgod	1936	728454	
Y Drum-boeth	1607	718464	
Y Manod	1378	718450	

THE FFESTINIOG HILLS

Once upon a time the little group of hills that rises to the E of what is now the grim slate town of Blaenau Ffestiniog must have been as fresh and rewarding to climb as the Moelwyns, across the vale, are to this day. No longer – now they are scarred beyond redemption by quarries and spoil heaps. Worse still, beyond the immediate desolation lies an unsightly penumbra of rusting equipment, derelict power lines, litter and noise, where the dull thud of muffled explosions replaces the song of bird and brook.

Fortunately the ravages of industry can be ameliorated, though not entirely eliminated, by judicious route selection. Whereas Manod Mawr (the highest of the three Ffestiniog peaks) and its nameless acolyte to the N are most conveniently approached from Blaenau Ffestiniog, you have only to opt for a slightly more circuitous routing from Cwm Teigl for a thoroughly enjoyable day. Similarly it is well worth driving to the top of the Crimea Pass to start the ascent of Moel Penamnen.

Viewed from across the Migneint or from the Rhinogs, when the quarry workings are hidden, Manod Mawr is a striking sight – its squat dumpy demeanour conveying a sense of power. Moel Penamnen is equally distinctive, even inspiring, with a leonine profile that always makes it seem a bigger challenge than it actually is, especially when a dusting of snow adds lustre to the scene.

A glance at the map reveals a generous sprinkling of lakes. Sadly few have survived unscathed to offer the opportunity for restful contemplation. Llyn y Manod is an exception. Despite being so near the centre of industry it nestles in a quiet little hollow that hides it from all but the most intimate gaze, a haven of peace.

As if to compensate for their scars all three hills repay the walker with sound turf and long, lingering views. On a sunny day even the slate tips lose their grimness as the sea shimmers around Criccieth and the Rhinogs blend into the haze over Cader Idris. Late summer is especially evocative with the purples of the Migneint tapering away to the distant Arenigs over the glitter of the rockbound Llynnau Gamallt and Llyn Conwy. Furthermore there is always the timeless grandeur of the giants: the Moelwyns and Moel Siabod so close you feel you could almost reach out and touch them; the Glyders, with Tryfan's gnarled summit peeping over their crest; the lofty Carneddau; and Snowdon itself.

Note In view of the above comments I only describe the more scenic routes from Cwm Teigl and the Crimea Pass. (The Crimea Pass, 700487, is not named by the OS; it is the highest point of the A470 between Blaenau Ffestiniog and Betws-y-Coed.) However, it should be noted that routes **FG2**, **FG3** and **FG5** could all be joined at Llyn y Manod by walkers starting from Blaenau Ffestiniog. To do this leave the A470 at 705444 and walk down the road towards Cae Clyd and Bron-Manod Farm. A variety of paths, some shown on the map, can then be used to approach Llyn y Manod from the S. In addition a quarry track runs from near the middle of Llynnau Barlwyd to the N outskirts of Blaenau Ffestiniog, and this provides an alternative approach to Moel Penamnen.

My routes do not encompass all of the listed lakes, namely Y Drum-boeth, Du-bach and Glas. However, ardent llyn-baggers have only to make short detours from Llyn y Manod to rectify these omissions.

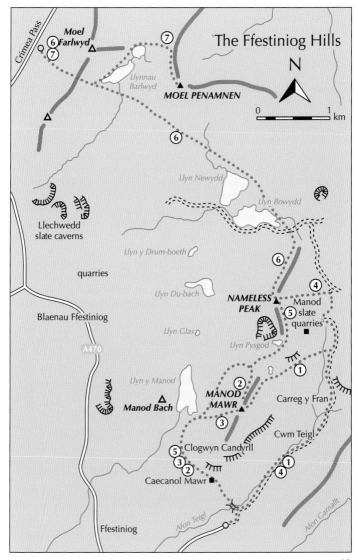

Manod Mawr

Were it not for its unsightly quarry workings Manod Mawr would be a popular peak. When viewed from S or E, with the quarries hidden, it is still a fine-looking mountain. Its stern, steep slopes (a mix of crag and scree) and above all its compactness convey an impression of great bulk and solidity. By the same token it calls for respect in mist when the only safe way off is N to the col and then down on **FG1** or **FG2**.

The trig point is almost entirely hidden by a large nettle-infested windshelter which surrounds it. Just N is a second shelter, unusually deep and narrow – good for loners, cramped for a party!

Cwm Teigl route (FG1)

Cwm Teigl is wild and desolate, almost oppressively so.

From Ffestiniog proceed up the minor road that branches off the A470 at 704423. You could drive all the way to the Manod slate quarries, but if you are planning a round trip combining **FG1** and **FG2** it is best to park just beyond a gate at 715431 where there is space for a few cars.

Manod Mawr and Manod Bach

In Cwm Teigl massive screes bear down from Manod Mawr and the fierce, almost malicious-looking crags of Carreg y Fran lie in wait up-valley. However relief is only a glance away as you plod up the long mountain road for behind you, resplendent in its greenery, is the sylvan softness of the Vale of Ffestiniog and the distant blue of Tremadog Bay.

After a long mile the road levels off and you pass between a rocky knoll L and what is now a much tamer and more friendly-looking Carreg y Fran. You even get a brief glimpse over Llynnau Gamallt to the Migneint. Such joys are short-lived as the harsher medicine of the Manod slate quarries starts to desecrate the scene. This is your signal to abandon the road and take to the purity of the hillside. Scramble up to the nameless lake at 727451. Here you will find a medley of playful little tracks, weaving between boulders and bilberries, and in minutes the top is yours.

Llyn y Manod route (FG2)

Leave the summit cairns N, but bear slightly W after a few minutes to avoid the quarries. Soon, coming down the slope, you meet a quarry path, green with age, descending the mountain's W flanks. The grim sight of Blaenau Ffestiniog is tempered with the quiet, mirrored calm of Llyn y Manod as it gradually unfolds below. Y Manod is a remarkable lake. Tucked in a hollow between Manod Mawr and Manod Bach, it is sheltered not only from viewers on the nearby hills but also from the ugliness that totally surrounds it – truly an oasis of peace and tranquillity.

Near the foot of the slope at 718446 is a prominent sheep-fold where the path becomes sketchy for a time. However it soon returns, good as gold, hugging the cliffs of Clogwyn Candryll to drop down to the derelict homestead of Caecanol-mawr (720439). It bears R just after this and then, just short of a stone barn, bears L. From here you can freelance back to Cwm Teigl and **FG1**, but if you do be sure to locate the little stone bridge over the Teigl at 723436.

This is described in descent because it dovetails neatly with **FG1** to provide a complete circuit of Manod Mawr (the round could just as well be done the other way).

W face direct (FG3)

From the sheepfold mentioned in **FG2** it is possible to gain the summit by a rough scramble straight up the hillside, following

A cruel test of wind and limb!

a broken line of quartz. This is conspicuous from a distance (less so nearer to hand) where it seems to start along with a vague zigzagging grassy rake.

Nameless (Manod Mawr)

Names count for a lot in this world, and a peak to be nameless is almost to condemn it to oblivion. This only goes to show how unfair the world can be for there are three nameless peaks in my lists (Berwyns, Glyders, here) and all of them are well worth climbing. Indeed the view from this little top is scarcely inferior to that from Manod Mawr itself.

Note Be sure to consult your compass if the weather thickens. There are deep quarry workings nearby. The safest course is N to the quarry path skirting Llyn Bowydd; but if you must go the other way trend well E of S for Llyn Pysgod to avoid the quarries.

Cwm Teigl route (FG4)
Walk up Cwm Teigl as in **FG1**, but this time continue on to the quarry gates at 733456. Do not enter the quarry; instead turn sharp R (almost a U-turn) to join a slaty path that skirts round the E flank of the hill on its way to Llyn Bowydd. After a few minutes, where it levels off at 735459 just after passing an abandoned excavation, strike W up the hillside direct for the top. This is a few paces W of where a wire fence makes a R-angled turn. A short distance N, along the fence, is a curious stony edifice rather like an altar.

Llyn y Manod route (FG5)
Follow the green track mentioned in **FG2** until it gets lost in the desolation of the quarry workings separating Manod Mawr from the nameless peak. Carry on E, skirting the N slopes of Manod Mawr, until you can climb up via Llyn Pysgod.

Crimea Pass route (FG6)

Park just below the top of Crimea Pass at 700487. Cross the road, go through a rusty old gate and stride out on 140° for a green track that is clearly seen rambling up the hillside. It narrows after a while but just about manages to keep going, leading round the flank of Moel Farlwyd to Llynnau Barlwyd. So far a very ordinary walk – then in a flash it comes alight as Moel Penamnen's leonine crest suddenly arcs the skyline ahead, a dashing sight that transforms the view at a step.

It is 1.5 miles to the foot of the nameless peak. Either aim direct for the E shore of Llyn Bowydd across trackless heather, brilliant mosses and spasmodic bog (much frequented by flies in muggy weather), or strike out E of S to pick up a quarry road along the S shores of Llynnau Newydd and Bowydd (**FG6,1**). The final rise presents no problems.

Moel Penamnen

Moel Penamnen is a striking sight with its shapely leonine profile. On top its broad grassy back is more typical of the Howgills than Wales, neither fence nor wall nor rock intruding on a fine green sheen.

Moel Siabod towers majestically N and you will find few better viewpoints for the scarped ridge of Yr Arddu and the placid Vale of Lledr. The stretch of heather and marsh trailing away to Manod Mawr is like a mini-Migneint enhanced, on a sunny day, with just a glint of the elusive Llyn y Manod. That apart, however, the view is slightly disappointing with featureless moors, forest and quarries pre-eminent. Even so it is worth a 2hr foray from the Crimea Pass – when you have 2hr to spare!

Crimea Pass route (FG7)

There is little to add to **FG6**. From Llynnau Barlwyd stay with the track until you reach a fence beyond the more N of the two lakes. Cross this over a stile for a short, sharp slog up to the long summit ridge where a tiny slaty cairn perches right on the very tip.

High-level Walks

Manod Mawr/Nameless (FG H1)

Ascend the nameless peak on **FG4**. Leave the cairn, staying on about 160° until Llyn Pysgod comes into sight just beyond a quarry road, then proceed S to the nameless lake at 727451. The descent does not involve much height loss and it is then little more than a simple stroll to claim Manod Mawr. Return to base on **FG2**.

Ffestiniog Hills complete (FG H2)

There are numerous options. One of the best is to climb the nameless peak via Cwm Teigl on **FG4** and then make a return trip to Moel Penamnen, setting out direct across the 'mini Migneint' and returning along the shores of Llyn Bowydd and Llyn Newydd as in **FG6,1**. Cross from the nameless peak over to Manod Mawr and then coast home above the blue of Llyn y Manod on **FG2**.

The grand slam of the Ffestiniog Hills cannot easily (or pleasantly) be done without some backtracking.

Lower-level Walks/Easier Days

Llyn y Manod (FG L1)

See **FG2**: what more need be said?

OS maps
1:25,000 – Sheet 11, 1:50,000 – Sheet 160

Peaks (by height)	Height (ft)	Map Ref	Page
Fan Fawr	2409	970193	22
Fan Gihirych	2379	881191	27
Fan Nedd	2176	913184	29
Fan Llia	2071	938186	26
Fan Frynych	2063	957228	25
Craig Cerrig-gleisiad	2060	961218	24
Fan Bwlch Chwyth	1978	912217	29

Mountain Lakes (alphabetically)
None

FForest Fawr

Visit Fforest Fawr and you will be among the forgotten hills of S Wales. For every 100 ramblers who tramp the Black Mountains or the Brecon Beacons probably no more than ten explore Mynydd Du (Black Mountain), and of them perhaps only one ever sets foot in Fforest Fawr. This is all the more surprising considering Fforest Fawr's strategic position, nicely tucked between the Beacons and Mynydd Du, and its claim to at least as large a share of the higher ground as its peers.

Fforest Fawr is bounded in the W by the Crai and Tawe valleys and by Bwlch Brynrhudd. The E limit is marked by the A470 as it follows the beds of first the Tarell and then the Taf. To the N the hills gently succumb to the pastoral charms of the Usk whi' S, sad to say, it is the harsh realities of the S Wales industrial belt that supplant the

Two valleys encroach upon the hills: the Senni from the N, the Mellte from th' Both are beautiful. The Mellte is generously endowed with waterfalls, pothole' wooded canyons while the Senni retains a simpler, more rustic loveliness. A r' mountain road links them, thereby splitting the area in half.

Of the six heathery, grassy hills that top 2000ft, four are in the E half and two in the W. The E sector is dominated by Fan Fawr, doyene of the range, whose flat decapitated top is a familiar landmark. Unlike Fan Fawr, Fan Lila is the culmination of a long whale-backed ridge and has little immediate appeal. These two peaks are perfectly balanced in the W: Fan Nedd (the custodian of another long ridge) which parallels Fan Llia, while Fan Gihirych is another headless giant.

The NE tip of Fforest Fawr protudes like a dwarf's head from a neck created by two cwms (Cerrig-gleisiad and Du) that thrust deeply into the hills. Nearby are the two remaining peaks, Craig Cerrig-gleisiad and Fan Frynych, though 'peak' is scarcely the word, for neither has sufficient presence to justify the title. Yet though these two peaks have little appeal, do not write off the cwms where Fforest Fawr sheds its usual austerity and displays its lofty soaring crags among prettily wooded slopes and timeless pastoral tranquillity.

Austerity is the key to Fforest Fawr's neglect. The highlands are bare, windswept fells devoid of secrets. Scarcely a wall, hardly a trace of rock, obtrudes upon the smooth uniformity of the moors. Few trees survive, even on the lower slopes, and no tarns reflect the sun's rays. On a dull day, or in winter with a bustling wind, it is a bleak and cheerless landscape without the slightest semblance of shelter. Even Fan Fawr and Fan Gihirych, imposing as they are, impress more by the stark, simple severity of their lines than by shapeliness.

Austerity does have another side – remember, even deserts have their admirers! Fforest Fawr still manages to lay claim to the hearts of those who derive pleasure from striding wild open places with only the wind, the challenge of far horizons and the munching sheep for company. There is but one inviolable rule: choose a fine day. Fforest Fawr has few landmarks and is a hard taskmaster in mist when route-finding ability of a high order is required. What would be the point anyway? Pick a clear bracing day in winter, or a sun-dappled day with the clouds scurrying overhead, and you have a day to remember!

Fforest Fawr is considerate to hillwalkers. Gradients are easy, many of the walks start fairly high and the prevailing terrain is firm, short-cropped grass and heather with little bog and few tussocks to slow you down. Miles flow easily, giving ample opportunity to admire the views. The best of these are N and S; N to the Usk Valley with the bleak uplands of Mynydd Eppynt and the hills of mid-Wales rising hazily beyond; S to

Note Restrictions on rights of way must be observed even more carefully than usual in the W half of Fforest Fawr because the whole area is part of the privately owned Cnewr Estate. There is only one permissive route across the estate and this is open all year round except for the period 15 April–10 May when it

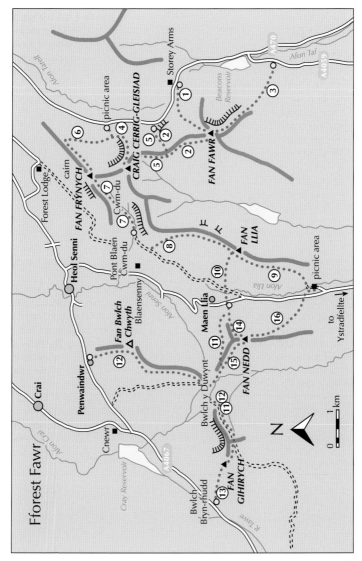

is closed for lambing. At the time of writing this route is roughly equivalent to my routes **FF13**, **14** and **15**. My routes **FF11**, **12** and **16** are not covered by the agreement. Please, therefore, check your route before setting out and if you are in any doubt, or wish to apply for special permission, write to The Estate Office, Sennybridge, Brecon LD3 8SP.

the boundless moors and foothills that gradually decline to the coast and Swansea Bay. The Beacons are all but obscured by Corn Du, and it is the silhouette of the Black Mountain that claims pride of place among the major hills to the W.

Fan Fawr

Fan Fawr is a shy mountain, denying the viewer from the A470 all but the most fleeting of glimpses. Its immense sprawling bulk is best seen from Fan Llia, asserting itself aggressively and with more than a hint of malice when mist swirls around. The top is a plateau of desolate moorland, tilting gently from the highest point overlooking the Storey Arms to the trig point 0.5 mile away SW. Sadly there is no cairn worthy of the senior peak of the range; just a small cluster of flat stones, unmistakable in clear weather but easily missed in mist or snow.

The view of the Beacons from Fan Fawr is disappointing. Although Y Gryn – for once – looks a worthy hill, the bulk of Corn Du precludes any wider vista. More striking are the views W, where the great whale-backed ridge of Fan Llia hogs the scene with Fan Nedd in the background. In marked contrast a short stroll N from the cairn reveals the green pastures of the Tarell Valley.

Storey Arms route (FF1)

Cross the stile by the car park across the road from the Storey Arms and follow a track that climbs the rather dreary hillside on 270°. Where it levels off, and just before it descends into a gully at 973202, break away L on 190° to mount the hillside near a couple of isolated outcrops. Fan Fawr rises abruptly

Fan Fawr from near Corn Du

ahead with a well-worn path climbing directly up its NE face to the summit cairn.

Alternatively (**FF1,1**) leave the stile on 230° and head directly across country until you meet the path up the NE face to finish as before.

Craig y Fro route (FF2)

This route also starts from a car park on the A470, this time at 971208. A short sharp pull up the broken slopes, keeping the stream and waterfalls L, leads to the broad saddle backing Craig y Fro. From here a narrow but quite distinct track contours across to the N and Craig Cerrig-gleisiad (**FF5**). For Fan Fawr head first SW and then SE over easy grass to ensure the gentler gradients.

S ridge (FF3)

This little-known route keeps the objective firmly in its sights all the way and follows the edge of the long, elegantly sculptured escarpment that gradually builds up from the SE. Park along the stretch of road around 988175, S of the Beacons reservoir, and from there make a beeline across the pathless fells for the ridge.

Craig Cerrig-Gleisiad

As a height Craig Cerrig-gleisiad is nothing, an insignificant grassy mound distinguished from its environs only by a few feet in altitude and a small cairn surmounted by a pole. Yet its ascent provides one of the most rewarding walks in the region in a colourful setting far removed from the bleak moorlands that characterise so much of Fforest Fawr.

E ridge (FF4)

Cross the stile by the picnic area at 971222. Pass through the coppice, keeping the stream L, and carry on for 200yd to a tumbledown wall where the full splendour of a hidden cwm is revealed. The splintered crags that stand guard L rear up as fearsomely as any in Wales. The slopes are dotted with trees and generously carpeted with bracken and heather. Yet despite the severity of the crags this is S Wales, not the N, and the cwm is a haven for quiet contemplation. Sure enough, as if in assent, the crags gradually moderate to ever more benign grassy slopes as the eye roves round to the N and the gentle ridge that rises to Fan Frynych.

Three tracks leave this delectable spot. R a path follows the wall en route to Fan Frynych (**FF6**); straight ahead a faint track leads into the cwm (**FF L1**). For Craig Cerrig-gleisiad strike out half-L to a wall breasting the crags. Despite appearances a playful track makes light of the climb, wending its way through the spiky cushions of heather that edge the dizzy depths R. Nearer the top the path veers R with a wire fence for company L. The cairn is then a short distance away over the fence.

If you follow the rim of the cwm N you will eventually meet a stone wall coming in from the W, joining the wire fence on your L at an iron gate. The bulldozed road referred to in **FF6** starts here. Follow it, passing a couple of tiny tarns L, and you will soon spot Fan Frynych's lonely trig point 5min away through the stubby heather.

Craig y Fro route (FF5)
See **FF2**.

Fan Frynych

Fan Frynych is uninspiring. Only the trig point, alone in a dreary waste of coarse heather, tired grass and struggling mosses indicates a top at all, despite the contours on the map. No one is likely to make it a prime objective. The views are the one redeeming feature. Craig Cerrig-gleisiad stands out well but it is Fan Fawr that claims the S skyline, displaying a surprisingly elongated top. Corn Du is prominent E, but the best views are W where Fan Llia impresses by its sheer bulk and Fan Nedd and Fan Gihirych both beckon. If it is clear you can also distinguish the long sleek lines of the Black Mountain.

NE ridge (FF6)
Take the track along the wall mentioned in **FF4**. This crosses a couple of lively little streams and skirts some pretty glades

Fan Frynych

R where many a happy hour could be whiled away. When the wall falls away R, shortly before the woods of Coed Ty-mawr, be sure to stay with the track as it bears L by a lone waymark sign. Soon you come to a stile and intersect a bull-dozed track at 967236. Turn sharp L here and then be prepared for a dull plod up the ridge of Twyn Dylluan-ddu, with only an ancient cairn R and the green of Glyn Tarell behind you to relieve the monotony before the trig point at least breaks the skyline R. The bulldozed track can also be joined from a brace of minor roads just S of Forest Lodge (**FF6,1**).

SW ridge (FF7)

There is no path from Pont Blaen Cwm-du to Fan Frynych, but strong walkers should have no difficulty in scaling the ridge at almost any point.

Pont Blaen Cwm-du (943215) provides an entrée to several unfrequented routes including this ascent of Fan Frynych, Fan Llia (**FF8**), and the exploration of Cwm-du itself (**FF L2**). It is most easily reached by a footpath that climbs up the prettily wooded hillside behind the farmstead of Blaensenny at 933215. This meets the bridleway that crosses Pont Blaen Cwm-du just 200yd to the S of it. The bridleway can also be joined at 925185, where it branches off the mountain road that links the Senni Valley to Ystradfellte, or by walking S down the lane from the crossroads at 939238.

Fan Llia

Fan Llia is a neglected mountain, its elephantine bulk, unmatched by any shapeliness of profile, giving it a dull appearance. But appearances can be deceptive: Llia's long N–S ridge, where the 1800ft contour line stretches for over 2 miles, might well have been made to order. Firm short-cropped grass and heather create perfect fellwalking conditions. The views are superb too. The Fan Fawr plateau curves away dramatically at either end; Fan Nedd and Fan Gihirych are backed by the Black Mountain's shadowy profile; meadows fringe the Usk and the distant outline of the mid-Wales hills while purple rolling moors beckon beyond the Ystradfellte Valley. A truly rewarding top. Tired walkers toiling up the S ridge should note that several hundred yards remain beyond the cairn before the highest point is reached.

Pont Blaen Cwm-du route (FF8)

A short walk S along the bridleway from Pont Blaen Cwm-du (see **FF7**) brings you to a gate where a fence struggles up the hillside. You can follow this for a quick but steep pull up to the N ridge. Alternatively continue along the bridleway for a few more minutes until you see a green path sidling away L. This is helpful for a time but gradually peters out. Even without a path it is still easy going and you should not be panting too hard when you finally breast the ridge. Either way look out for the mini rocky outcrop around Fan Dringarth; quite a rarity in these parts.

S ridge (FF9)

Cross the concrete bridge over the Afon Llia near the picnic area at 927165. Next climb a stile to join a track that runs beside the stream for a moment before turning R to scale the ridge alongside a wall. A dreary plod, but under 0.5 mile and well rewarded once you gain the ridge with springy turf and fine views the rest of the way.

Maen Llia route (FF10)

You can gain the N ridge at Fan Dringarth directly from the standing stone of Maen Llia. There is no path, but the slope is gentle and the only obstacle is a wire fence near the start.

Use as a quick descent or when crossing to / from the Fan Nedd ridge.

Fan Gihirych

Fan Gihirych is an imposing peak, especially from the E where the huge cwm that burrows into its N face gives it a charisma lacking in its peers. The summit plateau, a sea of tangled heather, is so large that only by walking around it can you appreciate the full extent of the views (the Black Mountain W, the Usk Valley N, Fan Fawr and the Beacons E, vast rolling moors S). There is no cairn, just a solitary trig point.

Fan Gihirych

The Senni Valley is a memorable sight on cold winter mornings when the golden tints of autumn mingle with the dazzling white of early frosts.

Maen Llia route (FF11)

The finest approach starts from 924189 where a ladder-stile gives access to the fells. With care it is just possible to park on the grass verge nearby. Over the stile follow the remains of an old stone wall (which soon degenerates to a line of posts) until you meet another wall crossing your path. Turn L and follow this along a superbly engineered track that crosses the steep upper slopes of Fan Nedd. Below R lies the Senni Valley, an oasis of long bracken-clad slopes and scattered woodlands far removed in spirit – if not in distance – from the bleak windswept uplands.

Fan Gihirych is hidden at first but soon begins to swell on the W skyline. At the same time a prominent cairn (shaped like a shark's fin) comes into view half-R across a boggy depression where the track fades in the mire. Pass through an iron gate at the far end of the bog, and it is then but a short climb up to the cairn where you meet a noticeably pink bulldozed road. You are now at Bwlch y Duwynt with the Penwaindwr route (**FF12**) coming in from the R.

Stay with the road until you come to another iron gate. Either follow the road for another 0.5 mile before scrambling up the slopes R or, better, advance through the heather by the edge of the cwm, keeping Fan Gihirych in view the whole way.

Penwaindwr route (FF12)
Little guidance is needed. Simply follow the wall that climbs the hillside next to the dwelling of Penwaindwr at 907229 and let it lead you, via the minor top of Fan Bwlch Chwyth, to Bwlch y Duwynt from where you finish as in **FF11**. The views are all you would expect from an isolated finger: Fan Fawr and Fan Llia on one side, the Black Mountain on the other and the Usk Valley behind.

All that prevents this becoming a more popular walk is the difficulty of fitting it into a round trip.

Bwlch Bryn-rhudd route (FF13)
This is the shortest but dullest route to Fan Gihirych. It is also the most difficult to fit into a satisfying day. It starts from a stile in the layby on the A4067 at 870195 from where it is a straight slog up the hillside.

Quick if you have good leg muscles, but unrewarding.

Fan Nedd

Fan Nedd has few pretensions. It can be walked up from any direction except N (where it is too steep for comfort) and its rounded, heathery top is always a strangely satisfying place from which to view the world. Perhaps this is because few other hills repay so little expenditure of energy with such a feeling of spaciousness and freedom. The views are similar to those from Fan Llia, but in a curious way the vista S is more inspiring than the high mountains as wave after wave of hillock and fell carries the gaze far and wide to the blue haze of distant horizons.

The highest point of what is essentially a shallow ridge running N to S is marked by a trig point. Just to the N is a neat little windshelter and, further N still, a large cairn. Another prominent cairn with a pole sticking up lies several hundred yards S of the trig point.

Maen Llia route (FF14)
Cross the ladder-stile as in **FF11** and then plod straight up the hillside to gain the ridge near the N cairn.

NW ridge (FF15)

This begins from the boggy depression at about 904193 mentioned in **FF11**, so is most likely to be of interest to walkers seeking to climb Fan Nedd on their way back from Fan Gihirych. From the bog a trail is clearly visible snaking up towards the N cairn. Where it becomes a little capricious higher up, head direct for the ridge through easy, short-cropped heather.

S ridge (FF16)

*This route is used in **FF H4** as a descent to the picnic area near the woods at 927165.*

The way is obvious, indeed the bridge at the picnic area can be seen quite clearly from the summit of Fan Nedd. The only decision is when to drop down L to the road – it is best left until just before the woods.

High-level Walks

The E edge walk (FF H1)

Climb Fan Fawr from the Storey Arms and then drop down to the depression near Craig y Fro, walking first on 315° and then on 45° to avoid the scattered crags that litter the peak's N slopes. Follow the edge N along a narrow path until, having crossed a wire fence, you join the path climbing up from Cwm Cerrig-gleisiad. Stay with this round the rim of the cwm and carry on to Fan Frynych along a bulldozed road. This starts near a gate where the cwm trail meets a wall coming in from the W (**FF4** refers).

You could regain the A470 by following **FF6** in reverse, but a shorter option is to retrace your steps a little to descend via **FF4**. Either way you visit the romantic Cwm Cerrig-gleisiad after which there is a 1.5-mile march along the road to regain your starting point.

Fan Fawr/Fan Llia semi-circular walk (FF H2)

This route maintains height, giving good varied views all day.

From the map a circular walk round the Ystradfellte reservoir seems tempting, starting and finishing near Fan Fawr and crossing Fan Llia on the way. In reality the S half of this walk is a dull grind with little to sustain morale. Much better is the double semi-circle suggested here.

On leaving Fan Fawr work round to Fan Llia in a N arc, crossing the upper reaches of Nant y Gwair and Nant y Caseg but taking care not to cut the corner too fine because – apart from losing height – you will get embroiled in some unpleasantly rough, tussocky grass lower down. Having sampled the view from Fan Llia advance N to the edge of Craig Cwm-du. Follow this along E, admiring the lush green of the cwm below, and then cross the neck of the plateau to the rim of Craig Cerrig-gleisiad. You now have two choices (plus an optional extension to Fan Frynych).

- The first is to descend down FF4. This gives a chance to explore the attractive Cwm Cerrig-gleisiad but necessitates a long haul back along the road.
- The second option is to hug the edge to Craig y Fro and then drop down to the A470 there (see **FF2**). This misses the cwm but reduces the road work.

It sounds a lot, but the easy terrain permits rapid progress and ensures a fairly 'middling' sort of day. What the round has in abundance is variety. You take in all the 'sights' of the E half of Fforest Fawr – the two cwms, the Senni Valley, Fan Fawr itself – with wide open vistas all the way.

Fan Gihirych/Fan Nedd (FF H3)
This is a natural for the W half of the range, giving an easy half-day. Climb Fan Gihirych as in **FF11**. Return over Fan Nedd using **FF15** for ascent and **FF14** for descent.

Fan Nedd/Fan Llia (FF H4)
Here is a route that straddles both halves of Fforest Fawr, taking in two of its finest vantage points. Scramble up Fan Nedd from Maen Llia (**FF14**) then follow the S ridge down to the picnic area at 927165, enjoying glorious views of the S Wales foothills (**FF16**). Next it's up the springy turf of Fan Llia's S ridge (**FF9**) and down to Maen Llia (**FF10**) in the evening shadows.

This could easily be done in a shortened day when rain dictates a late morning start.

Fforest Fawr hills complete (FF H5)
Dedicated peak-baggers will have little difficulty in claiming all six Fforest Fawr tops in a single day. The bridge at Heol

Try this on a good clear day and you will never again listen to the doubters who write off Fforest Fawr.

Senni (925233) is as good a place as any to start, and it neatly divides the road work between morning and evening.

Walk up the road to Penwaindwr and claim Fan Gihirych along the long N spur leading to Bwlch y Duwynt. Next climb Fan Nedd via the NW ridge, drop down to Maen Llia and pull up to Fan Llia. Curve round the plateau to Fan Fawr, taking care not to lose too much height (as much to avoid the jolty tussocks in the valley as anything else). Carry on along the E edge first to Craig Cerrig-gleisiad and then on to Fan Frynych. From there tired walkers can descend to the bridleway near Pont Blaen Cwm-du as in **FF7**, or follow **FF6,1** to reach the minor road by Forest Lodge.

Lower-level Walks/Easier Days

Cwm Cerrig-gleisiad (FF L1)

The cwm below Craig Cerrig-gleisiad (see **FF4**) is ideal for an afternoon stroll or a lazy day in the sun.

Escape the noise and hustle of the road to enjoy a haven of tranquillity and beauty with both the grandeur of crags that are unparalleled in S Wales, and the softer charms of the cwm itself – playful hillocks, the sheep, the stream, the colours of the heathers and bracken. While in the cwm try exploring the trail leading up to Fan Frynych (**FF6**). This leads to more pretty exhibitions of woodland and fell – Fforest Fawr at her most accommodating.

Cwm-du (FF L2)

Good for a rain-shortened day; a short brisk walk along the bridleway, and a foray into the cwm, might be rewarded with late shafts of sunlight.

Cwm-du bears more than a passing resemblance to Cwm Cerrig-gleisiad; a steep craggy face on one side facing pleasantly wooded slopes on the other. However the head of Cwm-du is narrower, and it twists itself more deeply and intimately into the curves of the engirdling hills with no crags, this time, to bar the way.

It takes longer to reach Cwm-du than Cwm Cerrig-gleisiad (see **FF7** for approaches to Pont Blaen Cwm-du) and it does not exhibit quite the same pristine freshness.

Craig Cerrig-gleisiad (FF L1)

Senni Valley (FF L3)

No directions are needed for an exploration of the Senni Valley. The map shows plenty of paths and lanes, and there are even more on the ground. The upper reaches of the valley, beyond Llwyn-Hydan, are splendidly wild and impressive.

Seen from the barren uplands of Fforest Fawr the Senni Valley appears like a jewel.

Mellte Valley (FF L4)

Start from Porth yr Ogof at 928124. There is a parking area close by. A valley path follows the densely wooded Mellte gorge for a time, later veering E to climb the slopes above the Hepste before descending to the riverside again, close to the waterfalls at Scwd yr Eira at 929100. The path actually continues into a recess behind the falls. There are numerous other falls and potholes en route.

This hauntingly beautiful walk cries out for inclusion, despite being some distance from the hills.

THE GLYDERS

OS maps
1:25,000 – Sheets 16/17, 1:50,000 – Sheet 115

Peaks (by height)	Height (ft)	Map Ref	Page
Glyder Fawr	3279	642579	47
Glyder Fach	3262	656583	39
Y Garn	3104	631596	57
Elidir Fawr	3030	612613	64
Tryfan	3010	664594	68
Foel Goch	2727	628612	61
Carnedd y Filiast	2695	621628	67
Mynydd Perfedd	2665	623619	66
Nameless	2636	678582	54
Gallt yr Ogof	2499	685586	55

Mountain lakes (alphabetically)		
Bochlwyd	1800	655592
Clyd (2)	2150	634597
Cwmffynnon	1260	649562
Cywion	1970	632605
Idwal	1223	645596
Marchlyn Bach	1600	608625
Marchlyn Mawr	2066	616619
Y Caseg-fraith	2430	670583
Y Cwn	2330	637584

THE GLYDERS

Snowdon apart, nowhere in Wales conveys the aura and majesty of the Welsh mountains with such authority and panache as the Glyders. There are wild inviting cwms, rocky spurs, sharp bracing ridges, mysterious threatening monoliths, savage grandeur, fresh sparkling lakes – a bonanza of riches. Here you are at the hub of the Welsh hills,

Glyder Fawr summit backed by the Snowdon massif (GL 7)

surrounded by mountains – the mighty Carneddau, Moel Siabod, Snowdon herself and the hazy blur of Cader Idris – with the skyline a breathtaking array of pinnacles and crests. Tramping the lunar-like, boulder-strewn tableland between Glyder Fawr and Glyder Fach you may glimpse five of Wales' most famous valleys: Nant Ffrancon, Ogwen, Conway, Llanberis and the hauntingly beautiful Nantgwynant.

The Glyders stretch, like an arm raised in greeting, from Carnedd y Filiast in the N to Gallt yr Ogof in the E. The elbow is at Llyn y Cwn, close by Twll Du (Devil's Kitchen), where the range suddenly swings E. There are eight peaks spanning a ridge which, in over 6 miles, never falls below 2300ft. Slightly askew of the main ridge, but linked to it by grand ridge walks, are Elider Fawr and the incomparable Tryfan. Both of these – along with Glyder Fawr, Glyder Fach and Y Garn – are members of the élite 3000ft club.

It is easy to appraise the Glyders from the road, bounded as they are by the A4086 and the A5. Llanberis makes a sorry start. Towering battlements of slate, inelegantly gouged from the mountainside, cast a sombre shadow over what must once have been two enchanting lakes, Padarn and Peris. Despite their scars, they can still charm you on a sunny day.

The mood changes as quickly as the weather. A couple of miles up-valley ushers in one of Wales' greatest spectacles, the Llanberis Pass, where the massive, lowering face of the Glyders (a Mecca for rock climbers) yields nothing in severity and grandeur to Snowdon's N flanks on the other side. Beyond Pen y Gwryd the mood changes again.

Now it is Moel Siabod that holds the gaze while the Glyders are at their gentlest in a flow of billowy moorland, dotted with crags and fledgling bluffs, white-ribboned by dashing streams.

And so to Capel Curig, the A5 (not forgetting the 'old road' of 1805 that parallels it much of the way) and the pièce de résistance. Thrills come thick and fast now. Cupped in the V of the valley, beyond Ogwen, are Y Garn and the plunging silhouette of Foel Goch. Nearer to hand Gallt yr Ogof's elephantine sprawl is but the precursor to greater things, that most perfect of mountains, Tryfan. Airy ridges, spiky spurs and fresh mountain lakes follow in breathless succession. Bristly Ridge, Llyn Bochlwyd, Y Gribin, Seniors Ridge, Llyn Ogwen, Llyn Idwal, the Devil's Kitchen, Llyn y Cwn, the twin ridges of Y Garn cradling shy Llyn Clyd… the names roll off the tongue like a hall of fame!

Few trekkers venture further N, but you have only to carry on to Bethesda – to end as you began, in the devastation of quarries – to find that the magic goes on. Not with quite the same might and splendour, perhaps, but superb walking country nonetheless, especially if you value solitude. Cwm Cywion, a hanging valley with a teardrop tarn; the flaky ridge of Creigiau Gleision and the teetering pinnacles of the Mushroom Garden; Cwm Coch and the menacing Yr Esgair ridge, great as a spectacle but too exposed for walkers and too crumbly for climbers; Cwm Bual, Cwm Perfedd, Cwm Graianog and Cwm Ceunant – undiscovered and unsung, all of them, but well worth cultivating in spite (or because) of that.

Tryfan from the east (GL 34)

The N arm of Cwm Graianog is heathery and wild and leads above a wall of slabs, smooth as silk, to the most N outpost of the Glyders, Carnedd y Filiast. From here dedicated walkers could walk the entire ridge to Capel Curig in a long day. And what a day! A rollicking tramp over a grassy saddle, big enough for a fair, soon leaves the slaty wastes behind. Mynydd Perfedd comes next; a name without a presence. The direct line of advance lies straight ahead, but only the most indolent would ignore the edge path that curls so delectably over the aquamarine of Llyn Marchlyn Mawr to the cone of Elidir Fawr.

Back beneath Perfedd is Bwlch y Brecan, high point of an old packhorse route that used to link Cwm Perfedd and Cwm Dudodyn and is one of three still navigable trails that cross the Glyders. These N highlands, over Foel Goch and Y Garn, are perfect striding country, blessed with helpful tracks and laden with atmosphere. With the exception of Cwm Las and Esgair y Ceunant, the S slopes facing Snowdon lack excitement while the neglected N flanks are full of potential with dramatic views across the neat, green meadows of Nant Ffrancon to Carneddau, Ogwen and the spires of Tryfan.

A rude awakening awaits anyone naïve enough to judge the Glyders on the evidence so far. A sharp drop to a marshy saddle reveals Llyn y Cwn and the head of the Devil's Kitchen. This is the key to the second 'low-level' crossing of the Glyders, up the Devil's Kitchen from Ogwen, down Cwm Las to the Llanberis Pass. More significantly it heralds a change both of direction and of style. This is the Rubicon; no more grass. The next 2 miles, presaged by a toilsome, near 1000ft slog up to the reigning peak, Glyder Fawr, are scree and boulder-hopping.

This is boulder-hopping on the grandest scale! Scabrous, posturing monoliths and spiky tors weave ghostly apparitions in mist and create a landscape of lunar abandon and wanton desolation. Wastes of boulders and rivers of rocky debris litter the narrow plateau that stretches to Glyder Fach in a highway made for giants.

Like good wine, the walk to Glyder Fach should be savoured gently and lingered over. Above all keep to the edge, for beneath the shattered N escarpment (replete with bulging crags, intimidating cliffs, and torrents of scree) lies the heartland: Llyn Idwal, the Nameless Cwm cupped between Seniors Ridge and Y Gribin, Llyn Ogwen and Llyn Bochlwyd, nestling in the shadow of Bristly Ridge and Tryfan.

To the S a myriad of peaks pierce the sky, but beware the slopes. They may look pretty and innocent, cloaked in a mantle of rich purple heather and dappled with knolls and rocky bluffs, but they are a nightmare – apart from a couple of established paths. The glitter of Llyn Cwmffynnon is one of the biggest snares of all, concealing a squelchy morass of glutinous bog.

Before long the dark citadel of the poetically named Castell y Gwynt (Castle of the Winds) builds up ahead, followed almost at once by the other-worldly piles of Glyder Fach. Here the desolation last witnessed on Glyder Fawr reasserts itself in a second outpouring of elemental power, even more intense than the first. Giant boulders randomly

The Devil's Kitchen (GL 8)

strewn create an impression of chaos, of disorder, of the insignificance of Man. No other top in Wales portrays Nature's architecture more magnificently, or casts such an overwhelming spell of mountainly grandeur.

E of Glyder Fach the land falls away to a broad spongy saddle where, on a still day, you may see Tryfan reflected in the waters of Llyn y Caseg-fraith. The third of the low-level passages crosses here, the miners' track from Ogwen to Pen-y-gwryd. Then a resurgence of vitality carries the ridge on to the bald moorland crest of the nameless peak. The passion is finally spent. The broad tongue of turf and heather that surges yet again over Gallt yr Ogof before declining to the wooded vale sheltering Betws-y-coed, is a far cry from the harsh, arid uplands of only an hour before. Gone is the drama of crag and cwm; this is pretty country made for late afternoon sunshine or the cool glow of evening when you can watch the shadows lengthen over the Carneddau and envelope the rocky crown of Siabod.

Glyder Fach

If you were to blindfold me and place me at random on any of the 170-odd peaks in Wales that exceed 2000ft, it would probably take me a little while to discover my whereabouts. Unless it were either of the Glyders that is, for they are unique, incomparable, unlike anywhere else in Wales!

Glyder Fawr and Glyder Fach mean 'Great Pile' and 'Little Pile' respectively, though there is little to choose between them. Glyder Fach is, if anything, the more rugged peak – a wild, chaotic plateau of gesticulating boulders crowned with two mighty tors. Glyder Fawr is marginally tamer; no less dramatic, yet very different. Its vast stony dome, littered with leafy, spiky quivers of rock, recalls the tor country of the NW Carneddau and has a curious beehive appearance when approached from Glyder Fach. In mist, or moonlight, both tops generate a weird, eerie atmosphere as their huge monoliths pierce the gloom.

To tramp the lofty tableland between these two giants is a unique experience. So let me give you a brief guided tour starting from 659584 which is where the top of Bristly Ridge and the path from Llyn y Caseg-fraith both mount the plateau. A cairned path is just discernible, steering a course on 230° through the rocky debris. It passes N of one massive pile (on the W side of which is the famous cantilever) before skirting N of a second even larger pile which is the (cairnless) top. It becomes difficult here to distinguish the cairns from the all-pervading bouldery waste, so follow the tell-tale sign of eroded, reddish sand until the cairns reassert themselves.

Directly ahead is the rearing citadel of Castell y Gwynt, a dark slabby pyramid of teetering rocks that only lacks distance from its neighbours to be accorded peak status itself. Rock-hounds will enjoy an easy scramble over the top while the path weaves round to the S. At 653582 a large cairn marks the top of the Bwlch y Ddwy Glyder route S (**GL5**) while the main path swings W to groove through a grassy bank, slightly

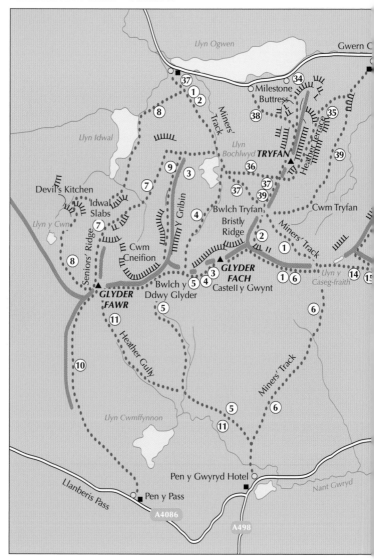

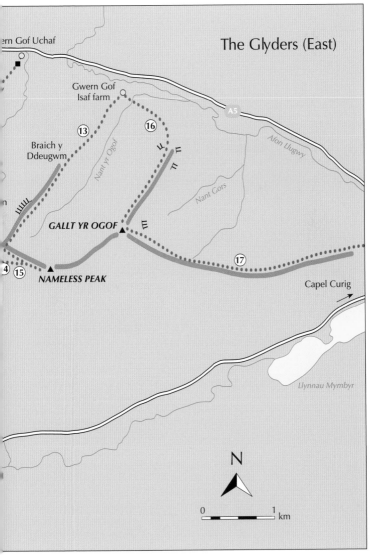

The Glyders (East)

ern Gof Uchaf

Gwern Gof
Isaf farm

A5

Afon Llugwy

Braich y
Ddeugwm

⑬

⑯

Nant yr Ogof

Nant Gors

GALLT YR OGOF

④ ⑮

NAMELESS PEAK

⑰

Capel Curig

Llynnau Mymbyr

N

0   1
          km

The cantilever rock on Glyder Fach (GL 1)

below the edge, before climbing up to the bare, desiccated scalp of Glyder Fawr and its flaky spires.

In clear weather it is best to abandon the path immediately after bypassing Castell y Gwynt and walk along the edge for a while. The view back to Castell y Gwynt, flanked by Glyder Fach's shattered front of buttresses, gullies and terraces, is impressive to say the least! Soon comes a cairn signalling the top of Y Gribin; then Seniors Ridge breaches the skyline while all the time the gaze is fed by a sweeping panorama of Bochlwyd and Idwal, Tryfan and Bristly Ridge, the long sinuous line of the N Glyders and the smooth lines of the Carneddau. With luck you should be able to pick out five of Wales' most famous valleys or passes: Nantgwynant, Llanberis, Nant Ffrancon, Ogwen, and even a peep of Conway. Only to the S is the tension relieved in the blue haze of endless ranges rolling on and on: Arenigs, Arans, Rhinogs, Cader Idris, Plynlimon...

You should return to the path now. Heavily cairned, it ploughs through jostling scrums of spires and boulders to land you just L of the highest tor of all – the crown of all the Glyders.

Miners' Track (N) (GL1)

The men who worked the copper mines in Cwm Dyli from Napoleonic times to the Great War showed extraordinary stamina. They used this same track week in and week out, fair weather and foul, to return to their homes in Bethesda from the bleak stone 'dwellings' that housed them during the week on Snowdon's E slopes.

The track starts nowadays beside the refreshment hut at Ogwen, across the road from a phone box, and quickly leads to twin stiles (they cater for crowds here!) and a bridge. The first 300yd, where it doubles up as the path to Llyn Idwal, are flagged with boulders, but such luxury is short-lived. Where the main path swings R for the lake you must strike out SE across dark, mirey ground (where stepping stones have been all but swallowed up) to a rocky man-made stairway that climbs above the ravine of Nant Bochlwyd to one of Wales' most enchanting lakesides.

For a track as easily graded as this to cross not only the main spine of the Glyders but also the high-level ridge linking Tryfan to Glyder Fach is truly remarkable.

> **Note** If the car park by Ogwen cottage is full you could set out from one of the other parking areas or laybys along the lake's N shoreline, though you then have a damp cross-country trek with little in the way of an established path to reach Bochlwyd.

Tryfan is awesome in its severity, its W face scree path revealed in distressing clarity. R is the serrated Gribin ridge, backed by Y Garn, impassive as always. Behind you is the heathery bulk of Pen yr Ole Wen, ahead the untrodden solitude of Cwm Bochlwyd (Valley of the Grey Cheek) squeezed between the stupendous, broken cliffs of Glyder Fach and Castell y Gwynt.

On resuming the track climbs above the E shoreline. After 100yd a faint path tiptoes away L for the col between Tryfan's S and far S peaks (**GL36**). The main track trends L to cross the high-level pass of Bwlch Tryfan near a brace of stiles over a wall at 662588. In season this is a major crossroads. Tryfan's

Glyder Fach from Llyn Bochlwyd

S ridge is L, Bristly Ridge R and, straight ahead, the greeny-brown marshes of Cwm Tryfan. The miners' track continues SE, the way never in doubt. It curls round the headwall of Cwm Tryfan, beneath the screes of Bristly Ridge, in scenery that is never less than riveting, and breasts the spongy saddle of Bwlch Caseg-fraith at 667583. Only a 750ft grind remains, up a well-cairned path that grows stonier and rockier with every step.

Bristly Ridge (GL2)

Experienced hillwalkers (though not family parties with children) may well be tempted to leave the miners' track at Bwlch Tryfan to tackle the Bristly Ridge, a rock scramble par excellence and one of the tours de force of the Welsh hills.

Despite its savage-looking spikes its bark is worse than its bite, so have a go!

Turn SW at the bwlch and struggle up the scree, along a trace of a path that parallels the wall. Then swing R to abut on the rock face at the entrance to a narrow gully. This is slightly above where the wall also embeds itself in the ridge. Squeeze up the gully as far as you can and then clamber up the rock face R to the crest. That is where you should stay, on the crest, guided by polished boulders and the tell-tale scratch-marks of the thousands who have gone before. Now scrambling up a little wall, now crossing a cleft between two pinnacles, now trending L, now dodging round to the R... So it goes on, sporting and challenging every minute of the way. Airy? Delightfully so. Exposed? No. Despite the succession of pinnacles and crags there is never a problem, given a modicum of care, in securing your flanks. In truth there is nowhere to go but the crest once you are launched. It would be far harder (and riskier) to try to dismount (unless you are a rock climber), until the final and sharpest notch that is. Now you do have a choice; either stay on the crest or settle for an easy bouldery rake W. Either way you soon have massive white slabs underfoot as the tension abates and a cairned path leads to the huge chaotic tor of Glyder Fach.

Walkers wishing to short-circuit the miners' track but not relishing Bristly Ridge could attempt the scree run that sweeps down to Bwlch Tryfan beneath its E battlements (**GL2,1**). However this is a brute, loose and slithery all the way.

Y Gribin (GL3)
See **GL9.**

Tryfan from near Llyn Caseg-fraith (GL 4)

45

Bwlch y Ddwy Glyder route (N) (GL4)

Remember that the word 'bwlch', which frequently does indicate a pass, more accurately means 'gap' or 'defile'. Never truer than here!

I give this route for four reasons. It is 'there'; it is direct (aggressively so); it is unfrequented, wild and rugged; it has magnificent close-up views of Glyder Fach and Castell y Gwynt. But – and it is a big 'but' – it is also exhaustingly steep and rough with only the most fleeting traces of a track. You have been warned! If you accept the challenge take the miners' track to Bochlwyd, then follow the lake's E shore leading into the brook that rises to the dip in the skyline directly ahead, past a tiny tarn. Good luck!

Bwlch y Ddwy Glyder route (S) (GL5)

Not recommended.

The descent starts from a cairn at 653582 on the track that circles round S of Castell y Gwynt. Any semblance of a path soon fizzles out and you should veer R after about 5min, along a heathery shelf banked by crags on either side. As the shelf loses its identity, follow a stream SE towards Llyn Cwmffynnon. Disjointed fragments of path appear, tempting only to deceive. There is no continuous track and what has been rough but bearable going hitherto (with Pen y Gwryd and tea hopefully only 30min away) suddenly becomes an ankle-twister worthy of the Rhinogs at their vitriolic worst. Large squirmy tussocks of heather, half-hiding (or hiding!) smooth slippery boulders and tiny rivulets treble the time and energy that would normally be needed. The frustration eases as you approach the lake, with conventional bog (a relief by comparison) the final challenge. Drier ground is to be found by contouring N of the lake and following the Nant Gwryd to the road at 661559.

Miners' Track (S) (GL6)

Dull? Maybe, if you are looking for non-stop drama, but not if you give the magic of Nantgwynant and Crib Goch time to work.

The miners' track that slants across the Glyders' S slopes from a stile at 661559, close by the Pen y Gwryd Hotel, is a far cry from its N counterpart. No mountainy grandeur here, just a simple track swathing through the heather of a rock-studded hillside. This used to be excessively boggy lower down, but strategically placed stepping stones and a 'walk-the-plank' type bridge now make light work of it.

Once you mount the boggy tableland, shortly after the falls at 667576, you are treated to the principals coming on

stage one by one, every step a revelation. Bristly Ridge, Tryfan, the nameless peak and Carneddau all appear, followed finally by the gentle Llyn y Caseg-fraith (Lake of the Dappled/Piebald Mare) and its diminutive satellites. Besides this lake you can pick up a black muddy path that soon turns to stone and leads unerringly (it is cairned to excess higher up) to the bouldery waste of Glyder Fach.

Mist clearing the southern slopes of the Glyders

Glyder Fawr

Most of what I want to relate about this evocative peak has already been told as part of the introduction to Glyder Fach. All that remains is advice on what to do in mist when one rocky spire looks very much like another. Without good compass work Glyder Fawr is one of the most disorientating peaks I know.

Assuming you are at the highest point – which is the more N of two adjacent and almost equal tors – the path to Glyder

Fach and Y Gribin starts on 90° and is so densely cairned as to be virtually foolproof. For Llyn y Cwn, and onward to Cwm Las or the Devil's Kitchen, a bearing of 280° leads into another line of cairns that again are unmistakable once you get below the topmost rocky cap. The Pen y Pass route is a bit trickier. Start on 220° and count the cairns. At the fifth cairn the track splits. One branch continues on 270° to give an alternative start for Llyn y Cwn. The other leads on 180° to another monolith, after about 25 paces. Red waymark signs begin here, plus cairns, and all is well, staying on 180°.

Note Seniors Ridge and the Heather Gully should not be attempted in mist.

Seniors Ridge (GL7)

One of the problems with a book like this is that there are no secrets. Everything has to come out – even pearls like this, which you would rather keep to yourself.

Take **GL1** to Llyn Bochlwyd where on still, sunny mornings Y Garn is reflected in its blue waters. Follow a narrow track above its N shoreline. Ignore the well-trodden path that strides off L for Y Gribin, but when the little path divides again, a few minutes later, bear L in the shadow of the ridge. (Pressing straight on leads down to Llyn Idwal beside a wall at 646596; worth bearing in mind as an alternative routing – **GL7,1**.)

The path splits yet again almost at once and it is important to take the higher fork that wends adventurously, yet safely,

Glyder Fach from Glyder Fawr

across the massive slopes of heather and scree that fall away from the spiky comb of Y Gribin. (The lower branch eventually fizzles out.) This is a walk in a million with Llyn Idwal, far below, cupped beneath the huge forbidding cirque of Y Garn and the Devil's Kitchen – from nowhere else as compelling as this. To gild the lily, ahead lies hanging Cwm Cneifion (Cwm of the Fleece, sometimes known as Nameless Cwm), wild and forgotten, a haven of secrets.

The path ventures over the lip of the cwm before abandoning you to the sheep. Only the tinkling of a tiny stream breaks an all-pervading silence. Seniors is the squat, rock-studded ridge forming the W arm of the cwm and is best tackled from its N tip at 645590. It soars aloft in a series of rocky bluffs and heathery shelves, not unlike the N ridge of Tryfan, but without the comfort of fellow walkers or polished rocks to highlight the way. There is no unavoidable exposure and, as the stiffest bits come first, there is no risk of being stranded through being unable to go on and reluctant to turn back. The views are superb, the purity of untrodden ground refreshing, and it is a disappointment when the stony plateau of Glyder Fawr signals the end of one of Snowdonia's forgotten treasures.

Note Not recommended for descent.

Devil's Kitchen (GL8)

Leave Ogwen along the boulder-paved track beside the refreshment hut. It begins as if aiming for Llyn Bochlwyd but soon swings SW (the Bochlwyd track carries straight on) to an iron gate on the shores of Llyn Idwal. What a transformation! After only 20min noise and bustle have given way to a scene that is the very quintessence of wild Wales; the jagged crests of Seniors Ridge and Y Gribin arcing the sky L; Y Garn; the shattered slopes of Pen yr Ole Wen behind you; the cliffs of Clogwyn y geifr (Goat's precipice) and the dark sinister cleft of the Devil's Kitchen directly ahead. At your feet is idyllic Llyn Idwal, sparkling and serene, yet rarely more than 10ft deep.

Assuming you follow the E shoreline (a path also follows the W shore) go past the famous Idwal Slabs (invariably dotted

Looking through the Devil's Kitchen to Pen yr Ole Wen

with climbers), up a man-made stairway, clamber across the rocky rift of a streambed and then, when the path gives up the struggle, scramble up the downfall of boulders to the cleft itself (Twll Du in Welsh, Black Hole in English). It is hard to reconcile the peaceful scene looking back over Idwal and Ogwen with the harsh, evil gash above. Even on a sunny day it is an eerie place, while in mist…

Beneath the cliffs a cairned trail forges SE up a shelf of splintered rocks to emerge on a broad marshy plateau with Llyn y Cwn (Lake of the Dogs) a stone's throw ahead. Few places are more desolate in winter. The gap in the hills channels the full fury of the wind, whipping the lake into a frenzy of rushing waves. To view the top of the Devil's Kitchen (uncairned) follow the stream that issues from the NW tip of the tarn. To locate the trail for descent take a bearing of 60° from the N tip of the lake and in 300yd you meet the cairned path.

It is time to move on. The key to Glyder Fawr is a stony gully by the NE corner of the lake. It starts sedately, albeit roughly, but later degenerates into a scree slither of the most wearisome kind. A sweaty treadmill climbing up, an unstable gritty slide coming down; a toss-up as to which is the least tedious. When the angle at last abates, lines of cairns appear to lead across a barren stony desolation to the weirdly gesticulating summit tors.

Note This slope is treacherous in snow and must be left strictly alone unless you are fully experienced and equipped for snow work. One unchecked slip could be your last.

For an alternative approach known as the Sheepwalk (**GL8,1**), cross the stream issuing from the foot of Twll Du and follow a sketchy path across a grassy ledge leading to the SE slopes coming down from Y Garn. Narrow, exposed in places and with a little unavoidable scrambling, this should only be attempted by experienced scramblers in good weather.

Y Gribin (GL9)

Y Gribin, the long serrated spur midway between Glyder Fawr and Glyder Fach, is one of the best scrambles in the area. Start

The Glyders are well endowed with challenging scrambles.

from the N tip of Llyn Bochlwyd where a track cavorts away W en route to Llyn Idwal (see **GL7**). Leave it L at 652594 where black peaty scars indicate the start of a much-used path. The going is easy at first, between soft pillows of heather whose playful innocence give little intimation of the savage gullies away R.

Before long you reach an open plateau of sheep-cropped turf, good enough for a cricket pitch. (You can also reach this by a rough scramble up a subsidiary ridge from Bochlwyd's SW shoreline at 654591 – **GL9,1**.) So far the day has been enjoyable without being remarkable – now for the fireworks. Ahead lies an airy tumble of rock and boulders, with occasional exposure L, requiring some easy gymnastics for its conquest. Grist for the mill for experienced hillwalkers, but no place for vertigo sufferers or victims of stiff knees! For them there is an alternative routing R, a badly eroded and crumbly path that avoids the scrambling (and the thrills) in return for a sweaty huff and puff.

The ways unite at the top on a bouldery tongue midway between the two Glyders which is dominated by Castell y Gwynt and the regimented, shattered crags of Glyder Fach. A large cairn at 651582 is the landmark to look out for in mist.

Pen y Pass route (the red route) (GL10)

Glyder Fawr is one of the last peaks you would expect to be able to climb almost all the way on grass, but life is full of surprises!

A fine route, threading attractively through a maze of hollows and humps liberally laced with marsh and islands of rock. It is also a scenic route. Crib Goch and Cwm Glas are the main attractions, but you also get an unusual prospect of Llyn Cwmffynnon and the shapely cliffs that girdle its S shoreline.

The path starts by the Pen y Pass Youth Hostel. A footpath sign directs you across a small garden to a stile over a wall daubed with a red waymark sign. It is wet and soggy at first across a boggy depression and the red blobs on the rocks are not easy to spot. However matters improve after a short sharp climb where the line of attack swings from being parallel to the road to N, and where you begin to tackle Glyder Fawr's S shoulder. By this time the waymarking is as dependable as any I can recall. It needs to be, because cairns are few and far between and losing the way, though not serious, would

Dinas Cromlech where the Glyders frown down on the Llanberis Pass (GL 12)

certainly be inconvenient. Avoi d the route in mist or snow when waymarks would be obscured.

If it is a clear day try contouring across to Esgair Felen, an exhilarating eyrie sprouting crags of a fine reddish hue. It rises a daunting 2000ft above the Llanberis Pass and is an ideal spot for viewing Cwm Glas and Snowdon's N battlements. You can also reach Esgair Felen direct from Glyder Fawr by starting out as if for Llyn y Cwn but then bearing SW down the bare stony finger.

Heather Gully (GL11)

Despite its attractive name this is not an easy route.

This descent entails a lot of uneven, trackless walking similar to **GL5**. It starts on a S course from the summit cairns, trending L at about 643575, beside a stream, into the gully that gives the route its name. After much hard labour you approach more open terrain surrounding Llyn Cwm Fynnon where the route merges into **GL5**.

Cwm Las route (GL12)

Walk up the Llanberis Pass from the car park at 607583. When you come to a footpath sign at 614576 with a campsite L and a postbox R, proceed down the stony, walled path which is indicated. After crossing a stile at the second of two white cottages the path momentarily fades and you should trend L to pick it up again near the Afon Las. Thereafter it is never in doubt as it shadows the stream's true L bank. The first 0.5 mile is attractive, climbing steeply above a shady glen and a succession of tumbling falls. Higher up you cross the bleak spongy saddle beneath the red-tinted screes of Esgair Felen to end by the shores of Llyn y Cwn. Regretfully the hardest work, the treadmill up the gritty screes to Glyder Fawr, is still to come (see **GL8**).

Nameless Peak

'Nameless' had a more romantic ring in the good old days of the 1-inch maps when it was known as pt 2636. However, despite the dark craggy face it shows to

Nant yr Ogof, and views which are well up to Glyders' standards, there is little of interest and this small peak is seldom visited except as a staging post on the long trek from Glyder Fach to Gallt yr Ogof. The best thing about it is the ascent over Braich y Ddeugwm, a breezy, open walk which never fails to engender a 'good-to-be-alive' feeling.

Braich y Ddeugwn route (GL13)

A stile beside Gwern Gof Isaf Farm gives access to a grassy crest that is too gentle and rounded to be called a ridge. This rises in easy steps and ledges mingled with knuckles of rock until, higher up, a more defined path leads to the marshy shoreline of Llyn y Caseg-fraith. The nameless peak is then but 10min E up bare, featureless slopes.

No other walk displays Tryfan's prodigious architecture to better advantage, especially when capped with a powdering of snow or frost.

Those are the facts. What they do not convey is the over-powering presence of Tryfan across the cwm. Towering aloft in splendid isolation, the massive gullies of its E face illuminated by the morning sun, it is the very epitome of mountainly grandeur. Yet, strange to relate, in over 30 years I have never once spied a fellow walker on this lovely route.

Miners' Track N or S (GL14/15)

You can also reach Llyn y Caseg-fraith by following the miners' track as described in either **GL1** or **GL6**, thus giving two more routes to the nameless peak – **GL14** from Ogwen, **GL15** from Pen y Gwryd.

Gallt yr Ogof

We live in a world that is all about coming first; runners up are all but forgotten. Who came second in the Derby? That is exactly Gallt yr Ogof's problem. It may be the second most charismatic peak along the A5 from Capel Curig but, rising in the shadow of Tryfan, what chance has it got? So, sadly, despite a lumbering elephantine sprawl that completely dominates until you round a bend and Tryfan comes into view, it is virtually neglected. Neglected, that is, except by connoisseurs who revel in solitude and the unspoilt freshness of a cairn surrounded by heathery dips and hollows which know nothing of the black peaty scars of fame!

As befits this most E outpost of the mighty Glyders, the view on a clear day is a memorable one. Carneddau, a glimpse of the sea and the countless ranges Siabod, you would expect. However, the scene is now beyond enriched by Llyn Cowlyn and a peep at the Vale of Conway; by Llynnau Mymbyr and the tree-clad hills surrounding Betws-y-coed. Glancing back reveals the splendour of the Glyders heartland and the long tramp to far-off Carnedd y Filiast, the starting point for those hardy souls who attempt all ten tops in a single day.

Direct but trackless approaches are possible from the basin of the Nant yr Ogof to the W, or via Nant Gors from the E. I have eschewed both of them as the former is unpleasantly wet and the latter laboriously rough with every step a battle. Apart from the two routes described below, the only other approach is along the ridge from the nameless peak, following a friendly track close to a brace of tiny tarns.

Cave gully route (GL16)

A route that is every bit as diabolical in descent.

The damp ferny cave that gives the mountain its name is clearly visible from the road about two thirds of the way up, and slightly L of, the prominent gully that rends its N face. The foot of the gully is best reached along the old road from the farm of Gwern Gof Isaf at 685600. Thereafter all you have to look forward to is a brute of a struggle up a treadmill of unstable scree and sparse grey grass. Rampant heather takes over as soon as the angle abates, but by then the damage is done with frayed tempers and dusty, aching limbs.

The Capel Curig route (GL17)

A stile by the side of Joe Brown's mountain wear shop at Capel Curig signals the start of the old road to Ogwen. Follow it for about 5–10min, past the farmhouse, then break away L up the rock-studded hillside to the crest of the ridge. The route used to be waymarked in red but the signs have long since disappeared and the simplest course nowadays is to follow your nose, dodging cliffs and bog as best you can. Once atop the ridge a path permits a relaxing walk with plenty of opportunity to enjoy the views.

Y Garn

Y Garn means 'cairn' or simply 'pile' (of stones); not a very evocative name for a member of the famous 3000ft club. Yet it is a grand peak, proud and aloof, as witnessed by its domination of Ogwen. To see it at its best you must first climb Tryfan. Only then can you appreciate its magnificent architecture and admire the two sturdy arms in the bosom of which nestle the twin lakelets of Llyn Clyd. Little more than a mile from the road, yet unsuspected, their secluded hollow is a haven of tranquillity where the hills enclose you in mighty splendour – a perfect spot for a sunny day.

The more S of the two NE-facing ridges is just on the wrong side of the exposure scale for mere scramblers. The other atones by offering two variants. Combining these gives a fine excursion for a short day. There is also a pleasant route beside the Afon Las from Nant Peris. Otherwise the grassy S and W slopes are monotonous.

Once Y Garn's scalp is in your bag it is a simple matter to capture Foel Goch too, a much less popular top. A gritty path leads down to a minor col overlooking Cwm Cywion, passing on the way the cairn which marks where **GL18** comes in. Before long a grooved path takes over to bring you to a stile. The main path trends L here en route to Bwlch y Brecan. For Foel Goch you must follow, instead, a little-used track beside a fence that forges straight ahead, N.

As far as views go, of all the riches on display none compares with the noble line that extends from Snowdon to the scarps of Moel Eilio, with Mynydd Mawr, the Nantlle ridge, the Rivals, Anglesey and the sea all peeping over. Beyond Ogwen the broken face of Pen yr Ole Wen leads the eye to Carnedd Dafydd, Carnedd Llewelyn, Yr Elen, the lonely tor country of Gyrn Wigau and the smooth slopes of Pen Llithrig y wrach. Finally there is a wonderful vista of the Glyders from Carnedd y Filiast to Tryfan. This is also a good place to appraise the complex lie of land supporting those three great ridges – Bristly, Gribin and Seniors. A keen eye can even discern the trace of the exquisite little path that curls round the foot of Y Gribin en route to Cwm Cneifion and Seniors Ridge.

NE ridge N (GL18)

From Ogwen take the well-used path to Llyn Idwal. Follow the N shoreline until you can cut across slightly N of W to the foot of the ridge at 638600 and a wide, badly eroded track. This climbs steeply to a little plateau where an untidy,

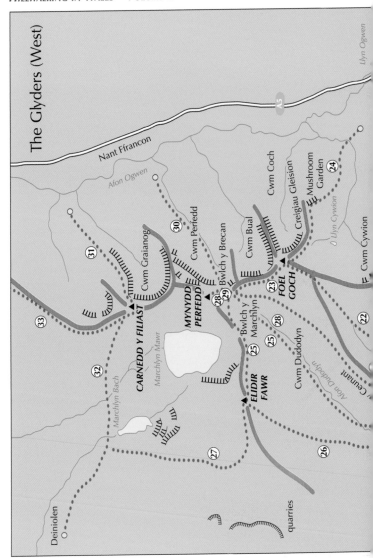

The Glyders (West)

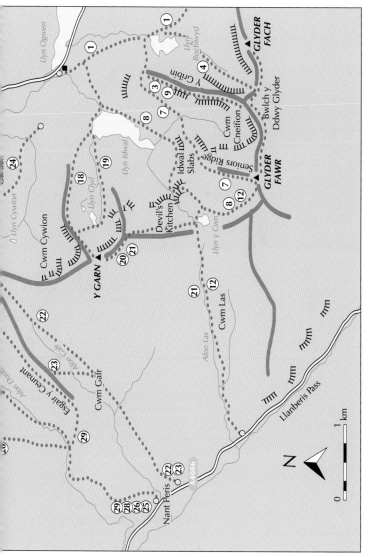

Y Garn

rambling cairn marks the junction with the main ridge just below the top. This is an airy rewarding route, with steep drops either side demanding care in snow and outstanding views of Cwm Clyd and Cwm Cywion.

Fisherman's Path (GL19)

The approach is similar to **GL18** except that this time you aim for the stony path above the true R bank of the stream that comes cascading down from unseen Llyn Clyd like a silver thread. However, the two routes could scarcely be more different in character. Where the ridge is breezy and open, this is intimate and secluded with no inkling until the very end of the hanging cwm and its twin delights – Llyn Clyd, where you can laze in the sun on heather-clad slabs, and its reedy acolyte nearby. Continuing N from the tarns gives you the NE ridge to finish as in **GL18**.

Devil's Kitchen/Cwm Las routes (GL20/21)

Take either **GL8** or **GL12** to Llyn y Cwn. Thereafter a massively wide path plods inexorably up the dull, stony slope to the edge at 634594 where the monotony is relieved for the

final 400ft by views of Llyn Idwal and beyond. It is much better, however, to avoid the path altogether and hug the edge right from the start. (For the record **GL20** is via the Devil's Kitchen, **GL21** via Cwm Las.)

Pen yr Ole Wen and the Carneddau from Y Garn (GL 18)

Foel Goch

The best of Foel Goch (Red Hill) is on its E side. Like Y Garn, dull grassy slopes make W approaches monotonous and many walkers avoid the hill altogether, a decision encouraged by the main ridge path which bypasses Foel Goch to the W. A far cry from the plunging arête that captivates the skyline ahead as you approach Ogwen from Capel Curig! The arête is Yr Esgair, the NW arm of Foel Goch and potentially one of the great ridge walks. Regretfully it is not to be. It starts attractively on grass that soon narrows to a fine scrambling edge. However, beyond a conspicuous notch where the angle really takes off, splintered flaky rock and crumbly turf banks, coupled with severe exposure immediately above the notch, render it out of bounds to mere scramblers.

The best route on Foel Goch is over the Creigiau Gleision/Mushroom Garden edge, and if this is combined with Cwm Cywion or another of the Glyders' NE cwms you are guaranteed a day full of fresh, dramatic scenery, well off the beaten track. The untidy pile of browny-red stones forming the summit cairn sits astride an airy promontory with calamitous drops into Cwm Bual and Cwm Coch. The fence that crosses the top leads sedately down to the ridge path, halfway to Y Garn.

Cwm Gafr route (GL22)

I include this route purely out of duty. It is easy and it gets you to the top safely, even in mist, but it is also deadly dull.

Start from Nant Peris at 608583 behind a cluster of houses set in an alcove. A lane leads to a group of white buildings before trending R up the hillside past a white cottage. Thereon the track plods above, but parallel to, the Afon Gafr for 2 miles of the bleakest, most featureless grassland you will find in many a long day. Even the gradient barely alters. After an eternity you meet a fence near the edge overlooking Nant Ffrancon that leads directly to the cairn.

Esgair y Ceunant route (GL23)

*More worthwhile than **GL22**, because it is higher with better views.*

Start with Cwm Gafr but pull up to the narrow finger of Esgair y Ceunant as soon as practical. Then, at about 620604, bear L onto a little-used path that slants across to Bwlch y Brecan. From here follow the ridge path to the foot of Foel Goch's shattered NW face where a steep zigzag up shaly screes leads to the top. Esgair y Ceunant can also be joined from Cwm Dudodyn (**GL23,1**) as described under Elidir Fawr (see below).

Criegiau Gleision/Mushroom Garden route (GL24)

I have never encountered another walker on this route.

Few walkers sample the E-facing cwms N of Y Garn and it is quite a surprise to find Criegiau Gleision (not to be confused with a peak of the same name in the Carneddau) sporting a shadowy little track.

Walk up the old road to the Yr Hafod hostel (644604), then follow a stream to the lip of the hanging valley above. This is Cwm Cywion (Cwm of the Chickens), a remote and sheltered hollow cradling the sparkling Llyn Cywion. One

Foel Goch across Llyn Ogwen

approach (**GL24,1**) is to climb above the lake on steepish grass to gain the col between Foel Goch and Y Garn at its apogee at 627603. You then follow the grooved ridge path to a stile where the path divides. The main track swings W of N, bypassing the summit; the lesser one follows a fence, due N, straight to the cairn.

For connoisseurs the more scenic option is to jump the stream as it emerges from a vegetated ravine and climb the long arm of the Mushroom Garden as it swoops down beside a tumbledown wall. A path, exiguous at first, trends W to the slender ridge of Creigiau Gleision proper. Speckled with flaky spikes of rock and soft tufts of bilberries, this is a wild gem, the land falling away sharply N in an intricate maze of gullies and fragile-looking pinnacles. Across Cwm Coch is the savage, dipping crest of Yr Esgair and its prominent notch. The ridge veers NW later to merge into the grassy nose culminating in Foel Goch from where, looking back, Creigiau Gleision rears as a fierce dark comb reminiscent of Cyfrwy near Cader Idris.

Elidir Fawr

Elidir Fawr is the odd man out of the Welsh 3000-footers – hard to fit into a short satisfying round. Without it the quest to capture all the 3000ft tops in a single day would be considerably easier! Above all Elidir is an elegant peak. To most viewers it displays a perfect cone; occasionally an undulating ridge (which it is); while to the blue ellipse of Llyn Marchlyn Mawr it reveals the crags of Craig Cwrwgl and the squattish Pillar in a scene as rugged as any in Snowdonia. The elongated summit ridge, forming a series of bouldery humps and hollows, culminates in a cairn and a windshelter. There are fine views of Anglesey, Snowdon, the Carneddau, and back to Y Garn and Foel Goch.

The best tramp on Elidir is along the ridge either side of Bwlch y Marchlyn, curving high above the lake, before breaking off to Mynydd Perfedd. S the mountain degenerates in vast steeps of grass and scree, with awkwardly scattered boulders that make walking a chore. N and W, where a shoulder falls away to a subsidiary top (Elidir Fach) the mountainside is ravaged beyond redemption by the slate works of Llanberis and Bethesda.

By comparison with this, the harnessing of Llyn Marchlyn Mawr for power generation is a masterpiece of sensitivity. While no one can pretend that the shoreline is the delectable spot it once was, a good job has been done of naturalising it as far as possible and the lake is still a lovely site when viewed on a sunny day from the edge almost 1000ft above.

Note Water falling from Llyn Marchlyn Mawr down to Llyn Peris in the valley below generates electricity; at off-peak times water is pumped back up to the higher lake which therefore acts as a power 'store'. In the course of this process Llyn Marchlyn Mawr's water level varies by up to 100ft.

Cwm Dudodyn route (GL25)

Leave the A4086 by a chapel just W of the Vaynol Arms and go down a lane, bearing first R then L, to a small white cottage at 606589. Pass through a gate L as directed by a footpath sign, but instead of carrying on to Fron break away R almost immediately uphill, past a barn, to a stile at the top of the field. Over the stile a path zigzags between banks of bracken and foxgloves whose quiet charm not even the massive spoil heaps can quite quell. Cross the Afon Dudodyn at a bridge with a single handrail.

The route follows the true R bank for about 1.5 miles when two choices present themselves:

- Scramble up loose scree L to Bwlch y Marchlyn – quick but rough (**GL25,1**)
- Or keep straight on up steep but easy grass to Bwlch y Brecan (longer but nicer).

Assuming the latter, follow the grooved ridge path round the vale head to Bwlch y Marchlyn (620615), where the track divides. Take the upper fork along the slender crest above the black, ribbed steeps that sweep down imposingly to the blue-green depths of Llyn Marchlyn Mawr. Sadly the path leaves the edge to cross a broad green saddle before wandering through a sea of boulders to the summit ridge.

SW approach direct (GL26)

Walkers in a hurry (perhaps attempting the grand slam of all 14 3000-footers) cannot afford the luxury of the leisurely and rather circuitous routing via Cwm Dudodyn. Their fate is to sweat straight up from the bridge at 608596. The best routing is almost due N, keeping the spoil heaps L and aiming for a stile at around 607602. This crosses the wall that straddles the hillside at roughly the 1600ft level. You should then slant diagonally across to the summit ridge. This route is also pretty hard in descent, especially after rain when the chaotically strewn boulders that litter the upper slopes are unpleasantly smooth and slippery.

A tortuous, energy-sapping grind.

> **Note** At all costs avoid the temptation to make a beeline direct from bridge to top (as I once did). The angle of attack is cruel and you are soon landed in an unholy jungle of screes and boulders.

Deiniolen route (GL27)

Park at the roadhead at 595631, go through the gate and march down the uninspiring reservoir road flanked by threadbare grass and building debris. Trend R as you near Llyn Marchlyn Bach and pull up the spur to Elidir Fach on cairned stony grass. Next head SE up easy screes to mount Elidir Fawr's main ridge. A path of sorts leads to the cairn, skirting just below the crest and thus avoiding what would otherwise be a laborious trek over large, bouldery humps each of which would persuade you it was the top. An alternative start (**GL27,1**) can be made from the end of a narrow quarry road at 595612 near Dinorwic. From here you can gain the spur by working round the side of the quarry workings.

Mynydd Perfedd

Mynydd Perfedd (Central Mountain) is unimpressive. Only a windshelter at the S tip of the spacious grassy saddle that stretches to Carnedd y Filiast 0.5 mile away N gives any inkling of a top. However there is plenty of good sport nearby, such as the stroll round the edge to Elidir Fawr above the blue shimmer of Llyn Marchlyn Mawr and the imposing Pillar that dominates its S shoreline. For a day with a difference you could always try exploring the lonely approaches through Cwm Perfedd and Cwm Bual. Wild gems, both of them, yet unaccountably neglected.

Cwm Dudodyn route (GL28)
Follow **GL25** to Bwlch y Brecan from where a short pull up easy grass, with a path to start you off, puts you on top.

Esgair y Ceunant route (GL29)
Follow **GL25** to the footbridge at 608596 but do not cross it. Instead steer N of E past two ruined barns and climb onto the ridge beside a wall. A blend of fledgling outcrops and rock moderates to grass by which time you should be looking out for a track L, beneath the crest, that sidles across to Bwlch y Brecan as in **GL23**.

Cwm Perfedd route (GL30)
No time to limber up today!

Leave the old road near Maes-caradoc at 635627. You are immersed at once in a gruelling uphill slog, keeping near the true L bank of the stream (but not so near as to get embroiled in the cleft). After crossing a wall trend SW into the piercing solitude of Cwm Perfedd, aiming for the head of the grassy tongue barring the way to Cwm Bual. Near the top a grey slaty track appears, all that remains of a packhorse trail that once linked Cwm Perfedd with Cwm Dudodyn. A small pinkish cairn marks the spot where this meets the main ridge path near Bwlch y Brecan. Mynydd Perfedd is then a short distance away R.

This whole region is more agreeable in descent (use **GL31** for the hard work) in which case it pays to stay on the tongue for a while. You can then decide which side takes your fancy to drop down to, provided you are careful not to leave it too late and get mixed up in the crags of Y Galan. A novel idea, if time permits, is to pick up a little track that curls round the tip of Yr Esgair into Cwm Coch. This leads into some very wild and remote country with striking views of the curious pinnacles of Creigiau Gleision and the vicious Yr Esgair ridge (**GL30,1**). A knee-jarring descent by a wall brings you down to the road by the footbridge at 638623. Once again you need to steer clear of the actual ravine, this time of Cwm Bual.

Carnedd y Filiast

'The Hill of the Lady Greyhound' is a melancholy place. Presiding over the N tip of the Glyders with heartwarming views (from Lleyn to Llandudno, Anglesey to the Carneddau and back over the Glyders) it ought to be a popular haunt. But the way-out position that makes it such an outstanding eyrie, coupled with the proximity of the largest slate quarries in the world, is too great a deterrent. So it is, instead, a haven of quiet, far removed in spirit from the bustle of its Glyder peers.

What visitors there are usually arrive across the crisp sheep-cropped saddle from Mynydd Perfedd. An easy, breezy walk with a splendid view of the smooth slabby cliff face that Carnedd y Filiast presents to Cwm Graianog. Near the same spot a stile over a wall ushers in the summit cap; a windshelter surrounded by a ramble of mossy boulders that are disconcertingly slippery when wet.

Of the three routes below, Cwm Graianog amply repays half a day of anyone's time; the others only if they fall into place as part of a longer round.

Cwm Graianog route (GL31)

Leave the old road near the elbow at 630637 and work your way across the marshy ground S of Cwm Ceunant, with crags L, to get onto the ridge almost directly above Tai-newyddion. Scraps of track gradually merge into a gritty path that takes a while to make up its mind, but eventually steers a heathery course between the grassy hollow of Cwm Ceunant R and boulder slopes containing Cwm Graianog L. Towards the top the latter coalesce into a wall of extraordinarily smooth, tilted, rocky slabs. These are clearly visible from the old road near Maes-caradoc. Easy angled, they are nevertheless out of bounds to walkers and even climbers are set a few problems as holds and belays are few and far between. Above the slabs a scree and bilberry slope goes straight to the top.

Deiniolen route (GL32)

Best used for a circuit of Llyn Marchlyn Mawr from Deiniolen (**GL H3**).

Walk down the reservoir road from 595631 as in **GL27.** Pause to admire Llyn Marchlyn Mawr and then, depending on your stamina, it is simply a matter of choosing where to cross some marshy ground before scrambling up to the NE ridge, dodging outcrops en route.

NE ridge (GL33)

A descent that is desolate and unutterably sad and, unless you love quarrying as well as hills, pointless.

In bygone times, long before the age of slate quarries, this must have been an enjoyable walk, facing the sea and the setting sun. The ridge starts NW before veering E of N in a gentle decline that enters the quarry works near the Glyders' last buttresses around 623644. Quarry roads then lead to the A5 by the layby at Ogwen Bank (627654).

Tryfan

Anyone not moved by Tryfan is unlikely to be inspired by any mountain. Of all the Welsh peaks it is the most brashly spectacular. Nothing prepares you for the colossal triangle of rock that leaps so dramatically into view on the road from Capel Curig to Ogwen. Narrow crested, unremittingly steep, isolated, generously garlanded in heather and bilberries, it is a scrambler's paradise to its very roots. Most striking of all is the E face, a massive edifice of precipitous rock, buttressed with frowning gullies that soar to a triple top. The W face is only marginally less steep; it rises from the placid Llyn Bochlwyd, over grassy steeps and scattered islands of rock, before merging into the topmost rocky crown.

The usual lines of ascent follow the N and S ridges. There is no better scramble than the N ridge, a long succession of rocky steps, shelves and giant boulders where the use of hands is obligatory. The S ridge is shorter and easier but no less rewarding. The W face is unfashionable, but if you can survive the early grind there is again an excellent scrambling finale. Curiously, for such a bastion of power, it is the E face that offers one of the easiest approaches – along a shelf known as the Heather Terrace that slants diagonally across it and is easily distinguishable from the road.

Of the three tops the one in the middle is the main top, the highest; a boulder-strewn platform where two famous monoliths called Adam and Eve (often mistaken for climbers by viewers in the valley below) stand in for the customary cairn. The spikier N top, 5min away across the scree gully that rends the W face, is the smallest and most rugged of the three tops. Airy and free of crowds, it is the most 'Tryfan-like' in character. The S top is flat and slabby beneath a tiny wall that can cause a minor problem for ordinary pedestrians. Finally, nearly 300ft below across a much-trodden col, is the far S top, a rocky eminence with a tiny tarn that from some viewpoints looks like a Tryfan in embryo.

Despite being overtopped by Pen yr Ole Wen and Glyder Fach, Tryfan is a first-class viewpoint, as befits a peak that rises over 2000ft from the road in under 0.5 mile. To the N the Carneddau stretch from the scarped slopes of Nant Ffrancon to the bald top of Pen Llithrig-y-wrach, leading the eye SE to the elephantine sprawl of Gallt yr Ogof and the lone elegance of Moel Siabod. SW are the threateningly sharp, even weird battlements of the Glyders beyond which a discerning eye can just catch a glimpse of Snowdon. Finest of all is the nexus of little-known cwms and hills to the W: the two arms of Y Garn, shy Cwm Cywion, Creigiau Gleision and the Mushroom Garden, the spiky arete of Yr Esgair falling away from Foel Goch, the slow curve of Elidir Fawr, and far-off Carnedd y Filiast. On a bright day you will be doubly blessed with the mosaic of greys, greens and mauves leavened by the glint of sunlight on the clear waters of Ogwen, Idwal and Bochlwyd.

Provided you stick to established routes Tryfan is safe in mist. The main paths are so well worn and nail-scratched that, with care, it is difficult to stray. In snow and ice, however, it is a different proposition and Tryfan should then be left to specialists who possess ice axes and crampons and know how to use them. In short, though Tryfan can be ruthless to the unwary, you have only to treat it with respect to be rewarded handsomely, time and time again!

Tryfan from the east in winter

Note The six routes on Tryfan described below start from one of four different points along the A5: Ogwen cottage for **GL36/37**, the car park towards the E end of the lake at the bend in the road at 660603 for **GL38**, the car park below Milestone Buttress at 664603 for **GL34**, and Gwern Gof Uchaf Farm for **GL35/39**. These are the most convenient starting points but it will be clear from the map that other permutations are possible given a bit of simple cross-country work. In particular I refer in the text to starting the Heather Terrace from Milestone Buttress and N ridge from the farm. To add to the variety, there are at least three other potential starting places: a stile on the A5 near the W tip of Llyn Ogwen, a layby at 656603 and a stile at 668606 opposite Glan Dena. The latter is especially useful once you know Tryfan well as you can pull up the slopes for N ridge, or follow a faint path round the E brow of the nose to reach the Heather Terrace, or follow a farm track to Gwern Gof Uchaf for Cwm Tryfan.

N ridge (GL34)

The N ridge is never exposed, yet 'nearly' exposed often enough to maintain challenge and excitement. You are always on rock but never far from restful cushions of heather. Surrounded by Tryfan's massive architecture there is never a dull moment in this scrambler's Valhalla.

Nature has excelled; this ridge is a hillwalker's dream.

Start from the car park at 664603 near the foot of Milestone Buttress. Walk up the man-made stairway across the stile, keeping near a wall R. After 5min bear L at a large cairn (straight ahead is for climbers intent on the buttress) and thread your way up a chaotic downfall of boulders in the shadow of a cliff. A heathery hiatus at 665600 invites the first rest, with views over Ogwen and the N Glyders. Continuing E from here would bring you to the Heather Terrace. However today's route is N, up a waste of boulders and scree. There is little to choose between a myriad of tracks; after a little easy scrambling they all seem to meet up on a cosy little terrace with a large cairn, another good resting place!

The main line of attack is now established, and you have only to follow the scratch marks on the rocks and their rounded polished edges to stay on course. A short scramble leads to a tilted shelf distinguished by outcrops of dazzling white quartz. Over to the R is the famous Cannon Rock (easily spotted from the road) with Y Garn and Foel Goch gloriously portrayed

Looking from Tryfan N ridge across to Y Garn (photo Steve Lewis)

beyond. The track meanwhile meanders over heathery, boulder-studded slopes to another shelf where Llyn Bochlwyd comes into sight for the first time and a soaring wall of gigantic boulders bars the way ahead. They may look formidable but experienced scramblers should have no trouble in shinning straight up, provided there is no snow about (**GL34,1**).

For something less taxing follow a cairned trail that twists round to the E. and descends briefly before regaining its composure to cross a gully. Leave it here and climb the gully R with a spell of easy foot and hand work. The top of the gully is the 'notch', just N of the N top, which is clearly visible from the road below and is where clambering directly up the rock wall would have brought you to.

More scrambling, high up on the W face, leads to a hollow separating the N top L from the main top R. There are easy scrambles up to each with the latter crossing over the W face gully route.

Stepping over the gully and staying with the path would bring you to a shallow cleft between the S top and main top, high above the E buttress, with an obvious finish for either.

Y Garn and Llyn Ogwen from Tryfan's N ridge

Heather Terrace/S ridge (GL35)

An easier route to
the top.

It is strange that such a manly giant as Tryfan should surrender itself so tamely to a thrust across its fearsome E face. Strange but fortunate, for how else but along the friendly Heather Terrace would the first-time walker not yet confident enough to take on the N ridge (or the family party with young children) get to enjoy this most exciting of Welsh mountains?

Park near the entrance to Gwern Gof Uchaf Farm. Follow a well-worn track that skirts the farm R before crossing a stile and making for open country in front of some smooth, tilted slabs known as Little Tryfan (a nursery for young climbers). The next objective, across a splash of bog, is the ribbon of white scree that scars Tryfan's otherwise inviolate ramparts. It is laboriously steep and loose but a newer path avoids the worst (until it too suffers the same fate) by arcing round to the L.

Up the slope a jot more and you would be on the N ridge. Otherwise join the ledge L as it climbs aloft through boulders lavishly dressed in heather and bilberry. Below, the mottled-green loneliness of Cwm Tryfan; above, buttresses and gullies speckled with climbers' reds and blues and an occasional glimpse of the wild goats that frequent these lofty heights.

Before long the angle abates and the terrace divides into two paths. Both trend W to a wall with two stiles that crosses the col separating the S and far S peaks. The lower path toils unadventurously up scree, while the higher gives a short but airy romp over the terminal boulders of the S ridge.

Heather Terrace is over; now for the S ridge. Scramblers looking for a challenge can take it head on, climbing virtually due N over huge blue-grey slabs of scabrous rock. Most folk will cross the wall and continue round the bend for 50, maybe 100yd, until a line of cairns reveals a more conventional scramble to the miniscule col separating the main and S tops.

Coming down is a bit more difficult. Starting off on 230° puts you on the cairned track just described, but staying on it is quite another story. In over 20 descents I doubt if I have ever followed the same line twice! I descended the S ridge twice in three days in July 1988. On the first occasion I reached the col in no time at all, calm and collected; two days later, using the 'same' route, I was stepping gingerly over yawning crevices, ensnared by awkward boulders, trapped by tiny cliffs just too high for comfort and forced to slide down shiny rock. It is magnificent scrambling nonetheless, and great fun!

Bochlwyd/S ridge (GL36)

Follow a band of scree falling away W from the col separating the S and far S peaks. It aims for the N tip of Bochlwyd and soon merges into a wet, squelchy path beside a stream before eventually passing between two little outcrops to join the miners' track about 100yd short of the lake's N shoreline. Halfway down you may notice a track creeping away E of N. This gives an alternative lead into the W face route.

A quick way down when time is of the essence.

Miners' Track/S ridge (GL37)

Follow **GL1** to Bwlch Tryfan. Do not cross the stiles; instead follow a well-used stony track heading N. This climbs a rocky knoll and then stays W of the wall before rising to the S col to finish as in **GL35**. Find time, if you can, to visit the far S peak to see the little tarn that lies cupped in its summit rocks.

West face (GL38)

On a grey, drizzly Ogwen morning the sight of the pink scree trail struggling painfully up the mountainside so very far above is as daunting as any I know. From the parking area at 660603 cross the stile, climb the steps and then make a beeline S for the stony path that curves round to the W of the knuckle known as Brag Rocks. (Do not stray L to the stone shoot that fills the gap between these rocks and Tryfan proper.) The best ways I know to survive the tumble of loose, wet bouldery debris that lies in wait are to enlist a congenial companion, or to concentrate on some knotty philosophical problem (or both!). The gradient relents when you at last cross a broad grassy saddle. But beware – this idyllic interlude is shortlived. The agony returns with unabated fury when the trail merges into the prominent scree shoot that culminates in the cleft between the N and main tops.

The first hour is a brute; slow starters should look elsewhere!

Now for the good news – at least for experienced hill-walkers. As you cross the grassy saddle look out for a faint path that breaks away to skirt the edge R, high above Bochlwyd. Stay with this until it embeds itself in the rock face at about 662594, then scramble up boulders W (**GL38,1**). A scattering

View across the Gwyder forest to the Glyders (photo Steve Lewis)

of cairns looks reassuring, but there is no established path. It is very much a matter of trial and error in a setting of heathery thickets, fresh rock-bound pools and little rock walls reminiscent of the N ridge at its best (with the added zest that comes from novelty and isolation). Trend L and you should come close to a bull's-eye on Adam and Eve; stray too far R and you will probably join one of the S ridge paths.

You can also reach the grassy saddle from Bochlwyd by following **GL36** until you can exploit a gap in the crags (**GL38,2**).

Cwm Tryfan/S ridge (GL39)

This lonely cwm has the freshness and serenity Tryfan is so often denied.

Cwm Tryfan lacks nothing in grandeur, cupped between the terraced outcrops of Braich y Ddeugwm and Tryfan's kingly spires. Nowhere is the triple crown more splendidly revealed, and when a powdering of snow dusts the tops the effect is truly magical.

Start along **GL35** (the Heather Terrace route) but break away S, keeping little Tryfan on your L, until you meet the wire fence that straddles the fells from W to E. At least five stiles cross this fence. The one you want is the highest, a new ladder-stile at 671599, so plod up alongside the fence to the crest and then cross over. The path appears at once, white and stony, keeping well to the W of the stream and heading for drier ground.

The shortest 'route' (**GL39,1**) is to grunt and groan up scree to the col below the S ridge. Feasible, but trackless and definitely not recommended. It is much better to imbibe the wild flavour of the cwm for as long as you can by staying with it until you meet the miners' track at 666584 (**GL39,2**). Best of all – a compromise – is to look out for a sketchy path that wends away R where the track crosses the stream at 667588. This swathes through rampant heather to Bwlch Tryfan and **GL37**.

High-level Walks

The lie of the land – a long curving ridge with an abundance of ridges and cwms – gives an embarrassment of riches for planning high-level walks in the Glyders. Little description is necessary, however, as once the routes for ascent and descent have been decided it is simply a matter of progressing along the main ridge.

N-based horseshoes (GL H1)

Most walkers will want to concentrate on the Glyders' central core, at least initially. Even then there are at least seven lines of attack: Y Garn, the Devil's Kitchen, Seniors Ridge, Y Gribin, the miners' track, Tryfan/Bristly Ridge and Cwm Tryfan. A minimum of road work is involved because (apart from Tryfan) all the walks can be started from Ogwen, and even the inclusion of Tryfan only leaves you with a longish mile. It is simply a matter of permuting any two from the seven possibilities.

Slightly off-centre you can combine Tryfan with a return down Braich y Ddeugwm. In the N half of the range you can construct an away-day by pairing any two of the Graianog route, Cwm Perfedd, Cwm Bual, Cwm Cywion, the Devil's Kitchen and the Y Garn ridges. Use the old road to regain base.

S-based horseshoes (GL H2)

The best two horseshoes from the S are miners' track/red route, and Cwm Las/Esgair y Ceunant ridge.

Marchlyn Mawr circular (GL H3)

Good for an odd half-day.

It is a combination of **GL27** and **GL32** based on Deiniolen, linked by a rousing high-level tramp along the edge high above the lake. The regular path from Elidir Fawr to Y Garn leaves the edge at Bwlch y Marchlyn, so break away L over Mynydd Perfedd to enjoy the best views.

Glyder ridge traverse (GL H4)

This classic is sufficiently outlined in the Glyders introduction.

You can either start on **GL31** with a side-trip to capture Elidir Fawr, or begin at Deiniolen on **GL27** and backtrack to capture Carnedd y Filiast and Mynydd Perfedd. Thereafter keep to the Glyders' spine until you finally drop down to Capel Curig on **GL17**.

Lower-level Walks/Easier Days

A glance at the map demonstrates all too clearly that easier days and the Glyders are not the most congenial of bedfellows. All I can do is indicate a few simple walks where you can capture the essence of the Glyders with minimal effort. As for lower-level walks, they seem to be squeezed out altogether. I could suggest the miners' track (either crossing the range or a there-and-back jaunt), climbing the Devil's Kitchen, walking the round of the arms of Y Garn including Llyn Clyd, or heading up scenic Braich y Ddeugwm. These are all walks that keep well below the tops, yet they also exceed 2000ft so to style them 'lower-level' seems a bit like cheating! I shall therefore stick to the 'easier days'.

Llyn Idwal (GL L1)

A wander round Llyn Idwal hardly raises a sweat.

You can savour more of the wild in an hour round Idwal than in a day in most other places. The famous Slabs, the Devil's Kitchen, Y Garn, Pen yr Ole Wen closing behind you, the all-pervading presence of the higher Glyders – what more could you wish for? There is a paved track from Ogwen and you can stroll right round the lake.

Llyn Bochlwyd (GL L2)

Much the same could be said for Bochlwyd, although reaching it is not so easy and you are likely to get wet feet if you attempt a circumnavigation. However the atmosphere lacks nothing by comparison for, if being cupped between Y Gribin and Tryfan were not enough, you also face the towering spires of Glyder Fach and Castell y Gwynt.

Inspiring and awesome.

Cwm Tryfan (GL L3)

Cwm Tryfan is rarely visited, but is full of charm and character with thrilling close-ups of Tryfan's E battlements. The ground dips and twists in a complex of heathery knolls and peaty pools. The soft murmur of the stream is the ideal lunchtime companion.

The old road (GL L4)

A walk along a road? Yes, but no ordinary road. Opened in 1805 to link London and Holyhead, the section from Capel Curig to Ogwen is now green and quiet, free of traffic, while still managing to nudge the toes of the hills. Beyond Ogwen it remains drivable – in theory – but so few people try it that here, once again, it makes a pleasant walk and a good aperitif to the N cwms.

THE HIRNANTS

OS map 1:50,000 – Sheet 125

Peaks (by height)	Height (ft)	Map Ref	Page
Cyrniau Nod	2185	988279	86
Foel Cwm Sian Llwyd	2125	996314	91
Pen y Boncyn Trefeilw	2119	963283	90
Stac Rhos	2066	969278	90
Foel y Geifr	2053	937275	84
Moel y Cerrig Duon	2050	923241	92
Cefn Gwyntog	2017	976266	89
Trum y Gwrgedd	2008	942284	84
Foel Goch	2001	943292	84
Foel Figenau	1910	916285	93
Mountain Lake			
Y Mynydd	1500	008252	

THE HIRNANTS

The Hirnants are a compact little range squeezed between the more expansive Berwyns – from which they are separated by the B4391 – and Lake Bala. They are heavily afforested and all but one of their nine tops lies within a 2.5-mile radius of the centre of Penllyn Forest. The exception is Moel y Cerrig Duon, an isolated moorland hump near Bwlch y Groes, which is more akin to the spongy tops of the E Arans than its Hirnant counterparts.

The main group of hills rises either side of Cwm Hirnant, a tight, narrow valley fringed in its lower reaches with pastures whose rustic charm not even the invasive man-made forests can dim. Up-valley a cascading brook is a happy foil to soaring slopes garlanded with heather and gorse. Over the top and down to Lake Vyrnwy there is a warmer glow, with bracken and tangled woodlands sloping down to the water's edge below impressive crag-hung steeps.

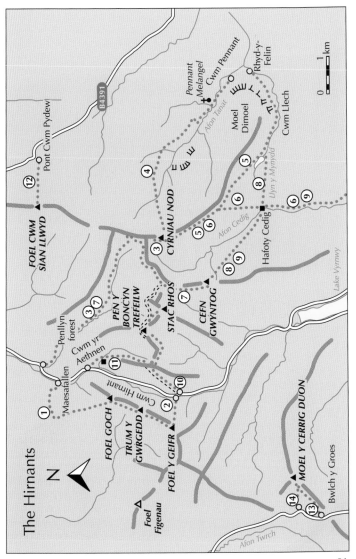

The Hirnants

N

81

The Hirnants across Lake Vyrnwy

Three of the tops – Foel Goch, Trum y Gwrgedd and Foel y Geifr – lie abreast the short, slender ridge that bounds Cwm Hirnant W. Cushioned with bouncy tussocks of heather and mosses and soft beds of bilberries, they reveal an expansive landscape of empty hillocks and lonely woods framed by the whale-backed Berwyns and dominated by the black, piercing splendour of the Arans.

Across the cwm the remaining hills arc the fringe of Penllyn Forest. These are more of an acquired taste. Pen y Boncyn Trefeilw and Stac Rhos are unassuming to the point of oblivion. Set in a vast tract of scrappy, boggy moorland, and virtually unmarked, careful map-reading is needed to identify their respective humps. Cyrniau Nod (the reigning peak of the group) and Cefn Gwyntog are both more colourful and more difficult. They are perched on shallow undulating ridges that oversee a squelchy, ankle-twisting wilderness of lonely fells that rarely succumbs to the walker's tread.

There used to be a time when these E Hirnants were virtually terra incognita, thanks to the daunting nature of the terrain. All that changed a few years ago when the local farmer bulldozed a path across the hillside from the head of the cwm to link up with one of the forest trails. This makes it much easier to get within striking distance of the tops. Masochists, tussock-hopping specialists and lovers of the wildest of the wild are still catered for, however, with a variety of old-style 'sporting' approaches from Cwm Pennant (a truly lovely valley in its secluded innocence) and the shores of Lake Vyrnwy.

A typical Hirnants scene taken near Cwm Pennant

That leaves Foel Cwm Sian Llwyd, aloof and alone. This hill lords it on the W sky-line as you cross the moors from Llangynog to Bala, and with the onset of late summer it is lavishly carpeted in a mantle of purple. Surrounded by virgin moors it is best approached direct from the road. There are no handy trails to relieve the toil this time!

The Hirnants are not popular hills, but for the occasional day with a difference, or when the lure of giants temporarily palls, they have a freshness – and a few surprises – that makes them worthy companions.

Foel Goch / Trum y Gwrgedd /
Foel y Geifr

These three moorland tops crown the short but striking ridge that forms Cwm Hirnant's W arm and it makes an enjoyable half-day – or at most a very easy full day – to visit them all. The sense of isolation on these modest, unspoilt little hills needs to be experienced to be believed. It is hard to credit that the bustle of Bala is less than 5 miles away. The E slopes are either steep, or covered in man-made forest, or both. Approaches from the W are possible but take you too far away from the main hub to be of interest. The usual approaches are therefore onto the N and S ends of the ridge.

The view from the summit of Foel Goch has an air of other-worldliness, with the dauntingly rugged face of the Arans as a centrepiece.

Maesafallen route (HN1)

The farm that gives this route its name lies at 948309 in a narrow break in the otherwise all-embracing woods. After passing through the farmyard follow a path that trends first R then L beneath an overhang of trees, gradually climbing the lightly wooded slope to reveal the verdant loveliness of the cwm. After crossing a forest trail the path fades and you must veer L for the corner of the woods at 939308. Next follow the boundary fence, preferably moving up-slope for the better views. The fence keeps well to the W of the highest ground so as soon as you have left the woods behind you must break away L across trackless tussocks for the twin summit humps of Foel Goch.

The view from the top is stupendous. Across a glint of Lake Bala are the Arenigs, while to the E more decapitated hills fringe Penllyn Forest, leaving the Berwyns leaning against the skyline. Yet the abiding impression is not of this peak or that, but of wild elemental isolation on a heroic scale. The gaze runs for miles across scattered woodland and green, crested hillocks, waves of purple heather and golden, peat-hagged moors. There are no roads or habitations; you are alone with wind and sky and a landscape where silence reigns supreme.

Dropping down S from the second hump, a vigilant eye may spot the cairn – a collapsed pile of stones slightly to the R. At the same time the tedium of the tussocks is relieved by the faint shadow of a Land Rover trail. Happily this carries on all the way to Foel y Geifr. It accompanies the fence for the most part, but to enjoy the views you will want to deviate either side. The beds of bilberries atop the W slopes are the softest and most luscious you will find in many a long day!

The Foel y Geifr ridge and Cwm Hirnant

The second top, Trum y Gwrgedd, has no cairn and could easily go unnoticed; until, that is, you glance back. Not so Foel y Geifr, the highest of the three with its trig point mounted on a platform of rock which you will miss in mist, if you rely on the fence, as it swings W just before the top.

E approach (HN2)

The easiest way to gain the ridge is from the top of the pass at 946274 where the ability to park at nearly 1600ft gives you a flying start. The Land Rover trail mentioned in **HN1** is clearly in view across a boggy depression and leads unerringly to the ridge N of the trig point. It is not too easy to spot from above, but that scarcely matters in a hillside totally lacking in venom.

Purists who like to claim their peaks direct and unde-filed, without crossing other tops en route, will doubtless discern the trace of a grassy shelf trending diagonally across the hillside towards Trum y Gwrgedd. This stops short of the actual top but if you think Trum y Gwrgedd merits such respect, then that is your way (**HN2,1**).

Cyrniau Nod

Cyrniau Nod is the highest of the Hirnants and, apart from the even more remote top of Cefn Gwyntog, the least accessible. Its small cairn, sprouting two wooden poles, is just visible from the Penllyn Forest road (and vice versa). Otherwise the view from its shallow, rambling crest of crisp heather is one of unbridled wildness and desolation, despite far-off friends in the guise of Arans, Arenigs and Berwyns. Only the softer greens of Cwm Pennant and a tantalising glimpse of Lake Vyrnwy intrude upon the monumental seclusion and silence of this lonely peak.

The simplest approach is from the Penllyn Forest road, but keen walkers have a variety of routes from the S to choose from. However these S approaches – from Cwm Pennant, Llyn y Mynydd, and the Afon Cedig – should not be taken lightly. Lovers of wild moorland scenery, seeking untrodden ways and guaranteed solitude, are well catered for. But a price has to be paid, and that price is some exceedingly rough going with knee-deep heather, bogs, occasional potholes and next to nothing in the way of tracks to sustain morale. Lone walkers should also remember the perils of going it alone; help would be a long way off.

Having said that, if you accept this unyielding terrain for what it is, you will find the experience wonderfully rewarding (and, I suspect, a trifle infectious!). A good idea is to combine the Llyn y Mynydd and Cwm Pennant routes in a horseshoe, taking in first Cefn Gwyntog and then Cyrniau Nod.

Penllyn Forest route (HN3)

The simplest, most straightforward forest walk imaginable (though not, perhaps, the most interesting).

Forest routes I do not know tend to worry me. Due to recent fellings or plantings the map may not be up to date. With the smaller 1:50,000 scale maps it is even worse as there is insufficient room to show everything, and you sometimes come across trails where it is total guesswork as to whether they are marked or not. In short it is easy to go astray, and when you do it is invariably a most frustrating experience with restricted views and trails that seem to circle round interminably without ever getting anywhere. You may even be tempted to make a beeline through the woods, though that is an error you are unlikely to make more than once!

Happily this route has none of those problems. It gets you to the tops with a minimum of the tiresome heather-slogging for which the Hirnants are renowned.

The trail starts at 953312; wide, plain and deadly dull apart from a vivacious stream that tries to atone with a display of tumbling falls. Keep L where the trail splits at 957308 and R where it divides again at 979293 with clumps of heather now brightening the scene. A gate heralds the forest boundary and a bulldozed road. It must be the ugliest such gash in Wales, wide enough for the motor racing that is occasionally staged there and so heavily banked with its own debris that you need to climb up the side to see the views!

When you can see them, both the Arans and the Arenigs look very imposing. Dduallt stands out well, as does the wedge-shaped Manod Mawr on a clear day. W are the Berwyns with Cwm Pennant glowing in the foreground; N the forest itself and the sumptuous heather dome of Foel Cwm Sian Llwyd, S a silence of rolling foothills and moors stretches as far as the eye can see.

Time to get back to work! It is not easy to claim these Hirnant scalps. The problem is that with so few distinguishing features one 'ridge' tends to look much like another. The only answer is good compass and mapwork. Cyrniau Nod is not too bad; you can see the pole marking its N top at 989290 as you emerge from the forest. For the main top stay on the bulldozed road until it momentarily swings S and then strike out S across the moor. It is funny country. One minute short-cropped heather, dry and firm; the next, huge heathery mounds, peat hags, squirmy moss and deep black pools. Even the occasional pasture appears! Fortunately the cairn is soon in sight with the last stage an easy walk beside a fence.

Cefn Gwyntog (**HN7**) can be captured in similar style. Stay with the road for another mile of twists and bends, check your ridge and then it's another –longer and tougher – stomp across trackless, tangled heather and peat hags. You could also go on to capture Stac Rhos and Pen y Boncyn Trefeilw, though a more direct routing for them is from the valley head at 946274 (see **HN10**).

Cwm Pennant route (HN4)

Parking is difficult in Cwm Pennant, though not impossible.

Stroll down the road, past the tiny church at Pennant Melangel at 024265 until, just before a gate across the road bars further access, a yellow waymark sign directs you across the fields R and a faint track takes you across the hillside to avoid the homestead further up the vale. Where it makes a sharp L turn (clearly waymarked) to return to the streambed and the tourist path to the falls at Blaen y Cwm, stay with a green drover's path that glides sweetly across the hillside to give magnificent views of the falls (which, for my money, are every bit as impressive as the justly famous Pistyll Rhaeadr in the Berwyns). The path fades above the falls and then some really hard work begins with a long toilsome plod across the fells on 270°.

The Cwm Pennant falls

Note I said 'stroll' above deliberately because Cwm Pennant, with its timeless charm, is made for dawdling. Every step is a joy. Even without the craggy eminence of Moel Dimoel and the silver sparkle of the falls cleaving the tree-clad slopes ahead, it is still a good place to be with its soft wooded pastures and air of innocence.

Llyn y Mynydd route (HN5)

The mountain road up to the lake from Rhyd-y-felin at 032254 ensures an easy start. An atmospheric start, too, with the road clinging adventurously to the steeps high above Cwm Llech and the chatter of the stream echoing plaintively through the forest below. Unfortunately the lake is a bit of a let-down, dull and rectangular, languishing in a prairie of bleak, open grassland. From its N shore a dampish trudge on 320° gives you Cyrniau Nod's SE ridge at Trum y Fawnog with a 1.5-mile gentle uphill plod still to come.

Afon Cedig route (HN6)

You can also gain the SE ridge from Lake Vyrnwy. Start from the lakeside at 998214 and follow the forest trail along the Afon Cedig's true R bank until it terminates across the bridge by the farm buildings at Hafoty Cedig. Cut across country on 20°.

Cefn Gwyntog

Cefn Gwyntog is a long, undulating ridge of virgin moors and dripping peat hags, enlivened by a scattering of tiny black pools. It is utterly featureless except for the two upright stone tablets that constitute the cairn and which somehow epitomise the immense solitude of this lonely top. Not even sheep come here.

Its capture poses quite a challenge. Even from the nearby forest road you are in for a good 30min grind while (see Cyrniau Nod above) the more 'sporting' routes from the S are only for experienced walkers who know what to expect and relish the challenge.

Penllyn Forest route (HN7)

See **HN3**.

Llyn y Mynydd route (HN8)

This route includes one of the most testing stretches of walking in Wales.

Take **HN5** to the lake. Next press on slightly N of W across desolate grassland to cross the Afon Cedig by the bridge at Hafoty Cedig (996250). A damp walk, but not exceptionally rough. A keen eye will even be able to detect the odd straggle of a path here and there.

However, once across the Cedig it's a different story. Continue up-valley a few moments until you come to a stream tumbling down from the W at 993253. Then set a bearing of 310° (for a bull's-eye on the tiny cairn) and grit your teeth. The next stretch may test your stamina, but it's beautiful too, in an undefiled wilderness where cushions of springy heather and soft mossy banks reign supreme. These provide the ideal bed for resting weary legs and admiring an endless panorama of windswept hill and fell.

You will jolt over tussocks, avoid potholes, seek out the odd stretch of innocent grass for blessed relief as crest follows crest. Then out of the blue a pair of upright poles appear carrying what look like the remains of a couple of small wooden containers, letterboxes (as on Dartmoor) perhaps? At least it proves someone has been here before you! The good news is that the final crest is now in sight, the heather less prolific, and you will soon spy the tiny cairn astride the skyline.

Afon Cedig route (HN9)

This is simply a combination of **HN6** to Hafoty Cedig and **HN8** thereafter.

Pen y Boncyn Trefeilw / Stac Rhos

These near-twins must be among the least charismatic of all the Welsh hills. Both are easily gained from the bulldozed road skirting the S fringe of Penllyn Forest. Both are broad rounded tops, artificially divided by a fence; bog and heather one side, rough pasture the other. The only difference is that whereas Pen y Boncyn Trefeilw is marked by a standing stone and what looks like the remains of a half-completed cairn, Stac Rhos is bare.

SW ridge (HN10)

This simple ascent starts from the head of Cwm Hirnant and follows the bulldozed track that leaves the road at 946274. This was blazed recently by the local farmer to facilitate reclamation experiments on the higher ground; hence the 'summit' pastures mentioned above. Apart from the noise of occasional motor racing it's a pretty uneventful walk, the main challenge being to identify the actual top. To do this note where the road swings in towards the forest, almost entering it before making a U-turn away again. At the bend of the U strike out S and in minutes the top is yours. For Stac Rhos stay with the track for a further short mile until it executes another U-turn. Then it's the same manoeuvre as before.

A bulldozed track makes mincemeat of what used to be a purgatory of deep uneven heather and bog.

Cwm yr Aethnen route (HN11)

Follow **HN10** in reverse, but switch to a secondary track that breaks away R at 954281. When this peters out keep going in the same direction, through a gate, then down glossy, grassy slopes to a tumbledown shepherd's house at 955296 from where a green path carries on to the road.

A quick way back to Cwm Hirnant.

Foel Cwm Sian Llwyd

No one who has seen Foel Cwm Sian Llwyd in high summer with the heather in bloom is ever likely to forget it. The entire hill is a picture, a glorious tapestry of pinks and purples, nodding sedately in the breeze. A solace for troubled minds, a scene to feast upon, a hill to admire but not a hill to climb; at least, not often! The heather that is so lovely to gaze upon is a harsh opponent, deep and tussocky, boggy and squirmy, not above hiding the odd pothole and quite intolerant of tracks. Its nearest companion, Cyrniau Nod, is nearly 3 tortuous miles away.

The summit is a straggly plateau sporting both a trig point and, at its N tip, the remains of a shepherd's hut. In between lies a sprinkling of dark peaty pools, bog mosses and coppery-red grasses. It is an excellent vantage point for both the Berwyns and the neighbouring Hirnants, with distant views of Arenig Fawr and Foel Goch prominent N.

B4391 approach (HN12)

Start from the derelict shelter at 009316, just N of the kink in the road. You can park there and a tiny track starts you off. It quickly merges into a grooved track (or is it a stream?) and gets you, maybe, halfway up before suddenly expiring. Then you are on your own and a beeline is as good as anything. A strong walker could do the return trip in little over an hour.

You could leave the road almost anywhere, but there is a lot to be said for making the agony as brief as possible.

Moel y Cerrig Duon

This little hill has a special significance for me because it was while I was climbing it, one frosty morning in December 1984, that I decided to write this book (although it was not until February 1986 that I first put pen to paper and started on the Rhinogs!).

It is a simple peak, a plain grassy mound, remote from its fellows but ideal when all you want is a quick blow after a day spent waiting for the sky to clear, or perhaps a quick farewell tramp on the way home. An hour should be enough, 1.5hr plenty. At that level it offers ample reward.

Bwlch y Groes route (HN13)

Cross the road from the parking area at 912233 and climb up a black marshy track beside a fence on a bearing of 60°. Moel y Cerrig Duon is not visible from the bwlch but soon comes into view L, just before you come to a junction of fences near a radio mast. Bear L here and let the new fence lead you directly to the top.

The neat stony cairn gazes down over a vast area of billowy moorland encompassing the main Hirnant range to the N, a tantalising glimpse of Lake Vyrnwy, the Arans at their awesome best, the Arenigs and, last but not least, the dramatic gash of the Afon Dyfi where a succession of ferocious cliffs and crags seem to all but envelop the tiny hamlet of Llanymawddwy.

W approach (HN14)

Leave the road at 915239 where it swings L in a dip as it crosses a stream. An intermittent path shadows the true R bank of the stream. Follow it while it is still useful and then make a beeline for the top.

High-level Walks

W ridge (HN H1)

Climb Foel Goch from Maesafallen (**HN1**), walk the ridge to Foel y Geifr, drop down to the valley head on **HN2**, then return along the road. It's a quiet road with plenty of atmosphere to soak up so there is no need to be put off. You could extend the day by diverting to Foel Figenau, the beautifully rounded hill that captivates the eye so forcibly from the N Arans.

A longish half-day should suffice for what, despite some road work at the end, is a very rewarding hike.

Cwm Hirnant horseshoe (HN H2)

Start as in **HN H1**, but this time when you hit the road at 946274 gird your loins for another bit of ascent and climb Pen y Boncyn Trefeilw on **HN10**. You then have a choice:

- Backtrack a little to regain the valley via Cwm yr Aethnen (**HN11**); or

If the weather is fine it would be a pity not to do a little more by combining the W ridge with some of the E tops.

Pen y Boncyn Trefeilw from the north (HN H2 and HN H3)

- Continue round the forest road on **HN3**. You can then peel off to capture as many of Stac Rhos, Cefn Gwyntog or Cyrniau Nod as time and energy permit.

Penllyn Forest walk (HN H3)

The title is a misnomer because for much of the time you are well above the 2000ft level, skirting round the forest's S perimeter with every opportunity, as in **HN H2**, to claim up to four scalps. It is essentially a combination of **HN3** and **HN11** using the bulldozed forest road as the link.

Cyrniau Nod circular (HN H4)

Dedicated enthusiasts of wild, untrodden country who accept bog-bashing and tussock-hopping as all part of a day's work might like to consider combining **HN4** and **HN5** on Cyrniau Nod.

Cyrniau Nod/Cefn Gwyntog circular (HN H5)

Better still, picking up the thread from **HN H4**, climb Cefn Gwyntog from Llyn y Mynydd on **HN8**, go on to claim Cyrniau Nod using the forest road for temporary respite, then drop down to Cwm Pennant on **HN4**.

Be warned: this and HN H4 are only for experienced walkers who know what to expect.

Lower-level Walks/Easier Days

Cwm Pennant (HN L1)

Ideal for a lazy day.

The secluded Cwm Pennant that hides so coyly up a by-road from Llangynog is every bit as lovely as its better-known namesake in Snowdonia. A variety of footpaths is shown on the map, but for a first excursion I would tramp up-valley to the falls at Blaen y Cwm (see **HN4**). Set in an amphitheatre of tree-hung crags flowing down to gentle pastures, the thunder of the cascades lends a hint of drama to a scene that is truly idyllic. Another idea would be to follow the mountain road to Llyn y Mynydd.

MOEL SIABOD AND THE MOELWYNS

OS maps
1:25,000 – Sheets 16/17/18, 1:50,000 – Sheets 115/124

Peaks (by height)	Height (ft)	Map Ref	Page
Moel Siabod	2860	705546	100
Moelwyn Mawr	2527	658449	120
Moelwyn Bach	2334	660437	121
Allt Fawr	2287	682475	116
Cnicht	2265	645466	105
Moel Druman	2218	671477	118
Ysgafell Wen	2204	667481	112
Ysgafell Wen (subsidiary top)	2165	663486	112
Ysgafell Wen (subsidiary top)	2132	664488	112
Moel yr Hydd	2124	672454	119
Moel Meirch	1991	661504	112
Y Cribau	1938	676537	104
Yr Arddu	1933	673507	114

Mountain Lakes (alphabetically)			
Arddu	1148	628466	
Cerrig-y-myllt (2)	1345	633472	
Clogwyn-brith	1575	665466	
Coch	2034	669478	
Conglog	2001	674474	
Croesor	1706	661457	
Cwm-corsiog	1772	664470	
Cwmorthin	1082	678463	
Cwm-y-foel	1476	655468	
Cwn (cluster)	2100	662487	
Diffwys (2)	1706	659468	
Diwaunedd (2)	1214	684538	
Dyrnogydd	1300	693488	
Edno	1804	663497	

Mountain Lakes (alphabetically)

Ffridd-y-bwlch	1080	695480
Iwerddon	1575	685478
Llagi	1247	649483
Nameless	2100	665479
Nameless	2098	664484
Nameless	2034	669474
Nameless	2034	675476
Nameless	1834	654488
Nameless	1300	722559
Nameless	1100	637467
Stwlan	1673	665445
Terfyn	1902	668479
Wrysgan	1476	677453
Y Biswail	1870	649474
Y Foel	1756	715548
Yr Adar	1886	655480

MOEL SIABOD AND THE MOELWYNS

There are 10 long miles separating the NE ramparts of Moel Siabod from the W slopes of Moelwyn Bach; 10 miles wherein the rugged grandeur of the giants that watch over Siabod gradually moderates to a scene no less grand, no less captivating in its breadth and serenity, but more relaxed. A scene of wavy blue horizons, green valleys, yellow sands and windswept sea. Quite a transformation! But then the region I have grouped together as Siabod and Moelwyns is vast: a huge, skewed quadrilateral bounded by the road from Betws-y-Coed to Pen y Gwryd, by Nantgwynant, by the lush vales of Glaslyn and Ffestiniog, and finally by the A470 as it winds over the Crimea Pass on its way back to Betws-y-coed beside the tumbling Afon Lledr.

In truth Siabod and the Moelwyns form an unholy alliance. Handy for constructing chapters, justified because a strong walker could tramp from one to the other without ever crossing a road, but totally ignoring character differences. (I also take a liberty in the use of the word 'Moelwyns' which, strictly speaking, applies only to the two peaks so named.)

Siabod is an isolated peak which is lofty, boasts fine ridges and harbours no secrets; the popular unquestioned king of all it surveys. The Moelwyns are harder to fathom. Despite Cnicht's all-pervading presence, and the shapely line Moelwyn Mawr and

The Moelwyns (SM H1)

Moelwyn Bach present to Tan-lan and Glaslyn, they are a family of more modest equals – a land of convoluted hillocks and hollows, replete with secluded lakes and knobbly tops.

In between lies the emerald green of the Lledr Valley and the lonely hills that nurture it. Neglected fells where the names have a welcoming freshness: Yr Arddu, Moel Meirch, Y Cribau, Bwlch Ehediad, Llynnau Diwaunedd, Roman Bridge. A glorious wilderness where you can greet old friends with new faces. The horseshoe from Yr Arddu round to Moel Dyrnogydd is long overdue for discovery.

Siabod has always been a popular mountain. Although adjoining Snowdon and the Glyders, it still manages to sustain a presence of its own. It stands alone and so is sure to command good views. In looks it is smooth and gently rounded, strongly suggestive of a hill offering high rewards for minimal effort. The classic route from Pont Cyfyng is justifiably popular, while the approach over Llyn y Foel and the Daiar Ddu ridge rates with the best in Snowdonia. The views, too, are superb: Snowdon, the Glyders, Moel Hebog and the Moelwyns, and a taste of the Carneddau all await you.

Compared with Siabod the Moelwyns are positively deserted – except for Cnicht. 'Matterhorn of Wales' may be an overworked cliché, but no one with red blood in their veins sighting that familiar soaring cone can fail to be stirred, even though it may be for the umpteenth time. As luck would have it, Cnicht is one of the easiest hills to capture. Easy yet exhilarating, offering a taste of all that is best in mountain walking

97

Snowdon from near Cnicht

with a narrow ridge, grand views and the summit in view throughout. Family mountain par excellence!

There is only one Cnicht, and although Moelwyn Mawr and Moelwyn Bach dance a striking duet, particularly in snow, the remaining tops shun the limelight. Smaller in scale, and lacking the sculptured finesse that produces such memorable skylines in Nantlle and Rhinog, they cast their spell in more subtle ways.

However, the views from Moelwyn Mawr and Moelwyn Bach are unparalleled, with the familiar colours of fells and tops enlivened by the orange-brown of the sands and the white-speckled blue of the sea. Then there are the lakes and tarns, so liberally scattered that a dozen can sometimes be spied all at once. Open, desolate sheets of water like Llyn Conglog, its surface usually rippled by the wind; secret, rock encradled lakelets like Llynnau Cerrig-y-myllt, where silence is king; the tiny 'dog lakes' (Llynnau'r Cwn) and dreamy Llyn Edno, the loveliest of them all. All set like jewels in a broken, undulating landscape that is dappled with sheltered hollows, little hillocks and knuckles of rock.

Cnicht, Ysgafell Wen, Moel Druman and Allt Fawr all lie along a gently curved ridge. (I use the word 'ridge' though, strictly speaking, the high ground is too broad to be classed as a ridge in the usual sense.) Moelwyn Mawr and Moel yr Hydd lie along another such 'ridge' to the S which curves round to the minor top of Foel Ddu before declining. (Moelwyn Bach lies on a subsidiary spur to the S.) Between these two 'ridges' lies what is most easily thought of as a plateau, albeit a highly irregular one! In reality it is a wide saddle – and a very rough and crude one at that – between two cwms, Cwm Croesor to the SW and Cwmorthin which curls round from the NE.

The 'saddle' contains a number of derelict workings (notably the Croesor and Rhosydd quarries) and there are more in adjoining cwms, although in many cases Nature is well on the way to reclaiming her own. Regretfully the Moelwyns' E flanks are also scarred by the dammed Llyn Stwlan, Tanygrisiau power station and Blaenau Ffestiniog across the valley. There is no denying the grim, sombre atmosphere this creates on a grey day, though fortunately most of the unsightliness is confined and whole realms of unblemished beauty remain.

The 'saddle' referred to above is one of the keys to the tops, encircled as it is by all but one of them. You can reach it by an old quarry road through Cwmorthin, while no less than three routes start from Croesor. One climbs up to the disused Croesor Quarry; another, a green path, slants across the cwm's S slopes to the old Rhosydd workings; the third, another green path, traverses the cwm's N flanks to Llyn Cwm-y-foel (one of the reservoirs the quarrymen used as a source of power).

The prettiest approaches start from the W and lead directly to the N rim of the saddle. The most popular by far is the exhilarating hike (for it is scarcely a scramble) up Cnicht's SW ridge. Three others originate from the narrow road that winds round from Nantmor to Nantgwynant. Each is a pearl with yet more joys along the way – Llyn Edno, the round Llyn Llagi or the refreshing wildness of Gelli Iago.

Note The Moelwyns (and Siabod too) can also be climbed from Dolwyddelan or Roman Bridge. These are long, lingering walks, way off the beaten track where the only certainty is solitude, and help would be a long way off in time of need. Reserve them for fair weather days (sound advice for much of the Moelwyn country – and you should certainly stick to the main highways up Cnicht whenever mist is about).

Moel Siabod

It is impossible to ignore Moel Siabod. On the road from Capel Curig to Pen y Gwryd it is 'there'. A vast rambling hill, aloof from its fellows, with a commanding presence, and gently curving slopes that promise easy ascents and splendid views. For once the promise is fulfilled; few tops can match Siabod and its spacious tapering W ridge for breadth of view. Nowhere else do you see the Snowdon massif revealed in such titanic splendour, the grandeur of pinnacle and crag leavened only by the glint of sunlight on Llyn Llydaw. N, across the crag-ridden Llanberis Pass, is the jagged line of the Glyders backed by the Carneddau, the squat wedge of Tryfan and Bristly Ridge. Further S Yr Aran captures the eye with a display of power that belies its modest height, while the familiar lines of the Hebog and Nantlle hills arc the sky beyond. Nantgwynant with its two lovely lakes introduces a note of serenity before the eye runs on to the rounded headwall of the Moelwyns (where even the usually shy Llyn Edno manages to raise a sparkle) with the Rhinogs, Ffestiniog hills, Arenigs and Arans framing the blue beyond.

Yet there are times when Moel Siabod seems just a bit dull. Despite the long, rocky summit cap the slopes look perhaps just a shade too smooth and easy for a really satisfying day. Such concerns are easily laid to rest! You have only to follow the A470 towards Dolwyddelan to become aware of a very different Siabod. This Siabod has an aggressively pointed top, serrated ridges and precipitous crags as you look up at it from beneath the cliffs that stand guard over Llyn y Foel and support the magnificent Daiar Ddu ridge. This is the most exhilarating of all the routes on Moel Siabod and rates as one of the best half-dozen ridge walks in Snowdonia. One final tip. Once you have taken the W ridge and Daiar Ddu on board, spare a day to tackle Siabod from Dolwyddelan or Roman Bridge (preferably both!) Away from the crowds, these routes offer wild and romantic insights into Moel Siabod's character that few suspect.

Daiar Ddu ridge (SM1)

Cupped in a hollow beneath Moel Siabod's massive crags, Llyn y Foel is one of the glories of Snowdonia.

Cross Pont Cyfyng (734572) over the gushing Afon Llugwy and follow the second of two footpath signs R up a narrow road that climbs steeply through a leafy glen. (A few cars can be parked between the two signs.) Keep the farmstead called Rhos R and continue along a stony quarry trail across a bleak moor. Moel Siabod's NE ridge looms ahead and as you draw

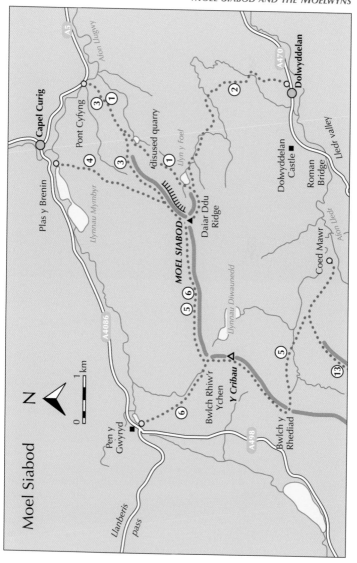

Moel Siabod

N

0   1 km

A5

Afon Llugwy

Capel Curig

Pont Cyfyng

Plas y Brenin

Llynnau Mymbyr

A4086

③
①
③
④

disused quarry

Llyn y foel

①

MOEL SIABOD

Daiar Ddu
Ridge

⑤ ⑥

Llynnau Diwaunedd

Bwlch Rhiw'r
Ychen

Y Cribau

⑥

Pen y
Gwryd

Llanberis
pass

A498

Bwlch y
Rhediad

②

A470

Dolwyddelan

Dolwyddelan
Castle

Roman
Bridge

Lledr valley

Afon Lledr

Coed Mawr

⑤

⑬

Moel Siabod emerging from early mist above the Capel Curig pinnacles

near a ladder-stile invites you to join it via a grassy ramp between two avenues of rocks (see **SM2**).

For Daiar Ddu stay with the quarry trail as it swings L at 723562, first past the nameless lake at 722559 and then on to a disused quarry at 716555 with a small pool (blue-black and man-made this time). The trail now swings SW over a small rise to Llyn y Foel. Rest awhile and enjoy this wild gem of the hills with its two rocky islets.

The ridge rises from the SW tip of the lake and is well cairned. It is exciting and airy, but never risky. Dizzy views R, plumbing the depths of the cwm, and with huge boulders seemingly blocking your way keep the adrenalin flowing. But holds are secure, easy and plentiful, and you will be sorry when the stony summit plateau ends a jolly romp.

Note When descending note that the Daiar Ddu route is signalled by a cairn on a bearing of 80° from the trig point.

Dolwyddelan route (SM2)

From the crossroads at Dolwyddelan walk up to the junction at 734525. Turn R as directed by a footpath sign. After a couple of minutes, beyond a gate, a second sign sends you across a field to a ladder-stile. The path shown on the map tends to come and go, so cut across to the forest edge as best you can (soggy!) and follow it to the stile at 736532 where the path marked on the map turns up as good as gold.

Cross the stile into the forest and bear L over a bridge after about 100 paces. After a similar distance turn L again on to the main forest road by another bridge. Press on to a concrete bridge at 732543 and turn sharp L just beyond, carrying on until the road ends at a turning circle at 725545. (Ignore branch roads going off first L and then R.) Cross the stream and follow a dark, overhung track that climbs through the forest on a carpet of pine needles and lichenous boulders before leaving it over a stile by a waterfall at 720546. The path now weaves through a flamboyant wilderness of heather and bracken, watered by many streams and liberally dotted with boulders and tiny outcrops. It culminates in a scramble up the side of some falls when the desolate depression cradling Llyn y Foel at long last comes into view. Next on to Daiar Ddu (**SM1**). What a day!

Don't be deterred by a scrappy start; after the first 10min this is a great walk. It also introduces a byway you might otherwise never discover.

Note In descent note that the track leaves the SE tip of the lake near the remains of a dam and a small, shingly beach.

NE ridge (SM3)

Climb the grassy ramp mentioned in **SM1**, with impressive views of the Glyders R, until the near mile-long girdle of rocks that straddles the summit ridge appears L. Then either scramble over the crest or, more sedately (**SM3,1**), keep just below on a blend of grass and stone-encrusted grass. The ridge is the more exciting choice with thrilling views of Llyn y Foel 1000ft below, but the boulders are very large and slippery when wet so it can be both slow and tiring. Why not compromise and opt for the ridge halfway along?

Plas y Brenin route (SM4)

The easiest way up Moel Siabod, but also the least interesting.

The route slants across the mountain's dreary NE slopes and denies you open views almost until the end. Follow the footpath sign at Plas y Brenin (716578), and cross the tip of Llynnau Mymbyr. Continue into the darkness of the woods, turn R on to a brighter trail at 716575 and then press on S, crossing a forest trail en route, to a delightful glade with a bubbling brook R. This becomes a heathery glen which abruptly ends where a ladder-stile heralds the transition to open hillside. Now comes a long slog up a slippery, peaty path until Moel Siabod's rocky crown at last comes in sight, a short scamper away across the stubby grass.

Roman Bridge ridge (SM5)

A glorious day in unfrequented country.

Roman Bridge may seem an odd spot from which to tackle Moel Siabod, but use it in descent, coupled with an ascent from Dolwyddelan on **SM2** (that way round gives the better views), for a wonderful day out.

Leave the trig point on 270° and follow the fence down the W ridge, admiring the magnificent views. The chaos of boulders soon yields to a fine striding ridge. Skirt round the cliffs cupping Llynnau Diwaunedd to reach Bwlch Rhiw'r Ychen (Pass of the Hill of the Oxen). Next follow the fence up to Y Cribau, an idyllic little top where a fantasy of bilberries, heather and rocks ensnares a tiny tarn. Down to Bwlch y Rhediad brings more tarns, white tufts of bog cotton, dips and hollows in profusion and evocative vistas of Snowdon and the Moelwyns.

The bwlch is marked by a cairn and an ancient, rather sad-looking, iron gate whose accompanying fence has long since passed away. Even the path now scorns the gate, slinking round the side instead. Head E now, guided by a line of stakes, over oozy grass. Bear R at a lone clump of trees and cross the footbridge at 678523 to join **SM13** and the road at 697515.

Alternatively (**SM5,1**) keep going beyond the copse, along a steadily improving path, to reach stepping stones and a stile into the forest at 686527. Advance into the woods to join the main forest trail at a fire station. There are two more of these on the way down, including one by the gate at 704519 next to the homestead of Pen y Bont where, after the inevitable zigzags, you join the surfaced road. Another possibility (**SM5,2**) is to gain the forest trail at source by scampering down to the lake at Bwlch Rhiw'r Ychen.

Note This leaves you with a stretch of road work if, as I suggested, you began from Dolwyddelan. You can reduce it by means of a footpath which starts from the bend in the road at 713519 and leads past the ruins of Dolwyddelan Castle to join the A470 at 723525.

Pen y Gwyryd route (SM6)

For a quick way to Bwlch Rhiw'r Ychen, and hence to either W ridge or Y Cribau, take to the slopes across the road from the hotel. Remember, though, that the ridge, with its incomparable views, is best in descent. Planning your walk that way would also, of course, increase the chances of arriving at the hotel at refreshment time!

Cnicht

'Cnicht', an old English name for a knight's helmet, well conveys the elegance of this fine peak. It is also known as the 'Matterhorn of Wales'. With names like that you are entitled to expect something special – and you will not be disappointed. Cnicht is among the most rewarding and popular hills in Wales, and no wonder! Who could fail to respond to the sharply pointed cone it displays to Croesor, Portmadog or the Vale of Glaslyn? Climb Cnicht from Croesor and you are spurred on along a slender rocky ridge that is airy but never exposed, exhilarating without ever imposing too strong a demand. Cnicht is the ideal family mountain; despite its robust appearance even a child can climb it and enjoy the views from Lleyn to Cader Idris.

Some purists complain that the thrill of this approach is not matched from other directions. This is unfair; Cnicht is no 'one route' mountain. Try the Llyn Llagi or Gelli Iago routes and you will experience the ethereal charm of the

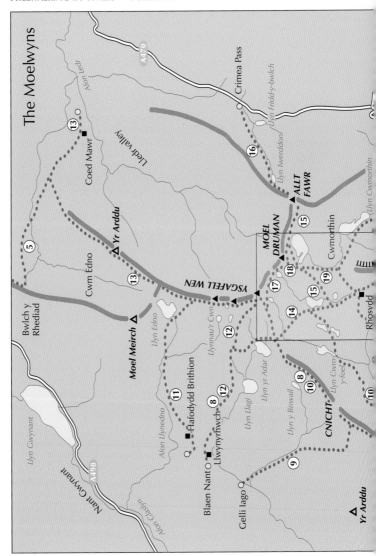

The Moelwyns

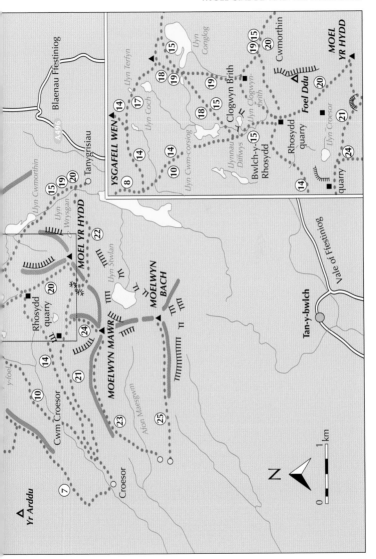

W foothills; a landscape of little hillocks outcropping everywhere, secluded lakes, secret places, all richly cloaked in the browns, greens and purples of rampant bracken and heather. Climb Cnicht via Llyn Cwm-y-foel and you will rub shoulders with the calamitous, fearsome slopes it throws down to Cwm Croesor.

Croesor route (SM7)

If Cnicht is a model mountain then this is the model ascent, with the objective displaying its most charismatic face almost all the way.

Turn R as you leave the car park in Croesor and follow the road until it ends at a stile. Step over the stile onto a stony track which climbs through a charming little glade. As you leave the glade, and the slope eases, turn R to join a bulldozed road. Stay with this until it peters out in bog near another stile.

Over the stile is the best natural 'lawn' in Snowdonia, a velvety stretch of fine-grained turf fit for bowls. (The NW ridge of Grisedale Pike in the Lake District is similarly endowed.) Watch the track; it gets a bit faint hereabouts (not that it really matters for Cnicht is now revealed in all its glory and the general direction is clear enough).

A further stile over a wall leads to a rough, bouldery track that runs alongside a rocky knoll before climbing through rocks and heather. This brings you to a grassy saddle at the foot of the final rocky pyramid, where the track temporarily divides. The R branch (which looks the more difficult) is the easier, especially in descent where a cairn indicates where the track divides. From now on it is sheer delight as the track twists and turns up the slender ridge, never exposed but with the sort of thrills you normally get only from exposed positions.

Llyn Llagi route (SM8)

Little Llyn Lagi could well lay claim to being the roundest lake in Wales.

The converted chapel at Blaen Nant (635490) is the start for this popular walk. Go through the kissing-gate as indicated by the footpath sign and descend slightly to the dwelling of Llwynyrhwch, keeping it to your R. A grassy path then wends through boulders and heathery thickets until more open, marshy ground heralds the approach of Llyn Llagi, spectacularly backed by dark cliffs and the white plummeting falls from Llyn yr Adar 600ft above.

Cnicht (SM 7)

The Nantlle ridge and Moel Hebog from near Cnicht (SM 7)

The easiest course is now L along a well-worn track that ascends a gully NE of the lake. This curves round to skirt the shores of Llyn yr Adar (Lake of the Birds) – a bleak, feature-less sheet of water with a tiny island that is an oasis of green in the yellows and browns of the encircling fells (and the invariable nestling place of a couple of seagulls). **Note** You can reach the same spot more adventurously by scrambling up beside the falls – **SM8,1**. From Llyn yr Adar work your way S to the rim of this spacious tableland where a well-used path leads to Cnicht. On the way you pass Llyn Biswail, attractively framed against a rocky bluff.

The scenery is on the grand scale. An immense panorama R is dominated by the Snowdon horseshoe, while L the gaze is held by the blue of Tremadog Bay, the towering Moelwyns and the far-off Arenigs. Cnicht itself gradually assumes the form of a long, tapering ridge with splintered slopes plunging precipitously into the chaotic abyss of Cwm Croesor.

Gelli lago route (SM9)

Leave the road at 632484, walk down the lane, go through the dwelling of Gelli lago and cross the tumbling stream over an old flagged bridge. Straightaway a gritty track appears, lonely and neglected now, though it was obviously in regular use once as stepping stones are still in place over boggy patches.

For a peak as popular as Cnicht this beautiful walk has a freshness that is as surprising as it is welcome.

Behind you the Snowdon massif is gloriously framed in the arms of the cwm while Cnicht looms impressively ahead. But wait awhile before launching your final assault. Stay with the track as it veers S into Bwlch y Battel and the nameless reedy lakelet at 637467. Next climb up the hillock to spot height 458m (635469) for one of the most hauntingly beautiful vistas in Snowdonia: Tremadog Bay, the Hebog hills, the Nantlle ridge, Yr Aran, the Snowdon horseshoe (less Crib Goch), the Glyders, glimpses of the Carneddau including Pen Llithrig-y-wrach, Moel Siabod, the Moelwyns, and of course Cnicht itself. But this is not all. Superimposed is a purple-green foreground of heathery humps, hollows and knuckles of rock, with Llyn Arddu and Llynnau Cerrig-y-myllt peering timelessly from their rocky cradles; flawless beauty, profound silence.

When the time comes to leave you have three choices:

- R to a scree slope and the final pyramid on **SM7**
- L to gain the ridge by a grassy rake S of Llyn Biswail (**SM9,1**) or
- A direct frontal which is easier than it looks (**SM9,2**).

Llyn Cwm-y-foel route (**SM10**)

Park at Croesor, return to the crossroads at 632447 and turn L up-valley. After a short 0.5 mile, at a group of cottages nestling in a shady glade, proceed sharp L down a cart track. After a few moments bear R at a gate to join an old quarry tramway. Stay with this until you come to a gate at 643454 where you must leave it L to cross a bridge and join a conspicuous green path snaking across the hillside.

The next mile is vintage stuff with panoramic views of the valley and the relics of bygone industries. The crags of Cnicht rear L, seeming much higher than they actually are and quite fearsome when wreathed in mist. Behind is the shimmering sea. Unfortunately Llyn Cwm-y-foel, when you reach it, is not up to the same standard. Service as a reservoir has taken its toll so you will probably not linger long by its gravelly shores.

A choice of two routes now awaits.

- Tigers can carry on N until a steep grassy rake at 657475 offers a direct pull up to the ridge (**SM10,1**).
- Much more pleasant, though slightly circuitous, is to work across country to Llynnau Diffwys, two sad-looking lakes trapped in drab little hollows high above Cwm Croesor. Next on to the enchanting Llyn Cwm-corsiog (good bathing) to pick up a track along its W shore. This takes you to a cairn at 657477, near Llyn yr Adar, to finish as in **SM8**.

Ysgafell Wen

Ysgafell Wen straddles a long, tapering ridge that juts between the Lledr Valley and Cwm Edno before declining beyond the minor top of Yr Arddu (673507). It is a remote untrodden area of coarse, undulating moors dotted with tiny tarns. Taxing to navigate at the best of times, it is best left along in mist. There has long been confusion over the highest point. In fact there are three tops, and to add to the muddle all are cairned and all are of a simiar height and shape.

The main top has an elevation of 2204ft and is sighted at 667481 with a teardrop tarn just to the W. A second top rises to 2132ft about 1 mile N at 664488. This is the most appealing, overlooking the three Dog Lakes (Llynnau'r Cwn). The third peak (2165ft) lies in between at 663486. Views of Snowdon and the Lledr Valley are outstanding from all three.

Llyn Edno route (SM11)

Edno is a lovely lake, a haven of peace where the only sound is likely to be the ripple of wave lapping on rock.

Tucked beneath the terraces of Moel Meirch with their bounteous cushions of heather, and with evocative views of Snowdon, few can resist the lure of this most queenly of lakes. But not all can find it! Even experienced walkers sometimes have difficulty in locating Edno in the surrounding maze of hillocks and hollows.

Park at the bend in the road at 637495. Ignore the footpath sign pointing N. Instead go through the gate and follow

Llyn Edno and the Glyders from Ysgafell Wen

the lane round to Hafodydd Brithion Farm (640495). Just before the farm bear E, trending NE, over a stream and along the N edge of a copse. When you come to a wall strike out N, then quite quickly NE again, and look for a ladder-stile over another wall at 643496. Cross this and you will see a path weaving up the bracken-clad hillside before you.

Up-cwm, across the noisy Afon Llynedno, tiered crags and tiny citadels of rock garlanded with heather and bracken engender a hint of romance. To the rear is the massive presence of Snowdon and its horseshoe, Hebog and Nantlle, the scene lit up on a sunny day by the glittering blue of Llyn Dinas.

About halfway you reach a gap in a wall. This is an important checkpoint in descent as you could find yourself on the other (N) side of the stream. If so – except in drought – this would probably be your last chance to cross to the S bank and the path. After the wall a sheepfold ushers in a splashy morass. However drier ground soon returns, and when it does the slopes close in in a manner reminiscent of the Rhinogs. There is the same sense of foreboding, the same purple slopes and, on Moel Meirch, the same striations as on Rhinog Fawr.

Despite such style it is still a relief when, on topping a final rise, Llyn Edno is at last revealed in all its idyllic simplicity.

Note Find time for a detour to Moel Meirch if you can. It is an excellent vantage point and would be high on everyone's list if only it possessed the extra 10ft needed for 2000ft club membership. Perhaps we ought to be thankful it does not. The tracks winding up its heather-clad slopes are faint and pure, the cairn undefiled by litter. Long may they remain so!

On resuming, follow Llyn Edno's shoreline and work up to the skyline ahead. This is the ridge of Ysgafell Wen. The two subsidiary tops at 664488 and 663486 seem uneventful, but pause and explore the intervening hollow, the home of the rippling Dog Lakes (Llynnau'r Cwn). Two of these which are especially evocative, framing Snowdon in their tiny cliffs. After the second top the path drops down to a trough cradling a peaty tarn (664484) before climbing to bear sharp L by a little pool just before main top at 667481.

Llyn Llagi route (SM12)
Follow **SM8** to the N tip of Llyn yr Adar. Ysgafell Wen is then due E. Alternatively (**SM12,1**) you could explore the heart of the Dog Lake country by heading NE from the top of the gully at 655486 when, in under 1 mile, you will gain the most N of the three tops. Note the isolated lakelet at 654488, perched so precariously on the hillside above Llyn Llagi that only magic seems to prevent it spilling away. Finish as in **SM11**.

Lledr Valley route (SM13)
The last time I parked by the banks of the Lledr where the metalled road ends at 696513, and walked the ancient trail that leads across the fells from Coed Mawr Farm to Nantgwynant, I was reminded of the delectable Newlands Valley in Cumbria. There, as here, a succession of flowing ridges encloses an oasis of softly wooded pastures. You would expect Moel Siabod to be the focal point, but it is not. That honour goes to Yr Arddu

which looks massively solid and rugged and, because of its remoteness, mysterious and enticing too. The ridge from which it rises culminates in Ysgafell Wen (which for once has real stature) before sweeping on over Moel Druman and Allt Fawr to decline in the grassy wastes of Moel Dyrnogydd.

Follow the trail until you come to a gate in a wall at 685520, just above the SW tip of a forest plantation. Strike out L for the ridge. A playful path urges you on through a wilderness of rocks and thickets of heather to the lonely cairn on Yr Arddu. The blue of Llyn Edno lifts your spirits but the show is stolen by the Snowdon horseshoe, by Tryfan soaring like a castle in the air, by the Llanberis Pass, the noble silhouette of Moel Penamnen and, last but not least, the heather-clad Moel Meirch.

It is not far short of 3 miles to Ysgafell Wen, but it is a jolly walk that keeps to the edge of the ridge with a line of old stakes for company. Landmarks come and go – Ysgafell Wen's first top, Llynnau'r Cwn (the Dog Lakes), Ysgafell Wen's second top, the nameless tarn at 664484 and finally, after a L turn by a tiny pool, the main top at 667481 (see **SM11**).

Croesor/Rhosydd Quarry route (SM14)

Start from Croesor and walk from the crossroads to a cluster of terraced cottages at 637449. The road veers R here and a lane sidles away L. Ignore both; instead proceed ahead through a gate and follow a farm road that peters out after about 0.5 mile. Now pull up the hillside, half-R, to a gate in a wire fence giving access to a green track (644453).

The path slants merrily across the slopes beneath Moelwyn Mawr to reveal the mottled greens of Cwm Croesor where only the chapel now recalls the communities that once toiled there. Across the vale Cnicht rules supreme, while on a sunny day the scene is lit by the glint of the distant sea. Harsher climes lie in store. Dark angular crags frowning down R herald Bwlch-y-Rhosydd where, after a R turn, a quarry tramway leads to piles of shattered slate and the derelict, forlorn-looking cottages that once housed the workforce. ▶

L along the tramway would bring you to a ramp, once used to bring slate down to the valley; a quick but knee-jarring way down.

Today Rhosydd is a forgotten land and yet, except on the dullest of days, it still manages to convey a wistful charm. An interesting few hours could be spent exploring the 'highways and byways' of this wrinkled plateau. When the time comes to leave the bearing is 320°, quickly veering N whereupon a cairned track leads round the rocky spur of Clogwyn Brith. After a short rise, completely without warning, you find yourself on the shores of Llyn Cwm-corsiog. An inviting stretch of water when the sun is out, it is divided by a rocky promontory along its S shoreline and the remains of an old dam.

The track continues to the skyline at 656477 above Llyn yr Adar whence a short walk on 70° (passing N of a lonely, nameless tarn at 665479) brings you to a dilapidated fence at 665481. Ysgafell Wen is then a stone's throw R.

Allt Fawr

The 'Big Height' towers imposingly over the grey slate town of Blaenau Ffestiniog, where it always seems to rain. Although it is easily scaled either from the Crimea Pass or via Cwmorthin, both these routes start near scenes of industrial desecration and are rarely used. (This is a little unfair because any unsightliness is soon left behind.) Consequently Allt Fawr is usually traversed as part of a marathon of all the Moelwyn hills (see **SM H4**). Even then its luck is out as it stands aloof at the end of a spur and so tends to be the first casualty if energy fades. However it repays every pant, for it is a superb viewpoint.

Moel yr Hydd, usually so tame and insignificant, looks a grand little peak as it dominates the S foreground with the sea and Lleyn beyond. Then, as the eye roams clockwise, the parade of giants includes Cnicht, Moel Hebog and its satellites, the Nantlle ridge, Yr Aran, the Snowdon massif, the Glyders with Tryfan well to the fore, Moel Siabod and the soft greens of the Lledr Valley. Penyrhelgi-du and Pen Llithrig-y-wrach represent the Carneddau while the Arenigs and Arans fill the SE skyline backed by the Berwyns, Cader Idris and the Rhinogs. On a clear day you can even discern the distant curve of Plynlimon.

Cwmorthin route (SM15)

Either park by the sports field at 687449 just after leaving the
A496 or, after a steep drive, at the road-head at 683454 where
Moel yr Hydd displays some of the fiercest crags in the district. Carry on along the quarry track amid immense, grim
mounds of slate waste. The ugliness may be overpowering but
at least it is short-lived for when Llyn Cwmorthin comes into
view it still manages to convey a fragile charm. Beyond the
lake the track passes the remains of an old chapel and then
climbs up to the Rhosydd quarry workings. On the way, by a
gate at 670466, you cross the stream that flows out of Llyn
Conglog nearly 1000ft above (see **SM19**).

You can easily
imagine what a lovely
valley this must once
have been in its
pristine freshness (and
still is on a bright day).

From the quarry, with its ghost town of derelict dwellings,
pick up a boggy track with the odd cairn here and there which
starts on 320° before trending N. Leave it after about 10min
when you have outflanked the crags of Clogwyn Brith and
take to the hillside R, steering between the S shores of Llyn
Cwm-corsiog and the rocky, heathery hideaway sheltering
Llyn Clogwyn-brith. Continue round the N rim of the slopes
enclosing Cwmorthin and be reminded once again of the
serenity it once enjoyed.

As you come abreast Llyn Conglog (The Angular Lake)
Allt Fawr lies NE across a barren moor. Alternatively you can
first wander round Llyn Conglog and its two satellites prior to
a quick scamper up Moel Druman, a mere 200ft above the
lake, from where a track darkens the grass on its way to Allt
Fawr. There is a profusion of lakes and tarns in the vicinity
and a good day can be had trying to visit them all. All you
need is the ability to use a compass; the going itself is easy,
with or without tracks.

Crimea Pass route (SM16)

Drive up the A470 from Blaenau Ffestiniog and, shortly after
leaving the waste tips behind, look out for the diminutive Llyn
Ffridd-y-bwlch nestling furtively in a hollow. A little further
on, just below the top of the pass at 698484, park by a gate
with a ladder-stile and follow a green quarry track until it ends
by a ventilation chimney for the railway tunnel connecting
Ffestiniog with Roman Bridge. Next plod up the sombre valley ahead to the bullet-shaped, reedy Llyn Iwerddon. The

Not a particularly
ripping walk, and out
on a limb geographi-
cally, but useful for a
quick half-day.

finale is a scramble up the shallow gully that cleaves Allt Fawr's NE slopes.

Moel Druman

Moel Druman (Ridge Mountain) is a minor twin-topped hill less than 200ft higher than Llyn Conglog, the wild lake below its S slopes. No one is likely to climb Druman for its own sake, but it is well worth a diversion if you are tramping the windswept uplands between Ysgafell Wen and Allt Fawr because the vista from this modest hill is scarcely inferior to that from Allt Fawr. The views of the strangely neglected Lledr Valley are especially memorable, and it is fun to see how many lakes and tarns you can spot.

Croesor/Rhosydd Quarry route (SM17)
Follow **SM14** as for Ysgafell Wen but then, at the last moment, freelance across N of the nameless tarn at 665479 to the even more diminutive Llyn Terfyn and its mini cliffs at 668479. A faint track leads on to Moel Druman passing near Llyn Coch, another tarn with a rocky backdrop.

Cwmorthin route (SM18)
See **SM15**.

S face direct (SM19)

Tough but, like all direct routes, satisfying.

Follow **SM15** through Cwmorthin and carry on past the chapel ruins until you cross the outflow from Llyn Conglog at 670466. Loins should be girded and sweaters removed for a really gruelling 30min sweat up beside the falls. Relief comes when you at last veer R to enter a tiny gorge. The slope eases and in a few moments you step on to a ramp with Conglog rippling before you and Moel Druman rising above its far shoreline.

Moel yr Hydd

The 'Hill of the Stag' is one of Snowdonia's least-known summits. The origin of the name is lost in antiquity but the peak does have a curiously twisted, pointed profile not unlike a horn when seen from Cnicht or Hebog, and this may account for it. The top is a small tilted table, mostly grass with a scattering of spiky rock and first-rate views of Cwmorthin. Moel yr Hydd, so benign from most view-points, is surprisingly fierce and craggy on its S and E flanks and, with old mine shafts also in the vicinity, is best given a wide berth in mist.

Cwmorthin route (SM20)

Walk up to the Rhosydd Quarry as in **SM15** and then prepare for a trudge up a damp tussocky hillside on a bearing of roughly 150°, keeping Foel Ddu well to your L and a group of ugly grey-black spoil heaps R.

If you can plan your day to use this in descent, so much the better.

Croesor Quarry route (SM21)

Walk up to the derelict quarry at 657665 and then steer an E course through the gloomy ruins to join a faint track that climbs a small rise to reveal Llyn Croesor. Set against a backdrop of huge, slaty waste tips there is no more desolate sheet of water in the whole of Wales on a grey day, but when the sun shines it sparkles away with the best as if trying to atone for the grim-ness all around.

Stay with the track as it wends across the hillside S of the lake and, where it fades, aim for the W lip of the massive (unfenced) excavation at 665453. Here a well-trodden path comes in from the direction of Moelwyn Mawr and leads up a gentle grassy slope, with cliffs R, to the summit.

Route-planners should note that an old mining track leaves Llyn Croesor's W shoreline on 40° for a quick cross-country route to Rhosydd.

Tanygrisiau route (SM22)

Park at the roadhead at 683454. Cross the bridge by the falls and march on up the Llyn Stwlan service road. Some 600 paces on you will find a derelict sheepfold R beneath a tow-ering rock face. A narrow track sidles away here, faint at first but doubling back into a rake of loose, wet scree that is clearly visible from the road if (having missed it!) you glance back. It climbs to the elongated marshy shelf that lies between the two bands of crags that buttress Moel yr Hydd S. The path fades in the bog but reasserts itself on 280°, rising to a prominent cairn at 667453 through a break in the upper line of cliffs. Finish as in **SM21**.

In descent it is all too easy to miss the rake and to follow a well-worn track NE beneath the higher crags. This brings you out overlooking Cwmorthin, atop the mountainous quarry workings at 678456, with a nasty slithery scramble over slate waste to get down (**SM22,1**). However it does give you the chance to visit Llyn Wrysgan, a lonely little tarn fringed with reeds and snuggly tucked beneath a ramp of tilted slabs.

Moelwyn Mawr

Aloof on the periphery of Snowdonia, Moelwyn Mawr and Moelwyn Bach are stirring viewpoints where hills, valleys, sea and sand unite in a breathtaking panorama. They turn a fine face to the Vale of Glaslyn and are best seen under a dusting of snow. I will not describe the view from Moelwyn Mawr as it is similar to that from Moelwyn Bach. How fortunate to have two such vantage points!

But these are no twins. Moelwyn Bach is a rambling top girt with pools and slabby rock, jealously guarded by crags. Moelwyn Mawr is taut and austere, though never lacking character. 'Pure' is the best word for it. Whichever way you approach, the trig point stays hidden until the very end, inviolate atop a convex dome of short-cropped, coppery grass without so much as a hint of a track. Then, suddenly, all is revealed; the full splendour of the view and the slender, unspoiled breezy crown.

SW ridge (SM23)

The best ascent starts along the gated road that runs SE from the Croesor crossroads towards Tan-y-bwlch. Just before the second gate, by the bridge over the Afon Maesgwm, turn L on to a Land Rover track. Where it peters out pull up to the ridge where a gritty path, steep in places, hugs the crest.

Seaward views improve with every step, while Cnicht rules the roost across Cwm Croesor.

N ridge (SM24)

From the top of the Croesor quarry road at 657456 take to the hillside R and gradually work round to the N ridge for a steep, relentless grind that is more pleasant in descent.

Moelwyn Bach

Moelwyn Bach is an attractive top, quite apart from its heart-warming views. S of the cairn is a little gully with a small tarn and, beyond that, rocky terraces with more tiny pools. Crags bar the way N and E and finding a way off, other than the W ridge, requires good navigation (see **SM H1**). However, provided you stick to the ridge Moelwyn Bach is ideal for a family outing with rewards out of all proportion to the meagre effort involved.

W ridge (SM25)

Park at Croesor, return to the crossroads at 633446 and walk up the gated road that swings across the toes of the Moelwyns. Stay with it until, after 1 mile, you come to some woods with a stile L. Cross the stile and follow a path to the NE tip of the woods at 639436. Next strike out SE across soggy moors to gain the delicate (and dry) little track that straddles the W ridge. (Alternatively – **SM25,1** – continue past the woods and go through the first gate L. The path you find there climbs to Bwlch Stwlan but is hardly more than a swamp in places so you should break away R to join the ridge as before.)

To say that the steady plod up the W ridge is uneventful, apart from the jutting prow of Lion's Head Rock L of the summit, would be to speak in navigational terms only. The coastline from Lleyn to Barmouth, indeed far beyond, lies framed against the drama of engirdling hills. From the distant Rivals the eye ranges over the Nantlle ridge and the thrusting wedge of Hebog to Mynydd Mawr, then on to Snowdon

A walk where feet can be left to fend for themselves, freeing eyes to revel in Nature's bountiful generosity.

and Moel Siabod (twin bastions of the N skyline) trying, but not succeeding, to hide the Glyders and the far-off Carneddau.

The unsightly workings around Ffestiniog cast but a temporary blight. Elevate the gaze and you have long tumbling vistas of Arenigs, Arans and Berwyns, while S reveals the noble lines of Rhinogs and Cader Idris. On a sunny day, when the sea sparkles to the bright yellow sands and clouds cast their shadows on the crags and vales of Glaslyn and Ffestiniog, Moelwyn Bach is a place apart.

High-level Walks

The two Moelwyns (SM H1)

Moelwyn Bach's W ridge (**SM25**) provides an inspiring start. However, having admired the view, you will find it is not the simple innocent it seems. Finding the correct line of descent to Bwlch Stwlan can be quite problematical as Moelwyn Bach is crag-bound N and E. So leave the cairn S and drop down to a shallow gully with a band of rocky terraces behind. Hug its near side and move forward on 100° to a cairn. This points

The Moelwyns

to a thin, shaly path that slants down to the bwlch. It is loose and requires a cautious step in snow. A slip could be nasty.

The green path crossing the bwlch is the boggy path referred to in **SM25,1**. It links into a mellow old miners' track, robustly banked, that contours round above Llyn Stwlan en route to Moel yr Hydd. However today's walk is over the spiky snout of Craig Ysgafn and up the steep grass of Moelwyn Mawr's S ridge. Finally back to base on **SM23**.

The two Moelwyns/Moel yr Hydd (SM H2)

At Bwlch Stwlan follow the miners' track mentioned above, passing some dark, dank quarry shafts in the hillside L. Cliffs seem to bar the way, but a break in the crags at 663448 turns their flank to give a grassy finale. The backtrack to Moelwyn Mawr is also on grass, and virtually flat until the final 600ft slog up its E face.

You can extend the previous hike over Moel yr Hydd.

The Croesor horseshoe (SM H3)

Start by collecting the scalps of the two Moelwyns (**SM H1**). Next drop down Moelwyn Mawr's E face for an easy 30min to Moel yr Hydd before a tussocky descent to Rhosydd leads into **SM14**, which you should follow to the skyline at 656477. Then bear L to take Cnicht from the NE. Return to Croesor down the popular SW ridge with, hopefully, the sea gleaming like gold in the evening sun.

A classic with grand views all day long.

The Moelwyns grand slam (SM H4)

Starting from Croesor you warm up on Moelwyn Bach (**SM25**). Then it's over Bwlch Stwlan and Craig Ysgafn to Moelwyn Mawr, on to Moel yr Hydd, down to the Rhosydd 'ghost town' and up to Moel Druman and Allt Fawr on **SM15**. (Being on a spur Allt Fawr can be omitted if energy flags.)

The return to Moel Druman begins the homeward half. From Druman take a bearing of 320° to identify Ysgafell Wen (easy to go astray here) and then be guided by the remains of a fence. The wire is gone, only the poles survive. (Another shortcut for tired walkers is to cut the corner here forgoing Ysgafell Wen.) Cnicht, a long ridge with two humps from this viewpoint, now beckons. Luckily it is easy going with a good track and you can wind down and enjoy the views. From

Another classic, but strictly for tigers because you will probably need a full seven or eight hours and end with aching limbs.

Cnicht it's all downhill (**SM7**) to the car park at Croesor – then off with your boots!

Gelli Iago/Llyn Edno (SM H5)

A pearl of a day, pairing two of the loveliest routes in the area.

Up Cnicht from Gelli Iago (**SM9**), along the skyline to Ysgafell Wen, then home (**SM11**) with the chance of a bathe in Llyn Edno if it's a hot day. That succinct outline says it all yet tells you nothing of the delicate charms of two of the most delectable cwms in Snowdonia with their silent crag-bound lakes and terraces of heather-clad rock.

Note Take care on leaving Cnicht to identify Ysgafell Wen properly as similar-looking tops abound. The correct bearing for the main top is 50°.

Siabod/Lledr Valley circular (SM H6)

No crowds, not even in the height of summer.

I am making an exception to my normal rule of not including couplings of routes on the same peak because this could easily be overlooked, and it is too good for that. It combines **SM2** and **SM5** on a grand tour of Siabod with all the highlights: Llyn y Foel, the Daiar Ddu ridge, the SW ridge with its incomparable view of the Snowdon massif, and finally a foray into the delicate charms of the Lledr Valley thrown in for good measure.

The Lledr Valley horseshoe (SM H7)

There is no better entrée to the verdant Lledr Valley yet it is seldom trod, except by sheep!

I had tramped Snowdonia for many years before I discovered this beautiful walk, and was amazed at how many new faces of old friends it revealed.

Follow **SM13** from the road-head at 696513 to Ysgafell Wen. Drop down to Llyn Terfyn with its tiny cliffs, then climb Moel Druman and carry on across the moors to Allt Fawr. Scramble down Allt Fawr's broken slopes to Llyn Iwerddon, then pull up the opposite hillside on 45° to gain the slender ridge that points a finger at Llyn Dyrnogydd. Rarely visited, Dyrnogydd shines like a jewel when seen from the uplands between Cnicht and Ysgafell Wen in the noonday sun. Nearer to hand it is a disappointment, huddled beneath dreary slopes of yellowish sedge and blemished beyond redemption by unsightly power lines. So cross it quickly (no cairn) and then descend to the green quarry road that skirts its N slopes.

The scenery now grows more delightful with every step. Bleak fells yield to islands of castellated rock, richly adorned with heather and bracken. Barren grassland succumbs to a rustic landscape of woodlands and falls, half-hidden dells and walls green with age, all lying beneath the watchful eye of the scarped Yr Arddu ridge.

The road completes the round. However, as the map shows, it twists and turns interminably so there is plenty of scope for corner-cutting, provided you're not averse to wet feet!

From Siabod to the Moelwyns (SM H8)

The title is deliberately vague. A galaxy of walks could be constructed linking Siabod with the Moelwyns and taking in the neglected yet hauntingly beautiful swathe of high ground that extends from Siabod's W ridge, over Moel Meirch, to Llyn Edno and Ysgafell Wen. Logistics is the problem. The lie of the land does not favour circular walks and the nearest you will get is a tramp over Moel Siabod from Dolwyddelan that lands you back on the road beneath Allt Fawr. Grand hike though that is, it leaves you with a tiring slog back along the road. Of course if you are not tied to wheels or can summon up a tame chauffeur... As regards route-finding little needs to be said. **SM5** guides you to Bwlch y Rhediad, while **SM11** takes over at Llyn Edno to feed into the rest of the network. They are linked by a springy track across the heather-cloaked top of Moel Meirch.

Lower-level Walks/Easier Days

Llyn Edno/Moel Meirch (SM L1)

I might even say a romantic day with its superb backdrop of Snowdon and the gentle Vale of Nantgwynant, tiered crags, terraces and slabs (worthy of the Rhinogs) and prolific heather. Then there is the lake itself – perhaps to cool off in – and solitude, for Edno is right off the tourist track. Finally there is

Llyn Edno is made for a lazy day.

always the possibility of a scamper up Moel Meirch, at 1991ft only 200ft above Edno (**SM11** refers).

Cnicht: the W lakes (SM L2)

Picnic spots abound – what more need be said?

I mean by this the cluster of lakelets nestling in the broken, rocky tableland beneath Cnicht's W slopes: Llyn yr Arddu, Llynnau Cerrig-y-myllt and the nameless little pool at 637467 in Bwlch y Battel. This is a region reminiscent of Haystacks in Lakeland or the N Rhinogs. (**SM9** refers.)

The Rhosydd plateau (SM L3)

Pottering among ancient quarries, mine shafts and derelict miners' barracks may not be to everyone's taste, even with the hills all around – but it takes all sorts. Approach the plateau either from Cwmorthin as in **SM15** or from Cwm Croesor as in **SM14**.

Llyn y Foel (SM L4)

SM1 says it all.

Moel y Dyniewyd (SM L5)

For such unassuming little hills the scenery is out of this world!

A footpath sign at 611493 invites you round a copse and across a bridge where the vivacious Afon Glaslyn leaves the placid Llyn Dinas. A green path rises playfully through the bracken before heading SW above the Afon Goch. Moel y Dyniewyd is SE and it is a simple matter of following the path, deviating L at Bwlch-y-Sygyn (603482) where a net of peaty little tracks cleaves the heather.

Llyn Dinas with its arboured, crag-hung slopes, arguably the loveliest lake in Wales; the Vale of Colwyn with its champions, Hebog, the Nantlle hills and Mynydd Mawr; Nantgwynant and Snowdon; the Moelwyns; a hint of the Glyders; the estuary, the sea and the far-off Rhinogs. All this plus hillocks and dips in countless profusion where many a happy hour could be lazed away on a sunny day. Who could ask for anything more!

MYNYDD DU (THE BLACK MOUNTAIN)

OS maps
1:25,000 – Sheet 12, 1:50,000 – Sheet 160

Peaks (by height)	Height (ft)	Map Ref	Page
Bannau Brycheiniog	2631	825217	131
Bannau Sir Gaer	2460	812218	132
Fan Hir	2400	830210	134
Garreg Las	2076	777202	135
Garreg-lwyd	2020	740179	137
Fan Foel*	2575	824221	132
Tro'r Fan-foel*	2500	821225	132

*subsidiary tops of Bannau Brycheiniog

Mountain Lakes (alphabetically)		
Y Fan Fach	1675	802218
Y Fan Fawr	2000	831216

MYNYDD DU (THE BLACK MOUNTAIN)

Do not confuse this spacious moorland prairie with the Black Mountains that rise 25 miles to the E above Crickhowell and Abergavenny. Mynydd Du is correctly known in English as 'The Black Mountain' or sometimes simply as 'Black Mountain', but always in the singular. The risk of confusion is all the greater because two of the individual hills in the Black Mountains are called Black Mountain and Black Hill.

There is little danger of confusion on the ground! Mynydd Du has none of the pastoral softness of the Black Mountains. There is no sylvan Vale of Ewyas, no Rhiangoll, no leafy glades to speed you on your way, nor any of the intricate mingling of ridge and cwm that you find in those E hills. No, in the N at least (for the S is a different story) this is a treeless wilderness of bleak rambling moors not unlike the bare grassland of Fforest Fawr.

In some ways Mynydd Du is even more austere than Fforest Fawr. The tops barely surmount the surrounding fells and there is nothing of the stature of the decapitated summits of Fan Fawr or Fan Gihirych to catch the eye. The balance is only redressed

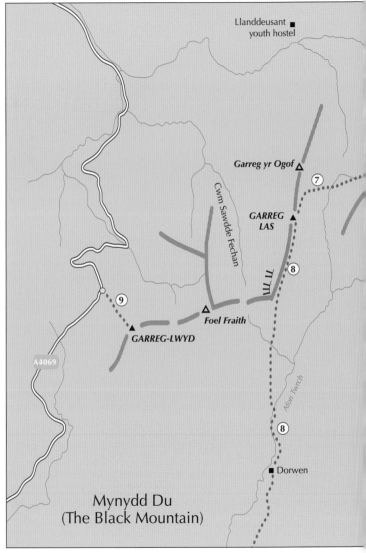

Llanddeusant youth hostel

Garreg yr Ogof

GARREG LAS

Cwm Sawdde Fechan

Foel Fraith

GARREG-LWYD

A4069

Afon Twrch

Dorwen

Mynydd Du
(The Black Mountain)

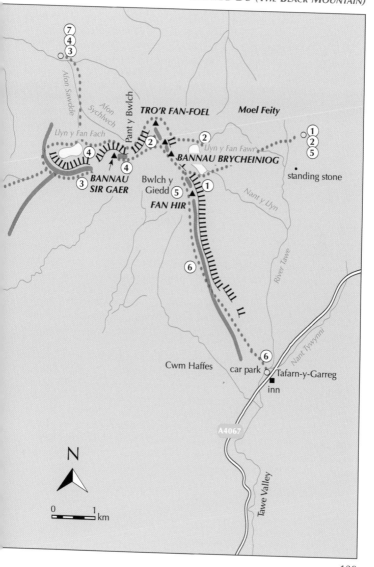

when you view Mynydd Du from the lowlands to N or E. Then the tops are seen in full regal splendour, borne aloft on the rim of a precipitous escarpment, 4 miles long, that extends from Llyn y Fan Fach to Fan Hir before declining by the banks of the Tawe. It is one of the glories of Wales, and there is nothing in Fforest Fawr to match it.

Llyn y Fan Fach is one of two lakes that huddle in the shadow of the cliffs. Mountain lakes are a rarity in S Wales and only Llyn Cwm Llwch in the Beacons can compare with these. Unfortunately Llyn y Fan Fach is cold and sunless much of the time, tucked away in a secluded N-facing hollow below the lowering heights of Bannau Sir Gaer. Its twin, Llyn y Fan Fawr, is more fortunate, cradled in a nest of tiny hillocks beneath Bannau Brycheiniog – a glittering jewel in the morning sun.

Mynydd Du is a large, tilted triangle. One foot rests on the A4069 N of Brynamman, the other on the A4067 near Glyntawe. The apex overlooks a vast expanse of soggy moorland which, within a couple of miles, spawns both the Usk and the Tawe. As it sweeps relentlessly N the ground rises and swells like a giant wave only to break and plunge, as if in the pounding surf, to create the dark towering escarpment. The two most popular peaks, Bannau Brycheiniog and Bannau Sir Gaer, rise either side of the apex where the cliffs change course from E to S. Fan Hir sits astride the edge 1 mile S.

A narrow stairway climbs the cliffs near Llyn y Fan Fawr. The other recognised approach starts from Llanddeusant and curls round Llyn y Fan Fach to join the escarpment as it tapers away in the W. One of the best walks is the edge high above the lakes, returning across the foot of the cliffs. This is just about the only part of Mynydd Du that is safe in mist – assuming you stick to established tracks. If the weather is kind you should enjoy grand views of Fforest Fawr and the Beacons, while on an exceptionally clear day you should also see the Black Mountains and maybe Swansea Bay and the Gower.

Most walkers draw the line there. They have 'done' Mynydd Du, peaks, lakes, the lot, but are oblivious of the two loners out W (Garreg-lwyd and Garreg Las) and know nothing of the rocky battlements and limestone terraces that transform the S half into another world. You could do a lot worse than visit these two outliers, and if you start from Dorwen you will get a taste of the limestone country too. Gazing from Garreg Las over a desert of hills and fells, and fresh from the limestone pavements of Esgair Hir and the sparkling Afon Twrch, you may wonder – as I do – at how much more is there to Mynydd Du than the treadmill round Bannau Brycheiniog. What might Carreg Lem and Castell y Geifr (to name but two) hold in store? One day I hope to find out.

Bannau Brycheiniog

I shall always remember a winter's day on Bannau Brycheiniog when, having eaten a hasty snack in the windshelter with my feet in icy mud, I staggered outside only to be blown headfirst into the trig point. It is not always like that, though being perched on the edge of a high plateau, open to all the elements can muster, it is likely to be bleak and 'challenging' more often than not. Yet on a calm, balmy day it is a place to linger; an eyrie for admiring the green fields of Llanddeusant, the bare orange-browns of Fforest Fawr, the blue-tinged outlines of the Black Mountains and the shapely Beacons.

Be sure to stroll round the finger that gazes out over the moors, first to Fan Foel and a view of Llyn y Fan Fawr, then, having passed two tiny tarns, to Tro'r Fan-foel and its elegant cairn. Steep descents can be made from both points.

Bwlch y Giedd route (BM1)

Drive down the Tawe Valley road from Trecastle and park just S of Glasfynydd Forest, around 856223. (You could also start further S and follow the Nant y Llyn to its outflow from Llyn y Fan Fawr – **BM1,1**. Either way a short diversion brings you to the standing stone at 854215.) Stride out across the featureless moors, aiming for the highest point and skirting the S slopes of Moel Feity. There is no continuous path, but no shortage of 'temporary' trails in roughly the right direction either. With any luck you should achieve a dry crossing.

One of those days when the objective is in view from the start – a gripping sight.

After a while you cross the infant Tawe. See if you can spot a lone tree (the only one for miles!) shading a tiny pool with the chance of a quick dip on a hot day (worth remembering for the return). Llyn y Fan Fawr hides until the very end, but when it finally appears you will not be disappointed. It is at once romantic and austere, wild yet welcoming. In summer it is a place to relax, to laze in the sun or bathe, but in winter the lake is all too often ribboned white by a gusting wind while the cliffs stand wreathed in grey mist.

A well-trodden path, the 'Staircase', inclines across the cliffs to Bwlch y Giedd. Loose and gravelly, it requires care in snow. On top bear L for Fan Hir. Otherwise stay with the path as it veers R for a final pull up to Bannau Brycheiniog's breezy cairn.

Pant y Bwlch route (BM2)

Stay with **BM1** to Llyn y Fan Fawr and then stroll round the shoreline to the higher ground N of the lake. The plan is to follow the foot of the escarpment so look out for a track fairly high up on the hillside going in the required direction. Quite soon you come to a sheepfold and clusters of rushes, near to a deep gash in the cliff wrought by the Nant y Cadno. A faint track struggles up the hillside here to Fan Foel (**BM2,1**). Further on, by the headland, a second track makes a direct pitch for Tro'r Fan-foel (**BM2,2**). However, these are routes for people in a hurry; it's much better to carry on beneath the cliffs.

On turning the headland you get your first glimpse of Llyn y Fan Fach beyond the striated slopes of Bannau Sir Gaer. Impregnable? Not quite. A breach in the cliffs, Pant y Bwlch, reveals a gully where the Afon Sychlwch tumbles down and a narrow pinkish track snakes up its far side to the col between Fan Foel and Bannau Sir Gaer. From the col, marked by a neat little pile of stones, the quickest way to the top is a beeline across the moors on 90°. The most rewarding way is along the edge, taking in Tro'r Fan-foel and Fan Foel en route (**BM2,3**).

Bannau Sir Gaer

An undistinguished sprawl of stones is all that marks this lofty belvedere. Perched on the very edge of a vast abyss, straddling the N escarpment, aloof and supreme, Bannau Sir Gaer conveys its message confidently enough. On a clear day the view is on the grand scale, but nowhere is it finer than over the vast 'desert' of rolling moors to the S that pushes on to the hazy outlines of the Gower and Swansea Bay.

Llanddeusant route W (BM3)

The only problem is that apart from the youth hostel at 777245 it is a fair way from other habitation and so a long drive is

Bannau Sir Gaer and Llyn y Fan Fach

needed to get started. The best place to park is by the banks of the Afon Sawdde at 798239 where the tarmac surface yields to a stony road used by the Welsh Water Authority. Follow this past the filter beds, with Bannau Sir Gaer looming darker and loftier with every step, until after a longish mile the road swings round in a semi-circle at 802221, first R, then L. This is your signal to break away R onto a path that curls around the top of the hollow cradling sun-starved Llyn y Fan Fach.

The scene is awesomely wild. The precipitous escarpment that bears Bannau Sir Gaer, its face ribbed by lateral outcrops of rock breaking the otherwise smooth drift of moss and grass, sweeps remorselessly on to the exposed promontory of Fan Foel, the N-most bastion of Bannau Brycheiniog. At the same time deep gullies, pink and raw, plunge 500ft to the moors below. Sombre in shade, eerie in mist, magnificent when emboldened by snow and enchanting in sun.

A solitary cairn and a tarn mark the top of the rise. This is where the route for Garreg Las, whose twin cairns prick the SW skyline, sidles away (**BM7**). It is now an easy stroll along the edge to Bannau Sir Gaer with dizzy drops L and windswept

Set amid undulating meadows and leafy glades, Llanddeusant provides a charming gateway to Mynydd Du.

moors R. The final rise is so gentle that I once strode right over the top in mist and only realised my error when descending the much steeper slope on the far side, down to Pant y Bwlch.

Llanddeusant route E (BM4)

Begin as in **BM3**, but this time stay with the reservoir road until it terminates by the shores of Llyn y Fan Fach. Next march E across the fells, beneath the towering cliffs, until you spot the fault where the Afon Sychlwch plummets down from on high. A sinuous path, pink and steep, shadows the stream up to the col and a tiny cairn, leaving you with a short, sharp climb on glossy turf along the edge to win the day.

Fan Hir

Fan Hir is more an edge than a peak, with the highest ground very much in doubt. There is no cairn and more than once, when climbing from Bwlch y Giedd, I have been lured from one small hump to the next by the nagging feeling of always being just short of the top! What is not in doubt is the allure. The long, dipping crest, girt with rocky slabs that take on a menacing pose when feathered in mist, totally dominates the grassy moraine E. On a sunny day the eye may feast on the distant Beacons and the glint of Llyn y Fan Fawr, the edge gently dissolving in delicately wooded foothills at the confluence of the Tawe and Tywynni.

Bwlch y Giedd route (BM5)

The hurried way most walkers visit Fan Hir.

A quick scamper up from the bwlch and then back to claim Bannau Brycheiniog (see **BM1**).

Tafarn y Garreg route (BM6)

It's better to tackle Fan Hir from the S. Arrange transport to meet you at Llanddeusant (see **BM H3**) or retrace your steps.

From the car park opposite the Tafarn-y-Garreg Inn follow a footpath sign over a wooden bridge (not shown on the map) and then walk beside the Afon Tawe for a couple of minutes until you are forced L through a gate on to a farm track between twin stone walls. This bears R by a little glade. Abandon it here and scramble up the hillside (very stiff!) to the S tip of

Looking east from Fan Hir towards the Beacons

Fan Hir's long, sloping ridge. The hard work is over now. It takes 2 miles to gain the remaining 900ft.

Alternatively (**BM6,1**) look for the footpath sign at 845165 and follow it to a ford across Cwm Haffes where a wall climbs the hillside R. This leads to open country whence the ridge can be gained as before.

Garreg Las

The long, stony ridge of Garreg Las is crowned by two enormous piles, prominent for miles around. A fledgling escarpment guards its SE slopes rising to a shattered tableland of rock adorned by an ancient, elegantly sculptured cairn. This is a top for quiet contemplation, lost in the immensity of the surrounding moors. Only once have I ever met anyone there, a shepherd looking for missing sheep. The only inklings of civilisation are the green and brown pastures of Dyffryn Tywi N, and the thrustful curl of the edge around Bannau Sir Gaer where you can imagine – though not see – your fellow ramblers. Elsewhere the gaze is lost in countless waves of rounded hills from which the empty plateaux of Garreg-lwyd and Foel Fraith emerge supreme.

Llanddeusant route (BM7)

Stay with **BM3** as far as the cairn by the tarn at 797215. Next strike out slightly S of W for the col between Garreg Las and the trig point on Garreg yr Ogof. A path materialises before long, passing a cluster of tiny, peaty lakelets and contouring round the drier higher ground at the head of Twrch Fechan. The ridge itself gives a pleasant tramp over boulder-ridden heather.

Dorwen route (BM8)

The S half of the Mynydd Du triangle has a lot going for it.

Starting from Dorwen in the deep S seems too far off the beaten track to be worthwhile, and I must confess that it was only after years of acquaintance with Mynydd Du that I discovered it. Lucky that I did! Despite lacking an obvious highlight it has an austere beauty of its own, like the call of the desert, with uncluttered wavy grasslands, vast skies, grey limestone pavements and terraces, peace, solitude and a great emptiness.

Park by the edge of the woods at 762125, which you can reach by turning off the A4068 at 750125 (easily missed). A Land Rover track leads to the decrepit farmhouse of Dorwen (773148), a damp, dullish walk to begin with but soon blossoming into a delightful foray above the narrow, twisting ravine of the Afon Twrch. Beyond Dorwen the path crosses a couple of pretty falls before dropping down to the water's edge. You must now cross to the W bank – easier said than done after wet weather – but not impossible if you make use of a long pebbly island to ferry you across (the ford marked on the map at 773162?).

Once across climb out of the streambed until you can maintain a N course. The track has given up the ghost by now, but with crisp short-cropped grass and springy heather underfoot who needs a track? A cairn breaks the skyline looking as if it might be the top – not so. It lies at about 780190 and appears to commemorate nothing. It is E, and a good 0.5 mile short of, the summit. Sitting astride a belt of broken limestone pavements, it is one of the most beautiful cairns in Wales – a real work of art, well meriting the short diversion.

To vary the return (**BM8,1**) drop down to, and cross, the Afon Twrch near some old quarry workings and a small pool at 784183. Continue S along the limestone escarpment overlooking the Twrch; a lofty, relaxing walk in the golden glow of evening, with wide-ranging views of windswept prairies and rocky citadels. However, it is best to rejoin the outward track at Dorwen if you want to finish the day with dry feet.

Garreg-Lwyd

This most W of all S Wales peaks is also the easiest scalp, being under 0.75 mile from the A4069 and a mere 400ft higher. It is a solitary boulder-strewn spot, too distant from Bannau Brycheiniog for all but dedicated hillwalkers, and too unfashionable to be awarded a day on its own. Yet for anyone satiated with the Fan Hir/Bannau Sir Gaer triangle and seeking new fields to conquer, Garreg-lwyd could be an excellent gateway, giving ready access to Mynydd Du's W fells (see **BM H2**).

A trig point, daubed white, adjoins a sprawling network of interlocking stone shelters, joint guardians of one of S Wales' longest views. On a clear day the vista runs from Swansea and the Gower to the distant Brecon Beacons.

W approach (BM9)

Park at 732185 where the A4069 levels off. Climb on a bearing of 100° up a slope where grass gradually succumbs to stones and boulders. Around 30min should suffice to reach the trig point. Just 0.25 mile NW is a most curiously shaped 'cairn'. Erected on top of an elongated block of stone standing on end it looks for all the world like a beckoning damsel as you approach it from the direction of Foel Fraith. It certainly fooled me!

High-level Walks

The N escarpment (BM H1)

A grand tramp that combines the best of peak and lake.

You can tackle it either from Llanddeusant or the Tawe Valley as in **BM1**; the distances are similar. Starting from Llanddeusant, circle round Llyn y Fan Fach to Bannau Sir Gaer (**BM3**), then drop down to the Afon Sychlwch gully and follow the edge to Bannau Brycheiniog as in **BM2,3**. Next, perhaps, make a diversion to sample Fan Hir's imposing cliffs – a good place for lunch.

The afternoon is totally different but nonetheless memorable. Descend the Staircase to Llyn y Fan Fawr (**BM1**). Next follow the edge, now in the depths below the same fearsome slopes that you were recently striding aloft like a king (see **BM2** and **BM4**).

The W fells (BM H2)

The lonely, untrodden W fells are ideal for a day 'away from it all'; this is just one of many walks in that vast sea of virgin moor and hills.

Park at 732185 and climb Garreg-lwyd (**BM9**). Such is the magic that within 30min the feeling of remoteness is complete, the silence profound. Carry on over Foel Fraith's bald top and drop down to inspect the yawning chasm of the Afon Garw. Follow this N for a while and then climb the crumpled, shattered limestone cliffs guarding Garreg Las's E flank for lunch in the shelter of its two ample cairns. For a varied return keep to the splintered pavements of Garreg Las's S ridge (not forgetting the beautiful cairn at 780190) before bearing R for Cefn y Clychau and home.

Fan Hir to Llanddeusant (BM H3)

Mynydd Du's soaring escarpment is a hill-walker's delight.

The first of two long traverses begins with Fan Hir's long S ridge (**BM6**), continues over Bannau Brycheiniog and Bannau Sir Gaer, then offers a choice of two relaxing routes (**BM3** or **BM4**) back to the tranquillity of Llanddeusant.

Garreg-lwyd to the Tawe (BM H4)

A long but rewarding trek including all five tops.

The second can be taken either way. W to E it looks like this: climb Garreg-lwyd (**BM9**); carry on to Garreg Las; cut across to Bannau Sir Gaer (**BM7** and **BM3**); follow the escarpment edge to Bannau Brycheiniog (**BM2,3**) and then coast down to the Tawe on **BM1** with an optional side-trip to Fan Hir if time permits.

Lower-level Walks/Easier Days

Llyn y Fan Fach (BM L1)

Leave the car where the road fizzles out by the Sawdde at 798239 and then stroll up to the lake. Afternoon is the best time, for by then the sun should be casting its spell on waters that are all too often doomed to cold and shade beneath the daunting precipice of Bannau Sir Gaer. Few scenes of such grandeur can be reached so easily.

A favourite Sunday afternoon outing with the locals.

Llyn y Fan Fawr (BM L2)

A walk that rivals **BM L1** features Llyn y Fan Fawr, Llyn y Fan Fach's twin beneath Bannau Brycheiniog (although the approach across the moors from the Tawe Valley might not be everyone's idea of an easy day!). The lake is at its best in the morning when sunlight brings the escarpment to life and tinges the lake a brilliant blue. Rocky slabs invite picnics and paddling/bathing while the more energetic can amuse themselves circling the shores.

THE NANTLLE AND HEBOG HILLS

OS maps
1:25,000 – Sheet 17, 1:50,000 – Sheet 124

Peaks (by height)	Height (ft)	Map Ref	Page
Moel Hebog	2565	564469	153
Craig Cwm Silyn	2408	525502	150
Trum y Ddysgl	2329	544516	148
Garnedd Goch	2296	511495	151
Mynydd Mawr	2291	539547	161
Mynydd Drws-y-coed	2280	548518	146
Moel yr Ogof	2149	556478	158
Mynydd Tal-y-mignedd	2148	535514	149
Moel Lefn	2093	553485	158
Y Garn	2077	551526	145

Mountain Lakes (alphabetically)			
Cwmffynnon	1300	538517	
Cwm Silyn (2)	1100	515506	
Nameless (2)	1375	519508	

The Nantlle and Hebog Hills

The Nantlle/Hebog hills are as different from their neighbours as chalk from cheese. Gone are the lofty, windswept ridges of the Carneddau and the bouldery wastes of the Glyders. Nothing recalls the rolling moors and lakes of Moel Siabod and the Moelwyns. As for Snowdon, well, Snowdon is Snowdon...

So what is their appeal? Partly a landscape softened by woodland and refreshed by the sea with the incomparable Nantlle ridge itself, the lovely Vale of Pennant and firm yet unobtrusive paths. Partly their good fortune in having been spared the industrial rape that has defaced the environs of the Moelwyn and Ffestiniog hills. Perhaps also, after the giants, their modest scale permits more varied days and greater intimacy.

With intimacy comes acute appreciation. The Nantlle/Hebog hills are full of little surprises that might well go unsung in a larger scene. Tiny rock-bound pools, dark lonely cwms, the Great Slab in Cwm Silyn, Owen Glyndwr's cave, the gushing falls of Castell Cidwm. These, and treasures like them, are what kindle and sustain their charm.

But enough of such generalisations! For though it is convenient to pair Nantlle and Hebog in the same chapter, they have their own distinctive sub-cultures with Mynydd Mawr, a solitary loner to the N, different again.

The Nantlle hills straddle a short ridge running NE to SW. Six peaks breach the 2000ft barrier, ranging from Y Garn, a bristly soaring eminence overlooking Rhyd-ddu in the E, to Garnedd Goch calmly gazing down over the Lleyn Peninsula in the W. (A seventh peak, Mynydd Craig-coch at 1996ft, just fails to qualify.) In between these two sentinels lie Mynydd Drws-y-coed, virtually an extension of Y Garn but requiring a fine little scramble for its conquest; Trum y Ddysgl, its smooth grassy top perched airily on the top of a mighty abyss; Mynydd Tal-y-mignedd of massive-cairn fame; and Craig Cwm Silyn, highest and rockiest of them all.

The traverse of the Nantlle ridge is one of the great experiences of the Welsh hills, fit to be mentioned in the same breath as the Snowdon horseshoe or Bristly Ridge, though vastly different in scale and character. Narrow, twisty, undulating, and grassy to begin with, the Nantlle ridge later moderates to a wide rocky plateau. S are the pastoral charms of Pennant, the Hebog hills, the sands of Tremadog Bay. N the dramatic pass of Drws-y-coed, the crumpled crags of Mynydd Mawr, the blue of Caernarfon Bay and the plains of Anglesey. Before you, the green meadows of Lleyn, to the rear the massive presence of Snowdon, and always the snaking, sinuous Nantlle crest itself, tempting you ever on.

Where else, in a mere 5 miles, are you offered so much for such a modest effort? Despite the sharpness of the ridge you are never exposed. The only time a steadying hand is needed is between Y Garn and Mynydd Drws-y-coed, and even then only momentarily. There is a good path all the way. There was a time when this exhilarating climb was the haunt of the connoisseur. Not any more! Gone are the wisp-like trails of yesteryear, replaced by well-trodden paths that are already, in places, degenerating into wide muddy scars.

With the Nantlle ridge the whole is so very much more than the sum of the parts that other routes often get short shrift. More's the pity! At the very least you should sample the rocky charisma of Cwm Silyn and the lonely climb from Braichydinas in the Pennant Valley. Pennant is a lovely vale, fortunate in having no through traffic to disturb its calm, an oasis of rustic simplicity in the lap of the fells. It is doubly blessed in playing host not only to Nantlle but Hebog as well.

Moel Hebog looks, and is, a real mountain, sporting a distinctive wedge-shaped top that is a landmark far and wide. It is a dominating peak too, towering not only over its native Beddgelert but completely dwarfing its two satellites, Moel yr Ogof and Moel Lefn. Yet how deceptive appearances can be! Viewed from Pennant it is Moel Hebog

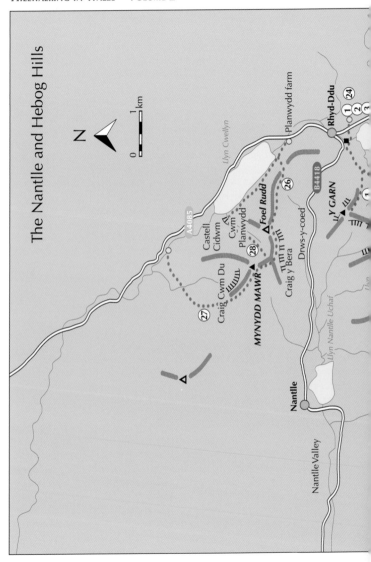

The Nantlle and Hebog Hills

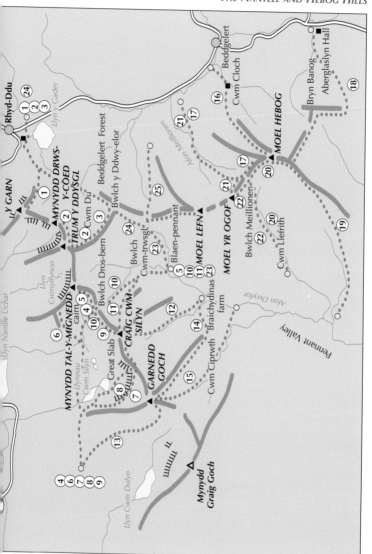

Y Garn and Mynydd Drws-y-coed at the start of the Nantlle ridge (NH 1)

itself that now lacks interest while the threatening black cliffs that command attention – so out of character with the rest of Pennant – are the W ramparts of Moel Lefn; lamb turned lion.

The Hebog hills are almost as much one-route hills as the Nantlle. The Cwm Cloch trail from Beddgelert is as much tramped as all the rest put together. Great hike though it is, why the others should be so overlooked is a mystery. A particularly fine walk starts with the rhododendrons in Aberglaslyn Pass, while others wind through the Beddgelert Forest. You can also attack Moel Lefn from the N, turning the flank of its W battlements. And so on. Nearly all these routes can be worked into rounds encompassing the high wold from Hebog to Lefn. This is one of the stars, a highland where thickets of heather lovingly garland a scattering of rocky outcrops.

Being on the seaward side of Snowdonia, the views are hauntingly beautiful. The coastline emerges from the haze way down the Lleyn Peninsula where the Rivals hold sway. You can follow it over the Black Rock Sands, round the Traeth Bach Estuary and on to Harlech, with glimpses of far-off Cader Idris. Then there is Anglesey, peeping through clefts in the Nantlle ridge, the calm of the sea complementing the peace of the valleys; the Colwyn Valley, home to the Beddgelert Forest; the ethereal charm of Nantgwynant; the Aberglaslyn Pass, and Pennant where the sylvan green of the lowlands merges imperceptibly with the purples of the heights.

Lift your eyes to the hills and you will see more old friends: the Nantlle ridge, Mynydd Mawr, Snowdon and its consorts from Moel Eilio to Yr Aran, Moel Siabod,

Cnicht and the Moelwyns, the Arans, Arenigs, and Rhobell Fawr. The Nantlle hills are equally fine viewpoints since, being further N, they also carry the gaze to the Glyders and Carneddau.

The story of Mynydd Mawr will sound familiar by now; a one-route peak (the Planwydd route) that is also isolated, with the result that it is sadly neglected. You have only to add Craig Cwm Du and Castell Cidwm to the repertoire, however, and the 'Elephant Mountain' becomes a worthy objective with fine rambling moors, forgotten cwms, spectacular crags and the falls of Castell Cidwm.

Note For many years the Nantlle ridge and Mynydd Mawr suffered from access restrictions that effectively put them 'out of bounds' to hill-walkers. These problems have only recently been eased, and the arrangements are still subject to regular review. Please, therefore, observe all access notices. When in doubt enquire and seek permission locally before setting out.

Y Garn

You can hardly fail to be impressed by the serrated, defiant-looking arête that dominates the tiny hamlet of Rhyd-ddu. It buttresses one of the many 'Y Garns' in the Welsh hills (of which the most famous is the 3000-footer in the Glyders). This Y Garn is a mere 2080ft in height, a fact it is hard to credit, such is the awesome sense of power it conveys. It can hold its own with the best and is the first port of call on the E–W traverse of the Nantlle ridge.

Y Garn commands a view of epic proportions. Snowdon and her satellites from Moel Eilio to Yr Aran; Cnicht and the Moelwyns; the scattered woodlands of the Vale of Colwyn; the Hebog hills; the sharp broken ridge to Mynydd Drws-y-coed; Anglesey and the sea; all gladden the eye and feed the spirit. Nearer to hand the shattered crags of Mynydd Mawr are framed in the clefts of Y Garn's equally splintered N face.

Y Garn and Mynydd Mawr

Rhyd-ddu route (NH1)

Cross the road from the car park at 571525, S of Rhyd-ddu, and follow the footpath sign. Tread gingerly over the stepping stones across a marshy field, skirt round the cottage of Tan y Llyn and then be guided by another footpath sign as you approach the B4418. Stay with this, initially along a wall, until after 0.5 mile a white arrow on a boulder (one of many) sends you off R. (Straight ahead leads to the Pennant Valley – **NH3**.)

From here on the path is obvious; too obvious as unfortunately it is now badly eroded. It is consistently and unpityingly steep, but plenty of rest stops are justified by the rapidly unfolding view. Higher up grass yields to rock out of which two enormous cairns have been built.

Mynydd Drws-y-Coed

Mynydd Drws-y-coed is really an extension of Y Garn, and it is from Y Garn that it is usually climbed. Indeed, when viewed from that peak it is one of Snowdonia's

Mynydd Mawr viewed from the ramparts of Y Garn (NH 1)

most gripping sights. The jagged teeth of its E arête, soaring above the yawning abyss of Drws-y-coed, endow it with a charisma worthy of Bristly Ridge itself. It comes as quite a surprise to find that the climb along the ridge – exciting scramble though it is – harbours no dangers (in good weather, that is; it would be a very different story in snow or ice.) Its teeth are completely drawn by the time you reach a top of gently undulating grass with only the merest hint of rock. Not even a cairn. It is magnificent nonetheless, and the views are stupendous.

Bwlch y Ddwy-elor route (NH2)
See **NH3**.

Trum y Ddysgl

Trum y Ddysgl is a silken, grassy finger formed where the narrow arête to Mynydd Tal-y-mignedd joins the ridge from Bwlch y Ddwy-elor (Pass of the Two Biers). It is a breezy, exhilarating eyrie. The land falls away sharply on every hand and the brow overlooks a vast chasm stretching across to Mynydd Drws-y-coed. Somehow it seems entirely appropriate that it retains a virginal purity – there is no cairn, no fence, not even a solitary stone. The sole adornment is an arrow etched in the springy turf and now fading with age.

Trum y Ddysgl means 'Ridge of the Dish', and you will be in no doubt as to the origins of this name should you ever have occasion to view the hill from the road running through Drws-y-coed.

Bwlch y Ddwy-elor route (NH3)
Go through the kissing-gate across the road from the car park at 571525 and follow the footpath past the cottage of Tan y Llyn to the B4418. There another footpath sign directs you through a gate, with frequent arrow signs to prevent straying. Before long a sign on a boulder heralds a parting of the ways; R for Y Garn, straight on for Pennant which is today's route.

After a squelchy trudge you enter the Beddgelert Forest and care is needed to steer through a confusion of forest trails, especially where only decapitated stumps remain. Keep to 205° as far as possible, aiming for the bwlch on the skyline ahead, but take care to spot the turn at 557509 where you must re-enter the forest from the ravages of the felling.

There is a glorious moment just after you emerge from the forest again when, at the top of the pass (marked by a gate and a stile over a wall), the scene is instantly transformed from dark forest to the greens of Pennant and the blue shimmer of the sea. Surely the promised land was never finer than this! Yet there is just a hint of the crags of Moel Lefn peeping over the shoulder of Y Gyrn to remind you that this is Snowdonia.

There are two tracks leading down into the Pennant Valley, but for Trum y Ddysgl bear R over rough grass and make for the edge of the woods where a path climbs the ridge. A long steep haul! A little over halfway up spot the track that inclines away R round the upper slopes of Cwm Du. It joins the Nantlle ridge midway between Trum y Ddysgl and Mynydd Drws-y-coed, providing the only direct approach to the latter peak (**NH2**).

Mynydd Tal-y-mignedd

Mynydd Tal-y-mignedd is strategically placed midway along the Nantlle ridge, but its main claim to fame is its huge chimney-like cairn which was erected to celebrate Queen Victoria's Diamond Jubilee and is a conspicuous landmark for miles. It is also one of the few places from where Criccieth, Caernarfon and Harlech castles can all be seen.

Oddly, for such an excellent viewpoint, there is no really satisfying direct route. The ways given below all have an air of artificiality. In reality this hardly matters as the timeless glory of the peak rests on its position as a staging post on the Nantlle traverse, and for that reason alone it will never lack visitors.

Cwm Silyn route (NH4)
Follow **NH9** to Bwlch Dros-bern and climb the SW ridge along the fence.

Pennant Valley route (NH5)
Follow **NH10** to Bwlch Dros-bern and climb the SW ridge along the fence.

NW ridge (NH6)

The least artificial of the routes.

Start on **NH9** but instead of following the slopes of Craig Cwm Silyn round to Bwlch Dros-bern, strike out across trackless country to gain the NW slopes of Mynydd Tal-y-mignedd at about 528516. The ridge itself is easy grass.

Craig Cwm Silyn

The stony top of Craig Cwm Silyn, its windshelter/cairn almost lost in a scrum of posturing boulders, is the highest point of the Nantlle ridge, a status the peak has no problem in living up to. Facing S, overlooking the Pennant Valley, are the frowning cliffs that give the peak its name. N is Cwm Silyn itself, as wild as anything Snowdonia can muster but transfigured on a sunny day by its glittering lakes. At 516502, facing NW, is the Great Slab, a Mecca for rock climbers. From the E the peak displays a softer face, a bouldery pyramid lavishly clothed in heather. Only from the W, where a stony waste leads to Garnedd Goch, does it fail to excite.

Some 99 out of every 100 visitors to Craig Cwm Silyn go there as part of the Nantlle ridge traverse, but this is a peak that deserves a day on its own. There is an enviable choice. Several routes start from Llynnau Cwm Silyn at 512507, a point you can reach by driving up the mountain road that ends at 496511, parking through the gate and then following a cart track. Other routes rise from the rustic calm of Pennant.

Rim route (NH7)

A well-worn track climbs the W rim of Cwm Silyn from 512507, making light of the 1000ft rise and giving dramatic views of the Great Slab. On top keep to the edge as you stride NW for the cairn, noting the rough crumbly head of the gully route at 518500 (the wall from Garnedd Goch makes a right-angled turn nearby).

Gully route (NH8)

From Llynnau Cwm Silyn look for the tell-tale scree trails that climbers use to get to the foot of the Great Slab. Just to the R you will notice a 'notch' in the skyline indicating a little gully. It is a slog up to the Great Slab – with a bit of the old 'two steps forward one step back' syndrome – but not too bad as the scree is mostly of the larger, firmer variety. From the Great Slab the gully entrance is straight ahead, leading into a mild scramble over rocks which double up as a waterfall in wet weather. Keep to the crest when the gully divides halfway up.

E face from Cwm Silyn (NH9)

Leave Llynnau Cwm Silyn and proceed on sketchy trails through the thickets of heather that decorate the N and E slopes of the mountain until you approach the wall that crosses Bwlch Dros-bern at 533508. En route you pass two nameless tarns at 519508. Avoid the scramble up the rocks beside the wall (unless you are adept at rock work) and go for one of the many tracks that zigzag up the heather/bilberry terraces ahead of the wall.

E face from the Pennant Valley (NH10)

Drop down to Bwlch Dros-bern, keeping L near the foot to avoid a little cliff near the wall. Cross the wall and then try and spot traces of the drovers' road that is reputed to have once linked the Nantlle and Pennant valleys. Keep N of the stream and it will not be long before you pick up the old quarry trail starting at 541504. Once in the valley a jumble of little trails leads to the road-head at 540493.

Breast route (NH11)

A direct, steep way down leaves the cairn on about 110° and follows the wall that straddles the SE ridge. When the slope gets too steep for comfort, bear diagonally L to join one of the many trails to the road-head.

Not recommended for tired legs.

Braichydinas route (NH12)

See **NH14**.

Garnedd Goch

Garnedd Goch is secure in the hillwalker's repertoire if only because it provides a higher and easier start to the Nantlle ridge than its counterpart, Y Garn, at the other end. Otherwise a top that is no more than a sprawling, bouldery waste would surely be forgotten. Having said that, the practice of terminating the ridge walk at Craig Cwm Silyn (if coming from the E) is to be deprecated for the views into Cwm Silyn as you continue on to Garnedd Goch are some of the best in the range.

NW approach (NH13)

The high start gives the quickest way onto the ridge and thus all the more time to enjoy one of Wales' finest walks.

A narrow road winds steeply up to the 850ft contour line at 496511 to give one of the highest starts in Snowdonia. There is parking space through a gate at the end, where the road becomes a cart track leading to Llynnau Cwm Silyn. For Garnedd Goch set out across the moors on 140°, with only the odd sheep track for support, and aim for the wall across the skyline. Follow this to the barren stony top. A more interesting though circuitous approach (**NH13,1**) starts along the rim route for Craig Cwm Silyn (see **NH7**), leaving it due S for Garnedd Goch about halfway up.

Braichydinas route (NH14)

This jolly route is little used and has a fresh appeal to hill-lovers seeking new ways to greet old friends.

Look for a stylish, rusty gate by a bridge over a stream, just S of Braichydinas Farm (534484). Go through it onto a path that swathes through the ferns, laying the Pennant Valley at your feet. The objective is to work round R of the rocky knoll ahead so where the path splits – as it does once or twice – choose accordingly.

The stream has gouged a deep gill R with gushing falls and foaming cataracts. At the top of the falls bear L along a wall to a sheepfold. You are now betwixt two streams. Staying with the R one (as you have up to now) gives a lonely, track-less route to Craig Cwm Silyn (**NH12**). However for Garnedd Goch switch to the L stream, following it across a flat bog to reach a 'micro canyon' at 527486, a good spot for a rest or a bathe.

Stay with the stream, maintaining a bearing of about 290°, first across more marsh and then up a heathery slope to a wall crossing your path. Look out for another wall, half-L, straddling a shallow ridge above you. Make for this and in under 30min Garnedd Goch is yours.

Cwm Ciprwth route (NH15)

When I last came down Cwm Ciprwth at the end of a hot, tiring day I sought solace in conjuring up all the epithets I would use to describe the route once I came to write about it. It starts in great style. Walking on 155° on crisp, springy heather you are soon facing the verdant loveliness of Cwm Pennant with Mynydd Graig-Goch's gnarled, rocky top R and Moel Lefn's lowering crags across the valley. So far so good – now the rude awakening. Easy heather changes to thick deep clumps, covering a haphazard assortment of smooth and slippery boulders. No more carefree striding; every step is now a step into the unknown – jolty and wearying.

However, after 1 mile (it seems forever) comes another transition, signalled by a rusting old waterwheel, a sad relic of a bygone age. Now, at last, a path appears, leading through pretty terrain where brook, pasture, rocks and woods exist in pleasing harmony. True the path fades when you reach the valley bed, near a bridge, but by then it is only a short step across the field to the road.

Overall verdict: committed hillwalkers who accept the toil because they are looking for new byways, by all means have a go; other walkers steer clear!

Moel Hebog

Moel Hebog (Hill of the Hawk) is the solid, wedge-shaped peak that stands guard over the charming little hamlet of Beddgelert. Seen from Llyn Dinas in the Vale of Gwynant it conveys a sense of power rather than beauty. Go to Rhyd-ddu, however, and a quite different Moel Hebog greets you. Now it is flanked by its two satellites, Moel yr Ogof and Moel Lefn, and together they form a soft flowing line whose challenge is well nigh irresistible when seen in the clear morning air.

Accept the challenge and you will not be disappointed. The classic Cwm Cloch route is but one of many that offer rich variety and complement a rousing panorama of Snowdonia with lingering views over the lovely vales of Gwynant and Pennant, and over the blue-white seascapes of Tremadog Bay and Anglesey. The trig point on Hebog stands near the junction of two walls on what is a rambling and mainly grassy top.

Moel Hebog and the vale of Gwynant

Cwm Cloch route (NH16)

Choose a cool, clear day as the angle is as steep as the views are fine!

Leave the Beddgelert-to-Caernarfon road at 584484 and walk down the leafy lane to Cwm Cloch Farm, passing under the old Welsh Highland Railway. Pass through a copse of pines. Turn R just beyond, as directed by an arrow on the wall of a derelict barn, onto what, except in the driest of seasons, is a quagmire of mud. Stepping stones soon come to the rescue and before you can say 'wet feet' a green path is happily swathing through slopes of bracken and heather.

The path swings L and begins its long upward haul, well cairned and never in doubt. The tiny hamlet of Beddgelert suddenly seems very far away while the blue of Llyn Dinas and the greens of Nantgwynant are framed in a magnificent V. Nantlle ridge, Moel Eilio and Snowdon raise one arm; Moel Siabod, Cnicht and Moelwyns raise the other (with a fleeting glimpse of Glyder Fach for the discerning eye). The temptation to linger is strong, but fair peak was never won as easily as this – so back to work!

The terrain is bleaker now with little rocky runnels and snakes of orange-brown screes threading up the broken escarpment (Diffwys) that is such a feature from the road, now more than 2000ft below. When the angle relents a stony track leads over sparse windswept turf to the cairn.

Cwm Meillionen route (NH17)

Use forest trails marked on the 1:25,000 map (the campsite in Cwm Meillionen at 578490 is as good a starting point as any) to reach the bridge over the Afon Meillionen at 569487. The trail proper starts here along the true L bank of the stream.

Delectable woodlands lie ahead as you wander on a cushion of pine needles beneath a dark canopy of branches, through dainty little glens, alongside the brook and round the tumbling falls. Occasional glimpses of the soaring crags of Moel Hebog and Moel yr Ogof whet the appetite for the lofty heights to come and the happy chatter of the Afon Meillionen, as it tumbles timelessly through its leafy paradise, accompanies you until near the end.

There are five forest trails crossed en route. No problem; just keep straight ahead. Before the first, and again

*The Hebog hills
(NH 16)*

between the first and the second, the stream divides. Keep L. Shortly after the fifth road (which you cross near a turning circle), leave the forest at a stile at 563479. The crags of Moel yr Ogof, topped by the cave where Owen Glyndwr is said to have hidden from his English pursuers, tower ominously above. The cave is not easy to find, so if you plan a visit this is the place to puzzle out the route. It is a bit of a scramble and care is needed round a couple of exposed spots.

Whatever your objective – Moel Hebog, Moel yr Ogof or the cave – you will need to pull up to Bwlch Meillionen and its scattering of peaty tarns. This is hard work over slippery boulders. A tumbledown wall helps in mist. From the bwlch the climb up to Moel Hebog is a good 800ft, but always seems more! An exhausting test of wind and limb in ascent, it is equally toilsome coming down, too steep either to walk or run comfortably.

Moel yr Ogof is a mere 350ft and gentler. Note the narrow cleft you pass through on the way. Dark, dank and fern-ridden perhaps, but nevertheless a welcome haven from the wind in winter.

Aberglaslyn route (NH18)

It begins at 594461, a few steps N of the entrance to Aberglaslyn Hall. No sign, no gate marks the spot, just a dark peaty path plunging into the woods. Follow it as it bears L through a gate to cross a stream and again as it rises to another gate marked 'Private' where it swings hard R.

The path levels off now, but you must leave it almost at once for a stony track L. This is not easy to spot as it bends back on itself nearly straight away and is thus almost hidden from view. However all is not lost if you miss it. The original path quickly comes to an effective end at a little gorge crossed by a pair of precarious-looking poles. If you get this far, simply go back and try again.

The new track is dark and moist, banked by mossy stones. It cleaves its aged way up rhododendron slopes where the silence is broken only by the chattering of the stream R. Eventually you leave the woods at a stile over a fence at 591461 with broken country ahead. Although there are fragments of

For the connoisseur this is a delectable – almost forgotten – route, amidst the rhododendrons for which the Aberglaslyn Pass is so renowned.

tracks, the best plan is to walk on 240°, aiming for the col between Moel-ddu and Bryn Banog (577456). A sharp pull up to Bryn Banog is rewarded by exquisite views with Snowdon, Cnicht, the Moelwyns, Arenigs, Arans, Rhinogs, Nantmor, Llyn Cwmystradllyn and the sea all on display.

Bryn Banog is the place to survey the rest of the route. Look for a grassy rake near 567464 that breaches Hebog's otherwise seemingly impregnable defences. There is a scattering of lonely tarns on the way over and an ancient cairn at the foot. The rake itself will test your fitness and you will not be sorry to find a cairned path at the top slanting across to the trig point. In descent begin on 180° and then bear L to pick up the line of cairns; alternatively aim for Moel-ddu.

The route can also be begun from the road-head near Plas-llyn, 562452 (**NH18,1**). Follow the farm track to the head of the valley and then scramble up to the col between Moel Hebog and Bryn Banog to join the rake as before.

SW ridge (NH19)

As a way up this is a bore, a grassy trudge up Moel Hebog's dullest side. However, used as a descent in the evening with the Rivals, Lleyn and the sea all bathed in sunlight, it offers the perfect finale. A succession of walls points to the telephone kiosk at 532454.

A good way down for tired legs, long but easy.

Cwm Llefrith route (NH20)

Start behind Cwrt Isaf Farm (540465). Early scrappiness – rough pastures, minor excavations – soon gives way to more pleasant scenery as height is gained. Surprisingly it is Moel Lefn that draws the eye, boasting a sharp rocky pyramid that totally upstages Moel yr Ogof (rugged but shapeless) and Moel Hebog (a dull grassy mound).

The mood changes completely at Bwlch Meillionen, the E skyline opening out to reveal a grand vista of peaks in which Snowdon and the Moelwyns are pre-eminent. It is as well to rest awhile to admire this enchanting view because the simple stroll up Cwm Llefrith is now replaced by a brutal slog up Moel Hebog's NW ridge (see **NH17**). Alternatively, a L turn along the wall that straddles the bwlch leads more easily to Moel yr Ogof (**NH22**).

Moel yr Ogof

Moel yr Ogof's chief claim to fame is the cave where Owen Glyndwr is said to have sought refuge from the invading English in the 15th century. Indeed the very name 'Moel yr Ogof' means 'Hill of the Cave'. The cave in question lies high up on the mountain's exposed E face and is not easy to reach for the average pedestrian (see **NH17**). The peak itself is a cluster of attractive outcrops most naturally reached along a well-used track from Bwlch Meillionen (560475). Crags bar the way W and E and the extension N towards Moel Lefn soon leads to unfrequented country. So if the weather clamps down, the safest retreat is back to the bwlch.

Cwm Meillionen route (NH21)
See **NH17**.

Cwm Llefrith route (NH22)
See **NH20**.

Moel Lefn

Moel Lefn is a deceiver. From the Colwyn Valley – where it stands in line abreast with Moel Hebog and Moel yr Ogof – it is no more than a little hump on the end. But what a change when you observe the same hills from the Pennant Valley! Moel Hebog is now a plain grassy dome and it is Moel Lefn that catches the eye. Dark brooding cliffs, topped by a rocky crown, not only stand in stark relief from the pastoral simplicity of the Pennant Valley, but prove beyond any shadow of doubt that here is a true mountain. The country N of Moel Lefn is relatively untrodden so, with crags around, it is best left alone in thick weather when the safest way off is over Moel yr Ogof to Bwlch Meillionen.

Pennant Valley route (NH23)

From the road-head cross the stone footbridge over the Afon Dwyfor and you are on course for Blaen-pennant and the Nantlle ridge (**NH10/11**). Step over the ladder-stile and a net-work of paths (plus remnants of an old quarry rail track) leads to Bwlch y Ddwy-elor and the vale head. This is today's route, through you do not go as far as the pass. Instead aim for Bwlch Cwm-trwsgl between Y Garn and Moel Lefn and spy out a path that begins near a quarry site at 550498, then winds over stone-studded grass along the N arm of the bwlch. When you come to a wall bounding the Beddgelert Forest, turn R and follow it past a stile (see **NH25**) and then over loose slate up to the disused Princess Quarry.

The path now plays hide-and-seek so work your way round the top of the crags defending Moel Lefn's W flanks. The bearing is 230°, later veering to 135°, after which the path reasserts itself. You end on a broad grassy plateau and only need to swing L to capture your peak.

The road-head at 540493 is a base for many fine hikes.

Rhyd-ddu route (NH24)

Follow **NH3** to Bwlch y Ddwy-elor. Take the L of the two paths that descend into the Pennant Valley, walking through a mix of quarries, spoil heaps and ruined quarrymen's huts until, at 550499, you pick up the track into Bwlch Cwm-trwsgl mentioned in **NH23**.

Beddgelert Forest route (NH25)

Descend from Moel Lefn to the forest stile at 554496 (**NH23** in reverse). Cross the stile into the forest. When you come to a forest road follow it L for 200 paces until a blue waymark sign indicates the re-entry point. After 300 paces leave the forest again over another stile and enjoy a colourful open 0.5 mile of mingled bog, boulders, heather and bracken. Enter the woods again at yet another stile, exiting onto another forest road at 567497. From here on it is best to use the forest roads shown on the 1:25,000 map to gain the Caernarfon/Beddgelert road.

A pretty route with variable scenery, and for once the blue way-marking is both clear and consistent.

Mynydd Mawr

Mynydd Mawr (sometimes known as the Elephant Mountain) is an inspiring sight from any direction. Yet it suffers the fate that befalls most isolated peaks that cannot easily be fitted into longer walks. 'Good for a half-day expedition without much excitement,' say the pundits. That may be true if you restrict yourself to the classic Planwydd route, but that would be to deny yourself many of the mountain's manifold riches. You have only to combine the three routes described below and the Elephant Mountain will repay you with as fine a day's sport as any, with grandiose views and solitude thrown in.

Note The cairn adjoins a sprawling windshelter set in a vast sea of stones. There is no inkling of the crags that lie in wait so when in doubt be sure to locate the Planwydd track (the only safe way off in mist) on 160°.

Planwydd route (NH26)

Pass through Planwydd Farm at 570539 and then straightaway turn L through a gate into a field. Cross the field on 280° to an iron gate on the edge of the forest. Follow the track that disappears into the darkness on a carpet of pine needles, keeping R where it splits almost at once. Clusters of bluebells and leafy glades provide a pleasant awakening in spring. You eventually emerge on the open hillside at 562540, whereupon a severe climb on grass brings the minor top of Foel Rudd and a much-needed flop by the cairn to admire the view which encompasses the Nantlle ridge from Y Garn to Garnedd Goch, Snowdon and her consorts from Yr Aran to Moel Eilio, and the great wedge of Moel Hebog. There are also the first glimpses of the sea, Llyn Cwellyn and the summit of Mynydd Mawr itself, still far away across the yawning solitudes of Cwm Planwydd.

The hard work is over. It is now a simple stroll round the lip of Cwm Planwydd with eyes focused on the vicious,

Mynydd Mawr across Llyn y Dywarchen

crumpled crags of Craig y Bera as they plunge to the depths of Drws-y-coed far below.

Craig Cwm Du route (NH27)

Leave the summit on 300° and pick up a track that curves round the edge of Craig Cwm Du, surely one of the loneliest and most forbidding cwms in Wales, whose stern N-facing cliffs know nothing of the warmth of the sun. All too soon the track deserts you to cavort away NW. No matter. The heather is short and crisp with freelancing no problem. You can forget your feet and feast on the lush lowlands that run on to Anglesey.

Aim for a gate in a wall at 536558 and then follow the forest boundary round to 541567, close to a cottage where a path leads to the footbridge at Salem. It is a pleasant ramble despite the trackless terrain, with a colourful mingle of woodlands and bushes, heather and bracken, boulders and bog.

The walk can be extended by staying with the course of the former Welsh Highland Railway, which you cross just before Salem, and rejoining the road at 547564. Alternatively you can work your way along the wall that contains Mynydd Mawr's NE crags to the vicinity of Castell Cidwm, and thence by forest trail back to Planwydd.

Castell Cidwm route (NH28)

Leave the road at Planwydd and follow the forest trail along Llyn Cwellyn to the disused quarry at its far end. Cross the stream and a wall and then climb up alongside the wall until it embeds itself in the rock face. A flagstone makes easy work of crossing the wall to join a well-trodden path (used by the occasional rock climber) that runs beneath the lowering crags of Castell Cidwm. The transformation from the scene of only a few minutes ago is remarkable. Gone are the valley flats, the green pastures, the lake. Now you are in a world of malicious overhanging cliffs where the thunder of the falls drowns all else, a world from which the only escape is a steep, slithery scree track that climbs damply beside the falls.

Stay with the stream as the gradient eases and bear L where it divides at 549552. The drama is spent. Cwm Planwydd is wide and shallow, featureless apart from two piles of aircraft wreckage. Yet it has an appeal; partly the appeal of the unknown, the untrodden, partly the appeal of isolation. The rim of the cwm is drawn so tightly that you could almost imagine you were walking in a crater. Work up to the rim near the W tip of Craig y Bera when only a short walk remains.

For a scenic variation (**NH28,1**) leave the cairn a little E of N, walk through prolific seas of heather and make for an ancient cairn at 543555 overlooking Craig Cwmbychan. Next follow the slope down to where the stream in Cwm Planwydd divides and so back to Castell Cidwm.

High-level Walks

Nantlle ridge (NH H1)

Beginning in the W with Garnedd Goch gives the higher, easier start. You will also be facing Snowdon, always food for the soul but a veritable feast in winter when the rays of the setting sun give the snow-capped tops a magical pinkish hue like icing on a cake.

No matter which way you tackle it, W–E or E–W, the Nantlle ridge guarantees an unforgettable day.

Climbing Mynydd Drws-y-coed from Y Garn at the start of the Nantlle ridge

Personally I prefer going E–W. Despite its rigours the climb up Y Garn is the ideal aperitif, with majestic views and an atmosphere of drama and excitement that will be sustained all day. It is an ascent of real character too, transcending the more prosaic trudge up Garnedd Goch. Best of all, do the round trip – there and back! It is well within the capability of a strong walker in a longish day and it also solves the transport problem.

This fine 'symphony' of a walk starts like many great works with a long slow introduction. There is no other way to take Y Garn, one of the stiffest tests of stamina in Snowdonia (**NH1**). Then comes the allegro, heralded fortissimo by the sight of Snowdon and the sinuous pinnacled ridge winding on to Mynydd Drws-y-coed. The scramble up the sharp rocky arête is airy, demanding hands here and there, but never dangerous. Keep to the edge for the easiest passage. As rock peters out, and drama fades, a stile leads to Mynydd Drws-y-coed's placid top.

Now for the slow movement. A simple walk, with little loss or gain in height, along a grooved path that stays slightly below the crest, brings you to Trum y Ddysgl's cairnless crown, an arrow in the turf the sole decoration. Be careful en route not to find yourself inadvertently taking the path that slants across to Trum y Ddyslgl's S ridge on its way down to Bwlch y Ddwy-elor. It is easily done!

Now another allegro. Down a sheeny grassy slope to a brief, but surprisingly narrow, rocky saddle with Llyn Cwmffynnon framed 800ft below. Next on grass again up another incline to the imposing obelisk on Mynydd Tal-y-mignedd.

Next a rumbustious scherzo; down along a fence, the path steep and eroded, to Bwlch Dros-bern, the lowest point of the ridge and the probable crossing point of an ancient drove road linking the Nantlle and Pennant valleys. Next up to Craig Cwm Silyn, king of the ridge. Unless you are a rock climber avoid the temptation to scramble up the rockface near the wall that supplants the fence. Detour R until the crags abate and a series of playful little paths rambles up a myriad of tiny ledges and terraces until the stony summit brings a welcome rest.

The finale is in quieter vein with a near flat mile to Garnedd Goch, stony at first, then grassy, the second half alongside a solid stone wall. Keep R to view the imposing cliffs of Cwm Silyn, the Great Slab and the sparkling lakes they cradle. Garnedd Goch itself is a waste of stones. The mood is finally one of peace as this great walk ends with the eye gripped by the green of Lleyn, the beauty of Pennant and the unending blue of the sea.

Ramblers wishing to reduce the ascent and descent of a complete two-way traverse have several choices. Having completed the ridge E–W, for example, you could drop down to the Pennant Valley on any of **NH10**, **11**, **12**, **14** or **15**. You would then regain Rhyd-ddu by working across to Bwlch y Ddwy-elor (553504) with a selection of easy valley paths to choose from, before following **NH3** back to base.

The options are more limited the other way. On reaching Y Garn you must retrace your steps at least as far as Mynydd Tal-y-mignedd where you can descend its NW ridge (**NH6**). Otherwise carry on to Bwlch Dros-bern then work your way round Craig Cwm Silyn's N slopes to Llynnau Cwm Silyn to recover your starting point at 495511 via the Land Rover track as in **NH9**.

Moel Hebog to Moel Lefn (NH H2)

To combine Moel Hebog with its two satellites is a natural. The usual routing is to tackle Moel Hebog from Cwm Cloch (**NH16**) and leave Moel Lefn through the Beddgelert Forest (**NH25**), making use of forest trails to minimise road work back to Beddgelert. The high-level tramp from Moel Hebog to Moel Lefn is a gem with wondrous views of Snowdonia, the meadows of Pennant and the long tapering coastline.

A walk for lingering over.

You can shorten the day by dropping down Moel Lefn's E slopes – slithery, lots of loose scree – and then following the forest boundary to 563479 to join the Cwm Meillionen route home (**NH17**). The walk can also be tackled from the Pennant side by combining **NH19/23**.

Pennant horseshoe (NH H3)

Having described separate traverses of the Nantlle and Hebog hills it is natural to think of combining them in a 'grand slam'.

A grand hike, but only for the super fit.

So here we go! There is little to choose between a clockwise or an anti-clockwise round. I will describe the former.

Climb Garnedd Goch from Braichydinas (**NH14**) and then set out along the Nantlle ridge to Y Garn. Backtrack to just beyond Mynydd Drws-y-coed and contour across to Trum y Ddysgl's S ridge for Bwlch y Ddwy-elor (**NH2**). The route is then across Moel Lefn and Moel yr Ogof and down to Bwlch Meillionen. Next comes the crippling haul up Moel Hebog, after which the gentle SW ridge (**NH19**) brings blessed relief.

Luckily there are plenty of shortcuts. For example you could omit Y Garn and avoid any backtracking, or even switch ridges from Trum y Ddysgl on **NH3**. On the Hebog side you could abort at Bwlch Meillionen, thus avoiding the hardest grind of the day and returning down Cwm Llefrith instead (**NH20**). More radically you could leave the Nantlle ridge at Bwlch Dros-bern (hopefully having got to Mynydd Tal-y-mignedd and turned round first!) using **NH10** to regain the valley before freelancing to join **NH23** for Moel Lefn.

The round of Mynydd Mawr (NH H4)

A round of Mynydd Mawr, combining the Planwydd and Cwm Du routes (**NH26/27**) and returning between the mountain's NE face and Llyn Cwellyn, has already been hinted at in **NH27.** It gives a good day in curiously neglected country and should nail once and for all the misplaced belief that Mynydd Mawr is a 'half-day mountain'. With luck you should have time for a side-trip to the falls at Castell Cidwm on your way back.

Lower-level Walks/Easier Days

Beddgelert Forest (NH L1)

A pleasant exception to the 'rule' that forest trails are dull.

The forest has a variety of tree and plant life, while the trails are open enough to permit seductive glimpses of the neighbouring peaks. You can break out to the attractive, heather-clad slopes to the W, or use parts of the Cwm Meillionen route (**NH17**) to help link the various trails. There is no point in describing particular walks; better to take the map (it must be the 1:25,000 version) and plan your own. Just two tips: Owen

Glyndwr's cave is well worth viewing, atop a daunting rocky tower near 563479, and the beautiful Llyn Lllywelyn (562500) makes a perfect lunch spot.

Pennant Valley (NH L2)

The upper Pennant Valley is criss-crossed by green paths, stony tracks, old quarry ways and a long-abandoned rail track that make for easy walking. What you will find are sumptuous banks of heather and bracken, burbling brooks and derelict mines. All of this lies beneath the mighty cliffs of Craig Cwm Silyn, the sculptured crest of Mynydd Tal-y-mignedd and Moel Lefn's fearsome cliffs. Lower down the valley has a pristine lushness and a rustic charm more reminiscent of the Border country than the high fells.

Cwm Silyn (NH L3)

If you park at 496511 and follow the Land Rover track mentioned in **NH7** you will have as easy a walk as it is possible to imagine for such a wild spot. With picnic spots in abundance, lakes to bathe in and (hopefully) climbers on the Great Slab to admire, a restful day is assured.

Braichydinas 'micro canyon' (NH L4)

I am not sure whether this is easy enough for an 'easier day', or even whether the objective is sufficiently attractive. Certainly it is novel. The way up is colourful and the 'micro canyon', when you get there, secluded and peaceful. On reflection I shall leave it in (see **NH14**).

Something for everyone here. Parking at the road-head permits forays either way.

THE PLYNLIMON HILLS

OS map

1:50,000 – Sheet 135

Peaks (by height)	Height (ft)	Map Ref	Page
Plynlimon Fawr	2467	789869	172
Plynlimon Arwystli	2428	815877	180
Y Garn	2244	775851	177
Pencerrigtewion	2201	798882	181
Plynlimon Fach	2192	787875	176
Carnfachbugeilyn	2041	827904	178
Plynlimon Cwmbiga	2008	831899	178
Foel Fadian	1850	828954	184
Carn Hyddgen	1850	792908	185
Banc Llechwedd-mawr	1837	776899	185

Mountain Lakes (alphabetically)			
Bugeilyn	1494	822924	
Glaslyn	1620	825941	
Llygad Rheidol	1700	792878	
Nameless (2)	2150	789862	
Nameless (3)	1500	779879	
Nant Ddeiliog	1450	861959	

THE PLYNLIMON HILLS

Tucked away in a lonely corner of mid-Wales is this range of hills that is strangely neglected by the hillwalking fraternity. They form a compact group bounded S by the A44 and the Wye Valley, W by the Rheidol, N by the Afon Hengwm and E by the Hafren Forest. Within these confines the high ground over 2000ft lies in the form of a rough zigzag, running SW–NE. Around the periphery no less than three rivers have their origins – the Severn, the Wye and the Rheidol. Strictly speaking the correct Welsh name

Plynlimon across the Dovey estuary

is 'Pumlumon', but the anglicised 'Plynlimon' now seems to have crept into general use and so for consistency I use that.

Plynlimon Fawr is the dominant peak, and such is the magic of its name – as one of the three chief mountains of Wales – that it is often treated as though it were the only peak in the range! In fact there are six other tops, all worth visiting. Strong walkers can tackle the lot in a long and varied day, while lesser mortals will enjoy climbing them in a series of shorter excursions.

The traditional way up Plynlimon Fawr is from Eisteddfa Gurig in the S. However other interesting routes exist, based on the Hengwm Valley in the N, which are largely unknown yet lead directly to some of the finest scenery in the area. Indeed when viewed from the N – from Llyn Rheidol or Pencerrigtewion – Plynlimon Fawr has all the rugged 'mountainliness' it so manifestly lacks when seen from the S, where it comes across as little more than a rather undistinguished mound.

You will not find high drama in the Plynlimon hills. The tops are vast, windswept expanses of grassy moorland with only minor variations in height and little naked rock. As for the valleys, they are mostly wide, shallow and almost treeless. On sunless days the mood can be one of bleakness and austerity, a feature which has led visitors over the years to describe Plynlimon in terms such as a 'sodden weariness' and a 'shapeless mass'.

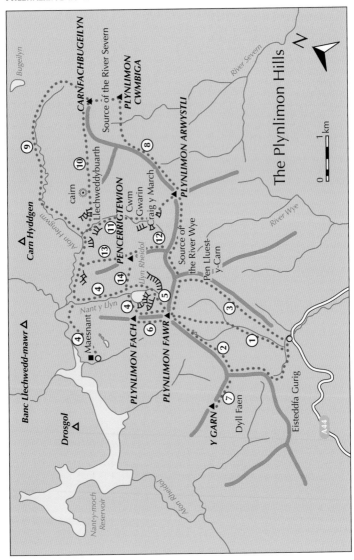

The Plynlimon Hills

En route to Llyn Rheidol (PN4)

Plynlimon is an acquired taste. It has little to offer in mist or poor weather and its main appeal will always be to lovers of solitude and the wide open spaces. Yet to dismiss it so abruptly would be an injustice. Far from being boggy the going around Plynlimon is mostly firm and easy underfoot (good striding-out country), and while excitement may not always be the prevailing emotion there are definite rewards nonetheless. Lacking the sharpness of crag and gully, the views delight us instead with rolling waves of hills as far as the eye can see – S towards the Cwmdeuddwr hills, N over Carn Hyddgen. Survey the scene from Carnfachbugeilyn or Cwmbiga on a sun-dappled day in autumn, when the heather is out, and you are in a world apart!

Significantly, many of these pearls are off the beaten track, for the truth is that the best of Plynlimon is away from accepted walkers' highways. Climb Plynlimon Fawr from the S, up the miners' track, and it is a long trudge. A trudge rewarded by the magnificent view that suddenly unfolds as the top is reached it is true, but a trudge nonetheless. Climb it from the N, on the other hand, and you are amongst scenery that would not be out of place in the Glyders.

Plynlimon does not display its charms lightly, but to those who seek they are there for the taking.

Plynlimon Fawr

Plynlimon Fawr is one of the three traditional mountains of Wales, Snowdon and Cader Idris being the other two. As such its conquest is the first objective of every walker in the area. The traditional route follows the old lead-mine track. However four alternative routes are given, each of which sheds new light on an old friend. Two of these are from the N and are virtually unknown. In return for rougher walking they reveal the true mountainy character of Plynlimon Fawr with imposing scenes of corrie and crag.

Note In mist it is important to keep to either the lead-mine route or the S ridge (see **PN1** and **PN2** below).

The lead-mine track (PN1)

The most popular way up Plynlimon Fawr; also the least interesting.

Start from Eisteddfa Gurig (797841) where cars may be parked in the morning and refreshments obtained on the return. Take the walker's path through the farmyard. It splits almost immediately. Ignore the slaty bulldozed road that breaks away L uphill for **PN2** in favour of the flat (usually muddy) grass track that soon makes a sharp R turn where the stream that will accompany you for the next mile must be forded. This has pretty waterfalls but regretfully lacks trees.

The trek up the valley is uneventful with gently contoured, bare and grassy slopes either side. Eventually the old lead mine comes into view, a veritable eyesore with its large spoil heap. Just before reaching it leave the valley and follow a line of stakes up the hillside. Despite the thousands who tread this way the stakes are easily missed. However, a well-trodden path soon materialises and all is well. Eventually the stakes give way to cairns while off L are the two small lakes (which, at around 2150ft, are the highest in these hills). Before long a large cairn appears ahead and the summit is yours.

The view is of epic proportions, particularly as you get no hint of it on the way up. Although the Nant-y-moch reservoir glitters enticingly below, it is the vast expanse of empty rolling hills to the N, beyond the Hengwm Valley, that first commands attention. Seen in their golden autumn colours they radiate an other-worldliness that always reminds me – difference of scale notwithstanding – of the Grand Canyon. Further away are Cader Idris, the Arans and Tarrens, while S wave after wave of the Cwmdeuddwr hills captivate the gaze. On a clear day you may even glimpse Radnor Forest or the S Wales peaks.

Note This is the safest and most direct way off Plynlimon Fawr in mist. To locate it, leave the trig point on 160° until you pick up the line of cairns and stakes that will guide you safely home.

The S ridge (PN2)

This route shares the high 1350ft start of **PN1** and is just as easy. It also gains height earlier and is more interesting. After traversing the farmyard at Eisteddfa Gurig take the L fork as described in **PN1** and trek steadily W towards the woods of Dyll Faen.

Combine this with **PN1** for a good round trip.

Once by the woods turn R and follow the fence for about 1 mile, gradually gaining height, until a flatter area is reached. (If you come to a stone wall with a gate in it you have gone slightly too far.) This is Plynlimon Fawr's S ridge and you must now strike off E of N along its crest until you find a well-trodden path through grass and sparse heather. This carries on to the top skirting the two little lakes R.

The S ridge is quite safe in mist. If descending leave the summit cairn on a bearing of 200°, keeping the wire fence that crosses the top initially to your R.

Pen Lluest-y-carn route (PN3)

Leave Plynlimon Fawr E along the wire fence and press on for 0.5 mile, down and up a dip, until you reach a large cairn and boundary marker where the fence makes a sharp R turn. Take a bearing of 170° and strike out for a conspicuous cairn

Not very scenic, but for tired legs this route has an innate appeal.

about 0.5 mile ahead. This is Pen Lluest-y-carn and your route is then down the shallow ridge on trackless, easy grass.

There are three choices:

- Keep to the ridge (**PN3**)
- Bear R early on to join the miners' track (**PN3,1**) or
- Veer L on to a farm road that joins the A44 just E of Eisteddfa Gurig (**PN3,2**).

If returning from Arwystli or points further E you can start the descent from the junction of fences at 802874 mentioned in **PN8**. Pen Lluest-y-carn is then clearly visible on 190°.

Llyn Rheidol route (N) (PN4)

Seen with a light dusting of snow the cwm holding Llyn Rheidol is a stirring sight.

Follow **PN9** down the rough track that continues from the road-head at 774880 near Maesnant. Cross the Nant y Llyn near a gateway in a tumbledown wall, then veer R along a damp sketchy track that accompanies the stream towards its source (with a circular stone wall enclosing a small group of trees to your L). Impressive views open out as height is gained with Plynlimon Fawr and Plynlimon Fach R both displaying

View across Cwm Hyddgen to the distant Cader Idris

craggy faces that few would suspect from the benign side they show to the S. Llyn Rheidol remains hidden until the end. When it too bursts into view the scene is worthy of Snowdon itself, with a cwm that is at once wild and sombre, desolate and beautiful.

Now is the time to survey the route ahead because, as so often, it is most easily detected from a distance. Look for a grassy rake that wends its way through gaps in the crags to the N of the lake. To find it on the ground walk 140 paces down the stony road at the lakehead, starting near a red lifebuoy station, until a grassy bank leads into the path where the road makes a sharp turn R. It is now an easy pull up to the col between the twin humps of Plynlimon Fach. From here Plynlimon Fawr is a mere 10–15min away, the route being obvious in clear weather and on 160° in mist.

There are two alternative beginnings.

- One (**PN4,1**) is to park about 0.75 mile before Maesnant and then follow the rough stony road that branches off R at 768875. This is the road that ends by the lifebuoy station at Llyn Rheidol. It keeps to higher ground above the Nant y Llyn and so offers wider views, and a better chance of dry feet! On the way you pass three attractive little lakes trapped in a ledge on the hillside.

- The other option (**PN4,2**) starts from the road-head near Maesnant as before, but this time you strike up the hillside, through breaks in the minor crags, to reach the stony road near the three small lakes. At the cost of a short, breathless start this probably gives the best of both worlds.

Note None of these routes is recommended in mist – least of all for descent – because of the risk of encountering the crags above Llyn Rheidol when leaving Plynlimon Fach. If you should be caught out the best advice is to walk on a bearing of 50° from the more N of Plynlimon Fach's two summit humps. This leads into a shallow grass gully between the humps from where the path down to Llyn Rheidol continues in much the same direction.

View from Maesnant to Carn Hyddgen on PN4

Llyn Rheidol route S (PN5)

A route for
red-blooded purists
who like to tackle
their mountains
head on.

There is no path, plenty of bog and some short stretches of steep scrambling over rough broken ground. On the other hand it is unfrequented and shows you Plynlimon Fawr in its wildest, most rugged mood.

Start from Llyn Rheidol on **PN4** and trudge along its E shore. There is a path of sorts but is quickly succumbs to the all-pervasive bog. When you reach the steeper slopes at the vale-head look out for an obvious grassy shelf that aims for the shallow col between Plynlimon Fawr and Plynlimon Fach. Once on the col a short stroll R leads to the Fach and L to the Fawr.

Plynlimon Fach

Overshadowed by its big brother, Plynlimon Fach is rarely visited. However it is a friendly little crest with two attractive humps, both of them sporting miniature rocky outcrops and covered with undulating heather. An excellent place to sun-bathe away from the crowds! The views are less commanding than from Plynlimon Fawr since the latter itself restricts the outlook S, but they are still extremely fine N.

Note A little care is needed in getting off Plynlimon Fach to the N in mist – the remarks in **PN4** should be noted. Indeed, if your logistics permit, it is preferable to make for Plynlimon Fawr and then descend by one of the better-known routes from there. There are two ways up Plynlimon Fach which have already been covered en route to Plynlimon Fawr (**PN4** and **PN5**). It therefore merely remains to describe the route from te senior peak to its satellite.

Plynlimon Fach from Plynlimon Fawr (PN6)

Leave the cairn on Plynlimon Fawr on a bearing of 340°, picking your way through some largish boulders at first, before dropping down a steep hillside of heather and mosses. The twin humps of Plynlimon Fach are now visible ahead with a distinct path skirting the W slopes of the first hump before curving round to climb the second hump on its E side. If in doubt keep well L to avoid any danger of meeting the crags above Llyn Rheidol.

Y Garn

Few of the crowds who tramp up Plynlimon Fawr ever think of tackling Y Garn. Yet, rising from an isolated spur, it is one of the best vantage points in the district. It is also one of the few places from where you can observe the shy little lakelets tucked away on Plynlimon Fach's NW slopes. Plynlimon Fawr itself is also seen to advantage, its reticent and craggy W face imparting a severity and dignity it so often lacks.

On its own Y Garn would only occupy a half-day, and an easy one at that, but if combined with the S ridge of Plynlimon Fawr and a return down the miners' track a more satisfying outing is the result.

E ridge (PN7)

Follow **PN2** to the Dyll Faen woods. Instead of diverting R to join Plynlimon Fawr's S ridge, stay with the boundary fence. The woods slope away L shortly before you reach Y Garn and the wire fence gives way to a stone wall, but by then the way is obvious. Now simply follow the wall. The summit boasts a large cairn complete with an inbuilt stone chair.

Carnfachbugeilyn / Plynlimon Cwmbiga

Because of their closeness in remote country it makes sense to consider these two peaks together. There are three routes given, all of them good-weather routes.

Note In poor conditions, particularly mist, these routes should be left strictly alone as there are few landmarks for route-finding and a clear day is needed to do justice to the scenery. If you are inadvertently caught by mist, the best plan is to walk from Plynlimon Cwmbiga towards Plynlimon Arwystli on a bearing of 200°, using the boundary of Hafren Forest as a safety net if need be.

The high-level route (PN8)

One of the classics of the Plynlimon hills, with varied views all day.

The round trip is a long one, a good 13–15 miles, although this is to some extent compensated for by the mainly easy going. Climb Plynlimon Fawr by **PN1** or **PN2** and then follow the wire fence along the summit plateau, NE quickly veering E. A sharp drop, followed by a similar rise, leads to a large cairn and boundary marker. The fence temporarily deserts you here, turning R. Ignore it and make a beeline on 80° for about 0.25 mile, glancing R to the valley cradling the infant River Wye. When you reach a junction of fences at 802874 cross a stile and follow the fence that carries on just N of E towards Plynlimon Arwystli, a quick uneventful mile away on the skyline.

You should not leave Plynlimon Arwystli without inspecting Cwm Gwarin, one of the most scenic of the local valleys. Above all be sure to survey the way through the network of peat hags that stands between you and Plynlimon Cwmbiga's two huge beehive cairns. Despite only an intermittent path it is possible to enjoy pleasantly firm walking most of the way. A line of old boundary stones starts you off and a good tip, when in doubt, is to trend E. Eventually, having jumped the fledgling River Severn and reached Plynlimon Cwmbiga, Carnfachbugeilyn is a simple heathery stroll away on 320°.

Although Cader Idris, the Dovey hills and the Arans are all visible N, the views are not spectacular. No lofty heights or serried crags capture the imagination. Instead there is a vast sea of rounded hills and soft distant woodlands, stretching in all directions to the bluish hue of the far horizon; a vista of solitude and peace, untrodden and unknown.

Hengwm Valley route (PN9)

Leave the A44 at 752813 near Ponterwyd and take the minor road to Talybont. Where it branches, near the reservoir, bear R and drive on until it ends just short of Maesnant (774880) where a couple of cars may be parked.

An entrancing foray into one of the least-known parts of Wales.

Go through a gate and advance NW along an obvious track which can be very muddy when wet. The open views across the valley to the bare grassy slopes of Drosgol and Banc Llechwedd-mawr contrast sharply with the craggy slopes R which unfortunately shut out any sight of Plynlimon Fawr. After 1 mile, having passed a derelict cottage and crossed the Nant y Llyn, you must decide whether to cross the bridge to the N bank of the Hengwm. Ultimately this gives the best track, but for the moment the most picturesque routing lies along the S bank (as shown on the map). The decision is an important one as the Hengwm is surprisingly awkward to cross for nearly another 2 miles.

After passing a gate near a fence that struggles up the hillside to Pencerrigtewion (**PN13**) the path becomes very boggy and it pays to hug the stream. Yet just when you begin to wonder if it is all worthwhile, the valley suddenly sparkles into life with scattered oases of trees while a copse all but hides a tumbledown cottage where in spring clumps of daffodils dance. This is where Cwm Gwarin comes in R and the Hengwm turns N in a deep ravine. When it veers E in another wide valley cross to a track on the N bank. Though this peters out near

Llechwedd-crin, bearing R round the crest of that hill puts you on the quarry track that crosses Bugeilyn on its way to Glaslyn.

Take a bearing of 135° and cross the valley to tackle Carnfachbugeilyn's heathery slopes. Once on top the cairn is prominent S and it is a pleasant stroll across heathery tussocks and a few mild peat hags for its final conquest. The continuation on to Plynlimon Cwmbiga is more of the same, on a bearing of 140°, until its two immense cairns dominate the scene.

This is the sort of walk that on a dull misty day can easily turn into a wearisome grind when everything looks drab. Yet on a bright day with sun and broken cloud, particularly in early autumn when the heather is in bloom, it is wonderful.

Llechweddybuarth route (PN10)

This starts with a short scramble and ends with a trackless, bracing walk over lonely breezy highlands.

Follow **PN9** to the second derelict cottage. Cross the vibrant brook issuing from Cwm Gwarin and climb easy rocks generously embellished with bracken, heather and a sprinkling of gorse to reach Llechweddybuarth's ancient cairn. Aim R for the rocky causeway that is so prominent from the valley and which, from above, provides a perfect frame for surveying the Hengwm Valley below.

There are no landmarks on this featureless moor so set your compass on 60°. It is fine striding-out country and it is not long before you spot a boundary marker from where, staying on the same course, you will soon be met by a wire fence which will accompany you to Carnfachbugeilyn. Plynlimon Cwmbiga is an easy 0.5 mile away on 140°.

Plynlimon Arwystli

Plynlimon Arwystli is usually visited as part of the high-level route to Plynlimon Cwmbiga and Carnfachbugeilyn (**PN8**). However a direct approach up Cwm Gwarin breaks new ground and is highly recommended for a day that shows the Plynlimon hills in a different light.

Note It is not suitable for descent or in mist when the best way off Plynlimon Arwystli is to proceed due S for 100–200yd until you meet the fence that leads towards Plynlimon Fawr as in **PN7**.

Cwm Gwarin route (PNll)

Whereas other valleys in the area tend to be shallow with smooth grassy slopes, often of a yellowish hue, Cwm Gwarin is bright green, its steep flanks generously studded with rocks.

Take the Hengwm Valley route (**PN9**) until the second cottage is reached, whereupon bear R beside a cascading stream. There is no path, but the turf is firm and there are no problems in threading a way between the tumbles of boulders, particularly if you keep well above the stream. The contrast with the spacious Hengwm Valley could not be more marked, heavy crags bearing down either side while up-valley the huge shattered triangle of Craig y March casts an awesome spell. The stream divides here and this is your signal to climb out of the valley on a bearing of 125°. This leads direct to Plynlimon Arwystli's three prominent cairns, each of which boasts a much-used windshelter.

Cwm Gwarin is wild and rugged, very different from the other valleys in the Plynlimon hills.

Pencerrigtewion

Pencerrigtewion's tall shapely cairn deserves better than to grace no more than a tiny hump lost in a lonely expanse of mosses, heather and grass. Yet despite that I must confess to a soft spot for Pencerrigtewion. It offers glorious views of the rolling hills to the N, while there is no better place for viewing Plynlimon Fawr than the W slopes here, from where it comes across as a peak of real stature. Add to this the fact that Pencerrigtewion is a frequent crossroads in circular walks, and inclusion of three routes is seen as well justified. These are all minor variations of other routes and so can be dealt with quite briefly.

S approach (PN12)

Follow **PN8** to the junction of fences at 802874. Bear L when a faint track follows the N fence to bring you within sight of the cairn. If approaching from Plynlimon Arwystli look out for another shadowy track that slants across the moors to Pencerrigtewion.

Hengwm Valley route (PN13)

The spot in the Hemgwm Valley where a fence runs up the hillside to Pencerrigtewion has already been described in **PN9**.

Llyn Rheidol route (PN14)

Use **PN4** to reach the N shore of Llyn Rheidol. From there it is simply a matter of toiling up Pencerrigtewion's W slope, using one or other of the two bands of grass on either side of the grey shaly outcrop.

High-level Walks

Eisteddfa Gurig circular (PN H1)

You might include Y Garn if it is a clear day.

Anyone thinking of climbing Plynlimon Fawr by the conventional lead-mine route should certainly consider this round. It gives a more interesting day, for no extra work, simply by combining **PN1** and **PN2**.

Plynlimon Fawr/Rheidol circular (PN H2)

An extension of the Eisteddfa Gurig circular.

For the cost of an extra 2.5 miles and a little more ascent and descent, this takes you to the very heart of this elusive range where desolate Llyn Rheidol lies cupped beneath the black crags of Plynlimon Fawr's N face.

Climb the S ridge (**PN2**) and then drop down to Plynlimon Fach on **PN6**. Next pick up the wispy track that wends down through the crags to the shores of Llyn Rheidol. To locate it leave the N hump of Plynlimon Fach on a bearing of 50°, then make for the shallow grassy hollow between the two humps where the track begins. From the lake a pant up grassy slopes gives you Pencerrigtewion (**PN14**). For home head first towards Plynlimon Fawr for the second time in the day (**PN12/8**) and then proceed either down the lead-mine track or via **PN3**.

Maesnant/Hengwm circular (PN H3)

One of the area's finest expeditions.

This route should not be countenanced on a dull day when it would be a pointless grind. However when the sun is out

– and especially in autumn with the heather in bloom – it has a wild appeal that whisks you along.

Follow the Hengwm Valley to Plynlimon Cwmbiga (**PN9**). Return along the high-level route (**PN8**) as far as Plynlimon Fawr. After that take the Llyn Rheidol route (N) in reverse (dropping down to Maesnant via Plynlimon Fach and Llyn Rheidol). **PN4,2** is probably the easiest course.

Maesnant/Llechweddybuarth circular (PN H4)
Replace the Hengwm Valley approach in the previous walk with the Llechweddybuarth route to Plynlimon Cwmbiga (**PN10**) and you have another fine round. It is a bit shorter and trades off the upper reaches of the Hengwm and Bugeilyn for a tramp across the spacious uplands beyond Llechweddybuarth.

Maesnant/Cwm Gwarin circular (PN H5)
This is a still further shortened version of **PN H3** which compensates for the loss of the lonely uplands around Plynlimon Cwmbiga by including Cwm Gwarin, the most attractive of all the Plynlimon valleys. You start with **PN11** to Plynlimon Arwystli and return as before.

Mile for mile one of the best, with varied terrain all day.

Plynlimon hills complete (PN H6)
Given their closeness and the lack of height variation, this is not as difficult as it might seem. Start from Eisteddfa Gurig and follow the high-level route (**PN8**) to Carnfachbugeilyn, using the S ridge of Plynlimon Fawr and ticking off Y Garn on the way. It is then just a question of diverting to Plynlimon Fach and Pencerrigtewion as the fancy takes you. This is probably best done early on before weariness intervenes!

Peak-baggers will no doubt want to capture all seven scalps in the same day.

Lower-level Walks/Easier Days

Foel Fadian/Pennant circular (PN L1)
Around a line joining Glaslyn (825942) to the village of Pennant (879977) are as many precipices as anywhere outside Snowdonia. Though they convey none of the high drama of their northern counterparts, to visit them all gives a good day in unusual

A glance at the map reveals some interesting country NW of the main Plynlimon spine.

surroundings. The junction at 832944 is as good a place as any to start.

Take the bridleway rising towards Foel Fadian (the highest point in old Montgomeryshire). Leave it where it begins to skirt round the top of the hill and strike direct up an easy slope of bilberries and heather for the top. Foel Fadian is one of those delightful little peaks it would be nice to carry around in one's rucksack for enjoying on a hot sunny day (Pen y Castell in the Carneddau is another). Undulating hills and dreamy pastures gladden the eye and there are soft heathery tussocks to rest on too! Be sure to see the awesome chasm of Uwch-y-coed before leaving.

Now make a beeline for the prominent tumuli at 842953, crossing the road at the junction near 837952 to join a farm track through a gate. Bear L after the tumuli to skirt another spectacular defile at 847960 before striking NW for the corner of the woods at 856966 and thence to the cliffs along the N edge of Mynydd Cil-cwm, where the easy short-cropped turf you have enjoyed so far gives way to deep heather. Soon you come to yet more cliffs, Creigiau Pennant, where a grooved track hugs the edge to give easy walking again. This is the highlight of the day with magnificent views across the Pennant Valley.

A diversion to Llyn Nant Ddeiliog is obligatory for llyn-baggers. It is too enclosed to rate amongst the more picturesque of the Welsh lakes, but you should certainly not miss the falls at 867953 where its clear waters plunge down to the valley. Keep to the edge as long as you can. Near the end bear W or SW to avoid the awkward problem of crossing the Afon Twymyn as it curls round to parallel the road. It is best to head for Dylife (864942) to gain the minor road at 862940. There is then a choice of homeward routes, all of them obvious from the map. On the way you can climb up to the site of the small Roman fort at 855935 if you have the energy.

Hyddgen horseshoe (PN L2)

One of the best is a horseshoe round the Hyddgen Valley. For the start drive down the minor road from Forge (763001) until, just after a telephone box and a steep rise, a stony road branches off R into open country at 776960.

The vast sea of hills N of Plynlimon Fawr offers challenges galore.

Before becoming committed it is essential to know how you will regain your base in the evening when you will have the Hengwm Valley to cross. There is a bewildering array of forest trails yet only two places, 776945 and 792959, where the Hengwm can be crossed with dignity. Anywhere else is absolute purgatory with steep impenetrable wooded banks and barbed wire fences to negotiate. The best plan – apart, of course, from studying the map – is to reconnoitre the lie of the land when you climb up in the morning. (**Note** The above is a different River Hengwm from that referred to hitherto. It is more to the N and a tributary of the Dovey, whereas the other flows into the Nant-y-moch reservoir.)

The stony road turns L almost at once, by a cottage, and then starts to climb the side of a secluded valley. Leave it just before it starts to zigzag at a second L turn and advance straight ahead through a gate to pick up a bridleway that leads you up to, and then along, some woods on the skyline. Almost at once you go through another gate where a rough track joins you from the R. This rises steeply through the woods to open highlands where lush grassland and a striking panorama await.

The N skyline is filled by the Tarrens, Cader Idris, the Dovey hills and the Arans, while farther away are Arenig Fawr and the Berwyns, with glimpses of Snowdonia beyond. Looking S the cliffs of Creigiau Bwlch Hyddgen and the head of Hengwm captivate the eye, with the rambling bulk of Plynlimon Fawr beyond.

After 1 mile the track starts to descend through woods. Leave it there and strike out across thick grass, almost due S, for Banc Llechwedd-mawr. Banc Llechwedd-mawr is a good place for lunch with excellent views of Llyn Rheidol and Cwm Gwarin. When you are rested it is a simple scamper down to the wide, featureless Hyddgen Valley. Nor is the pull up to Carn Hyddgen's twin cairns on the other side as tiring as it looks.

Next comes a rollicking walk across the fells to another of the wild cliffs that abound in these parts, Taren Bwlch-gwyn. Its harshness is accentuated by the green pastures below that sweep down to the Dovey. It is high time to make for home. Pull up to spot height 582m and Mawnog, glancing back for a rare glimpse of Glaslyn shimmering in its heathery cradle. There are then two options:

- Either drop down a bridleway R to reach the Hengwm at 792959, or
- Leave the ridge L to join a new bulldozed track that brings you down near 781949 where a farm road leads to the bridge over the Hengwm at 776945.

Either way leaves you with just over 1 mile along the valley trails to regain your car.

Llyn Rheidol (PN L3)

Stroll up to Llyn Rheidol. Either of **PN4,1** or **PN4,2** gives a drier walk than **PN4** (and better views too). You pass the three little lakes at 779879 and, with the widening views over Hyddgen, will doubtless be tempted to rest awhile. When you reach Llyn Rheidol a circuit of its shores looks enticing. Not so – the head of the cwm is very marshy indeed! Far better to picnic and admire the wildest scene in the Plynlimon hills.

Cwm Gwarin (PN L4)

Drive to Maesnant and then follow **PN11** into Cwm Gwarin. This has a real mountainly character, unlike the other Plynlimon valleys, and it should not be stretching the idea of an 'easy day' too far to lunch in the august surroundings of Craig y March.

Hyddgen Valley (PN L5)

Though not spectacular, this valley offers a quiet day when you will quickly be enclosed by the hills and captivated by the feel of the wild.

Follow **PN9** to the bridge over the Hengwm. Cross to the N bank and then walk along a faint track that keeps the marshy Hyddgen well to your L. You soon join a rough farm road which, depending on your energy, could take you up to the head of the valley, over and through the woods beyond, or even down into another more N Hengwm Valley on the far side.

N Hengwm Valley (PN L6)

Drive down the road from Forge as in **PN L2** until you can find a parking place near to where the road degenerates into a rough farm track in the Hengwm Valley. You can then progress on foot as far as the fancy takes you. The first couple of miles are the most spectacular, with steeply wooded slopes either

Cwm Pennant (PN L8)

side vying for attention with the cliffs of Creigiau Bwlch Hyddgen and the waterfalls of the nascent River Hengwm (the more N one). Eventually the track climbs through the woods to join up with **PN L5**.

Foel Fadian (PN L7)
It might seem like cheating to include a top of 1850ft in a list of suggestions for easier days, but if you leave the road at 838952 (from where the route is obvious) you are already at 1650ft. From Foel Fadian you can extend the day if you wish by wandering down the quarry road that takes in Llyn Glaslyn and Llyn Bugeilyn. Lonely, desolate country which is depressing on a dull day but has an ephemeral charm all of its own when the sun is out.

Foel Fadian is a charmer you will not want to leave (see **PN L1**).

Pennant Valley (PN L8)
This delectable valley, which is entered at 879977, is almost unknown. A variety of walks can be improvised from obvious footpaths and a foray to the head of the valley, starting from the farm at Pennant (875953), is particularly rewarding.

THE RADNOR FOREST

OS map
1:50,000 – Sheet 148

Peaks (by height)	Height (ft)	Map Ref	Page
Great Rhos	2166	182639	194
Black Mixen	2132	196644	191
Great Creigiau	2102	198636	193
Bache Hill	2001	214636	193
Whimble	1965	205627	191
Fron Hill	1715	193609	195

Mountain Lakes
None

THE RADNOR FOREST

N of the peaceful village of New Radnor, a mere 6 or 7 miles inside the Welsh border, lies a little-known outpost of the Welsh hills known as the Radnor Forest. It is a small, compact group that could quite easily be covered in a long weekend. Initially the auspices are not promising. The main valley, Harley Dingle, is used for ammunition testing and is thus out of bounds. Worse, the second-highest point, Black Mixen, is defaced by a transmitter station.

Luckily first impressions are not always right! There may be no sculptured ridges or rock encradled tarns, but there is plenty of good sport nonetheless. Sound tracks and gentle gradients abound, making these some of the easiest hills in Wales to capture and good for days when the spirit is keen but the flesh weak. (The most succulent bilberries are also to be found here.) The views are everything you would expect from an island of high ground, carrying on a clear day from the Shropshire hills in the N to the Brecon Beacons in the S, while to the E lie the green plains of Worcestershire and Herefordshire.

On first glance you may well be reminded of the Black Mountains. Of all the Welsh hills they are the nearest to these in character. Yet the similarities should not be exaggerated; there are none of the flowing escarpments or long whale-backed ridges you find between Talgarth and Abergavenny. The Radnor landscape is more convoluted;

Looking up Harley Dingle to Great Rhos (RF 5)

cwms twist and burrow to the very hearts of the hills, giving a unity between hill and vale that is not found in the S Wales uplands.

The atmosphere is subtly different too. To me the Radnor hills share with the Long Mynd, Wenlock Edge and the Wrekin – indeed with so much of the Border country – an elusive, almost wistful air. Perhaps it arises from a loneliness that is all the more poignant given their nearness to the adjoining lowlands.

The two main hills, Great Rhos and Black Mixen, rise on either side of Harley Dingle, a deep cleft that forms the main axis of the group. ('Dingle' means 'deep dell' and is a word frequently used in the Radnor area instead of 'valley' of 'cwm'.) The most popular walks are to be found around its perimeter, although there is also excellent tramping in the foothills N and W of Great Rhos. Close by Black Mixen are two minor tops, Bache Hill and Great Creigiau. All four hills are rounded moorland tops with prolific heather and a noticeable absence of rock. Not that rock is a total stranger, for Great Creigiau shows a craggy face to Harley Dingle and nearby is a curiously isolated outcrop known as the Whinyard Rocks.

Note The 'Danger Area' signs you will see close to Harley Dingle are concerned with ammunition testing, but so long as you keep clear of the dingle itself there is no problem. Over many years I have never once heard or seen any sign of activity, much less been deflected from my route.

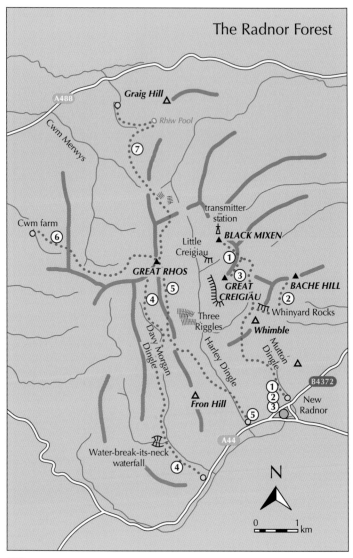

The Radnor Forest

Black Mixen

The most noteworthy feature of Black Mixen, apart from the view across Harley Dingle to Great Rhos, is the transmitter station that towers above the trig point and the flat expanse of the surrounding moors. It clearly says something about the ambience of these hills that not even this can spoil the pleasure of a day in their company.

Mutton Dingle route (RF1)

Join the route at 212610 where it leaves Church Street and tramp steeply uphill until it degenerates into two stony tracks, close to a Swiss-like meadow. Fork L (the R branch enters a forestry plantation) passing first under an archway of trees and then through a gate at 203618 to open country.

The track climbs round the edge of the woods, following a line of telegraph poles. Fron Hill and Harley Dingle are prominent L, but as height is gained it is the crags of Great Creigiau and Great Rhos – the latter displaying the three famous Riggles (narrow bands of scree) – that catch the eye. On a clear day you can even discern the familiar outlines of those S Wales stalwarts, Pen y Fan and Corn Du, on the SW skyline.

Whimble, a pocket mountain if ever there was one, rises enticingly from the corner of the woods at 202626 and is well worth a quick side-trip. Meanwhile the main track curls round Whimble's NW flanks, with a tributary of Harley Dingle burbling merrily below, to pass close by Whinyard Rocks. Crumbly and serrated, they too merit a short diversion. Facing them is a cultivated meadow – quite a feat of husbandry at over 1600ft!

On resuming, carry on up-valley, the scenery wilder and more desolate now, to a col at 204638 near a corner of the woods that cloak much of the hills' N slopes. Next pull up alongside a fence NW to the vast heathery plateau encircling Black Mixen, with splendid views of Great Rhos and countless foothills S and W. A peaty track leads across to the trig point which, like Bache Hill's, is set on a huge mound of bilberries.

Tramping up Mutton Dingle is a delightful way to start a day, especially in early summer when wild flowers speckle its banks in a riot of colour.

Coming down from Black Mixen (RF 1)

Bache Hill

Bache Hill lacks charisma and is too off-centre to be a common objective. Nevertheless it repays you handsomely with long lingering views over the mottled green pastures of Herefordshire and Worcestershire.

Mutton Dingle route (RF2)

Follow **RF1** to Whinyard Rocks and then bear E along a stony trail that runs beside the alpine-like meadow lying between the rocks and Whimble. Carry on to the tip of the woods at 210629 then strike out slightly E of N over a hillside generously carpeted in bouncy tussocks of heather and bilberries. There is no path but the ground is trusty underfoot and before long a gate in a fence leads into green pastures which extend to within a stone's throw of the top. Next it's briefly over heather again to the enormous mound of pure bilberries (a full 50ft in diameter!) that surrounds the lonely trig point.

   The path to Black Mixen is easily regained by making a beeline to the col at 204638 where there is a tarn and a small oasis of cotton grass (**RF2,1**).

Great Creigiau

It is all said below.

Mutton Dingle route (RF3)

Stay with **RF1** until you mount the Black Mixen plateau at about 203640, following the rise from the col. Cross the wire fence and tread carefully across a near-level expanse of deep, squirmy tussocks to the unmarked, unremarkable top. A tiring, jolty walk for which striking views of the Riggles and the deep cleft

Great Creigiau is an unfriendly place in mist, when it pays to beat a hasty retreat!

of the upper reaches of Harley Dingle are your only recompense. Alternatively (**RF1,1**) a track wends across the hill's SE slopes from the col and can be used as a springboard for the final trackless grind.

Great Rhos

Do not underrate Great Rhos. The map suggests a dreary moorland top devoid of interest. Superficially that is how it is, with only a solitary trig point breaking a bleak monotony of heather and cotton grass. What the map does not convey is the wealth of approaches to this neglected peak and their variety, the grandstand views of Harley Dingle, the Davy Morgan Dingle, the falls at 'Water-break-its-neck', the earthy silence of the N woodlands and the unknown Cwm Merwys. Good sport in abundance; but do not expect crowds!

Note In mist the paucity of landmarks can be a problem and the safest way home is then due E from the trig point to pick up the Land Rover track mentioned in **RF5** and **RF7**.

Davy Morgan Dingle route (RF4)

Leave the A44 at 194593 and follow a gravelly path NW. Keep R where it splits, but soon after entering Warren Plantation divert L to view the justly renowned 'Water-break-its-neck' falls. These cascade from a great height in slender rivulets half-hidden by trees to form little rocky pools in the depths of the dank, dark amphitheatre below.

Carry on along the main trail until it leaves the forest at a stile at 183619. Next slant half-R down into Davy Morgan Dingle. Follow this to its source, admiring giant cushions of soft green moss en route. On leaving the dingle stay on 20° until the trig point breaks the skyline, beckoning you on. Tracks are few and it is a bit spongy in places, but otherwise it's a simple walk.

For a more open route, with Great Rhos continually in your sights, stroll down the road through Vron Farm (195597). This parallels the E perimeter of Warren Plantation and then wends through a meadow between the forest and the W slopes of Fron Hill before leading into the Davy Morgan Dingle (**RF4,1**).

Davy Morgan Dingle

S ridge (RF5)

Steer E from the trig point for 200–300 paces until you hit a Land Rover track. This runs S, or slightly W of S, over moors ravaged by fire, keeping well clear of the slopes above Harley Dingle. You should, however, make a quick reconnaissance of the edge to view both the dingle itself and the bright red-dish/orange mosses that proliferate nearby. Your track, meanwhile, has become a green path, deeply banked by the heather slopes overlooking Davy Morgan Dingle before dropping down to a saddle beneath Fron Hill.

A steep descent through old quarry workings is but a temporary 'blip'. Before you can say 'green path' you are coasting down the sylvan slopes of Fron Hill with views across Harley Dingle to Whimble and beyond. A narrow plank at

This is described as a descent because with **RF1** it constitutes the core of the Harley Dingle horseshoe (**RF H1**).

Across Harley Dingle to Great Creigniau and Whimble

200611 affords a passage across a (fortunately) placid stream, and in minutes you are back to the bustle of the A44.

You can avoid the road by going L through a blue gate just after crossing the plank. This leads into a little glade and a footpath (marked on the map) that wends across the fields to the corner of Newgate Lane and Church Street in New Radnor (**RF5,1**).

Another possibility that is bright and breezy (**RF5,2**) is to maintain height from the saddle by continuing over Fron Hill. Tracks on either flank lead to the vicinity of the spot height near its SE tip, from where a steep descent down bracken-clad slopes leads once again to the plank. Fron Hill is a marvellous viewpoint. The gaze carries from Bache Hill and Whimble, over the crags of Great Creigiau, across the woods and meadows fringing Davy Morgan Dingle and on to a backdrop of foothills that extend to the shadowy outlines of the S Wales peaks on a clear day.

Cwm Merwys route (RF6)

The first objective on this fresh, lonely walk is the saddle at 162642. You have a choice of two paths. The first rises directly behind Cwm Farm at 155645; the second weaves up from the head of the lane at 155640. Either way, on breasting the ridge you are faced with a Cwm Merwys that is grand in scale yet wild and empty. Its monumental loneliness is relieved only by the musical tinkling of the brook that meanders through its virgin depths. Across the cwm Great Rhos, playing the giant, is seen at its impressive best.

From the saddle a green path, mossed and mellow, curves round the head of Cwm Merwys to put you on the plateau 0.5 mile W of the trig point. The path carries on NE along a fence to join **RF7** by the forest exit at 185650, but you must leave it here and cut directly across the fells.

Rhiw pool route (RF7)

Drive up the country road to 173673 where a couple of cars can be parked through the gate at the end. Follow the stony track that curls round Graig Hill to the oval-shaped Rhiw Pool where a gate gives access to a forest road. This climbs roughly parallel to the edge of the woods. Where it levels off near a patch of scree (177659) break away L onto a shadowy path that tiptoes into the forest beneath a dark tunnel of trees carpeted with pine needles. This widens to a soft green bridleway, engagingly edged with heathery clumps, that climbs through the forest to regain open country at a gate at 185650. (Keep R where the way divides, notably after passing a corrugated shed.)

As you leave the forest ignore the prominent track heading SW. This would take you to Cwm Merwys and **RF6**. Instead proceed virtually due S through the heather on a track that is faint at first but quickly develops into a fully-fledged Land Rover trail. This twists and turns a bit and eventually passes 200–300 paces E of the trig point, handing the summit honours over to a faint track R.

High-level Walks

Harley Dingle horseshoe (RF H1)

This route includes nearly all the 'sights' yet is well within the compass of the average walker. Leave New Radnor along

The area's most popular round.

197

Mutton Dingle and climb Black Mixen on **RF1**. Next work round the head of Harley Dingle to Great Rhos, an easy walk with virtually no height loss. A peaty track, marked by occasional stakes, leaves Black Mixen NW to start you off. Thereafter follow the edge of the woods to the gate at 185650 and finish as in **RF7**.

Cwm Merwys circular walk (RF H2)

You will be amazed how different this is from the Harley Dingle horseshoe.

If you have done the Harley Dingle horseshoe and want to have another go at capturing the spirit of these elusive, many-sided hills, then this could be the answer.

Climb Great Rhos from the Rhiw Pool as in **RF7**, then descend on **RF6** to the saddle at 162642 overlooking Cwm Merwys. The way home is then along bridleways more reminiscent of the Home Counties than Wales, with dreamy pastures and woodlands on every hand. From the col go N to 154662, then NE via Old Hall back to base, all along paths marked on the map.

Lower-level Walks/Easier Days

Whimble (RF L1)

Whimble is one of the best viewpoints in the district.

Black Mixen, Bache Hill, Whinyard Rocks, Great Rhos, Great Creigiau and the Riggles can all be seen from the gently undulating crest of Whimble (plenty of shelter from the wind!). Further afield the blue-green outlines of the Cwmdeuddwr hills and S Wales also make an appearance. Follow **RF1** to the corner of the woods at 202626 for a steep but exhilarating walk up Whimble's grassy W ridge.

'Water-break-its-neck'/Davy Morgan Dingle (RF L2)

See **RF4**.

THE RHINOGS

OS map

1:25,000 – Sheet 18, 1:50,000 – Sheet 124

Peaks (by height)	Height (ft)	Map Ref	Page
Y Llethr	2475	661258	220
Diffwys (S)	2462	661234	222
Rhinog Fawr	2362	657290	209
Rhinog Fach	2333	665270	214
Y Garn	2063	702230	225
Moel Ysgyfarnogod	2044	658346	205
Foel Penolau*	2014	662348	209
Clip	1937	653327	205
Moelfre	1913	626246	221
Diffwys (N)	1893	663351	208
Moel y Gyrafolen	1755	672353	208
Carreg-y-Saeth	1482	644302	213

*Foel Penolau does not rate as a 2000ft peak in its own right because of its proximity to Moel Ysgyfarnogod

Mountain Lakes (alphabetically)

Bodlyn	1250	648240
Caerwych	1300	641351
Corn-ystwc	1800	656336
Cwmhosan	1200	660277
Du	1825	657340
Du	1700	656294
Dulyn	1750	662244
Dywarchen	1700	654348
Eiddew-bach	1225	645345
Eiddew-mawr	1125	646338
Gloyw Lyn	1275	646300
Hywel	1750	664266
Irddyn	1050	630222
Morwynion	1400	658303
Nameless	2150	661255

Mountain Lakes (alphabetically)

Nameless (6)	1975	665243
Nannau-is-afon	1825	706228
Perfeddau	1500	659264
Pryfed	1775	665321
Twr-glas	1725	663325
Y Bi	1425	670264
Y Fedw	1075	625329

THE RHINOGS

Of all the mountains in Wales, none surpasses the Rhinogs in their rugged splendour. This is wild Wales at its wildest, a hillwalkers' Mecca, virtually unscarred by the works of Man and generously endowed with sparkling, lonely lakes. In the N the walking is as challenging as anything in Wales, and there are rewards aplenty for those who seek them. There is striking rock scenery, not on the grand scale of Tryfan but in the form of miniature cliffs, terraced pavements of heather-strewn rock set apart in their own wild, intimate, secluded settings. There is the untamed, 'twisted' lie of the land with often, it seems, no consistent grain. There are the vast expanses of heather, unexpected little lakes and friendly hollows for shelter from wherever the wind blows. Last but not least there are the views.

The views result from the Rhinogs' isolated position more than their height for even Y Llethr – the highest point in the range – only reaches 2475ft. Of the six peaks, five lie in an almost straight line running N–S. To the E is the Ganllwyd Valley and the Afon Eden which together divide the Rhinogs from the Rhobell country and the Arenigs. To the W the land rolls down to the sea in Cardigan Bay. To both N and S are major estuaries, Traeth Bach and Afon Mawddach.

With lowlands on all sides you would expect expansive views from almost anywhere on the Rhinogs' slender spine. And so it is, with the outlook N to Snowdonia especially striking throughout the N half of the range. To the E the Arenigs, Rhobell Fawr and the Arans command attention, while to the S Cader Idris dominates the skyline. To the W, always, is the sea.

Three valleys penetrate the Rhinogs from the W and these, together with three passes, are the key to many of the ascents. The Afon Artro, leading to Cwm Bychan, is the most northerly of these valleys. It leads directly on to Bwlch Tyddiad and the Roman steps, the first of the passes. Slightly S is Cwm Nantcol, the second valley, which opens

Rhinog Fawr and Rhinog Fach

the door to Bwlch Drws Ardudwy, a pass no less dramatic than the more famous Roman steps. Indeed these two passes, relatively remote, undefiled by roads and with crags closing in narrowly on either side, are among the most dramatic in the whole of Wales.

The third valley, that of the Afon Ysgethin, is wider and shallower than the others yet, curiously, more desolate. It gives access to the S Rhinogs. There is no corresponding pass in this case as crags above Llyn Dulyn and Llyn Bodlyn bar the way. The third pass is elsewhere and might well be termed the 'lost' pass for it is largely unknown although it leads to some of the finest walks in the area and provides one of the few approaches from the E. I refer to Bwlch Gwylim, over which there is a delightful path which skirts the E slopes of Clip as it links Cwm Bychan in the W with Cefn Clawdd in the E.

Just as dramatic as any of these valleys or passes is the complete change of character the Rhinogs undergo between Rhinog Fach and Y Llethr. To the N the country is rough and untamed. From Moel Ysgyfarnogod and its satellites in the far N as far S as Rhinog Fach the ridge is wild and broken with boulders strewn haphazardly around. Worse, these are often concealed under deep heather and every step must therefore be planned. Seldom can you afford to stride out and admire the scenery without halting first.

From the col between Rhinog Fach and Y Llethr all this changes. The lion gives way to the lamb and rocks give way to grass, so by the time Diffwys is reached a broad grassy ridge extends in one unbroken sweep all the way to Barmouth. You are now in real

The Rhinogs (North)

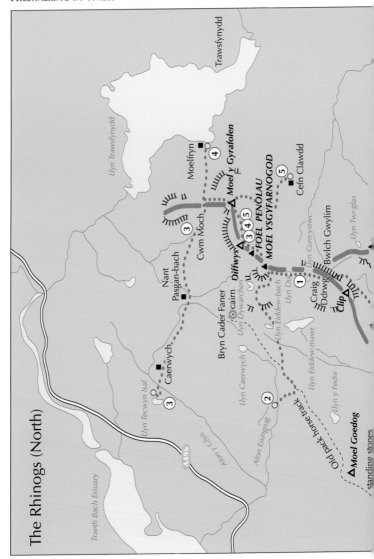

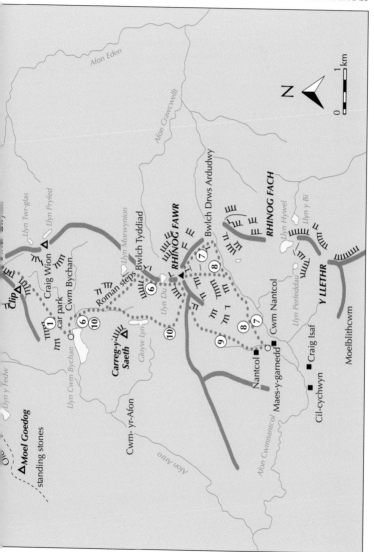

striding-out country, fit to compare with the best in the Carneddau, easy even in mist and with springy turf which rolls the miles quickly off your boots.

However nothing is quite that simple in the Rhinogs, and their change of character in the S has one important exception. This is the sixth peak in the range, the lonely outlier Y Garn. It lies off the main ridge and therefore usually has to be tackled as a separate expedition. There is some excellent sport to be had here, but you should go prepared because there are times on Y Garn when the easy walking so typical of the S Rhinogs is tempered by spells of rougher terrain more reminiscent of the N.

Rough walking? Yes, certainly the Rhinogs can offer plenty of that – especially in the N and around Y Garn – although the difficulty can be exaggerated. There is nowhere in the Rhinogs where the walker has to handle naked rock to reach the top as on the N ridge of Tryfan or on Crib Goch. The Rhinog tops are friendly places, generously endowed with grass or heather; fine spots for lazing on a hot day.

There are now tracks in most parts. Not wide gravelly or peaty tracks that leave an ugly scar visible for miles, but shy, delicate tracks which may not be immediately apparent but are there for the seeking. No one, therefore, should be put off the Rhinogs by their unsparing reputation. To lovers of wild scenery and solitude, they are second to none. So long as you go prepared, expecting challenging terrain, allowing more time than usual and confident of your track- and your route-finding ability (for to lose a track in the Rhinogs is not something to be countenanced lightly!) then you can expect as rich rewards as anywhere in Wales.

Note A cautionary word is necessary regarding mist. The N Rhinogs are best avoided in such conditions as the lie of the land can be confusing and there are few cairns to act as guides. Moreover once a track is lost there is a good chance of ending up in a sea of boulders half-hidden in deep heather. Broken ground like that is never comforting, least of all in mist! This advice applies anywhere N of Rhinog Fach, but particularly to Moel Ysgyfarnogod. The best plan on a misty day is therefore to keep to the S half of the range where the ridge is well defined with grass underfoot and stone walls to give direction.

Moel Ysgyfarnogod

With its companions – Foel Penolau, Diffwys and Moel y Gyrafolen – Moel Ysgyfarnogod (The Hill of the Hares) forms a striking silhouette at the N end of the Rhinog range. Yet it is largely unknown. This is partly due to its being off the beaten track, sandwiched between Snowdonia and the main Rhinog heights, and partly through its having acquired an undeserved reputation for inaccessibility and tracklessness. The reality could scarcely be more different! All around Moel Ysgyfarnogod is walking of the most exhilarating kind amid a profusion of heather, little lakes, rocky slabs and cliffs. Furthermore there are enough tracks, faint though most of them may be, to ensure pleasant going. Connoisseurs' country par excellence!

Because of its isolated position at the tip of the range, Moel Ysgyfarnogod offers unrivalled views. NW is the Traeth Bach Estuary and the Lleyn Peninsula; N is the Nantlle ridge, Moel Hebog, Cnicht, the Moelwyns, Snowdon itself and Moel Siabod; NE lies the mound of Manod Mawr and shapely Moel Penamnen; E you can see the Arenigs, Rhobell Fawr, Dduallt and the Arans; finally, away S, it is Cader Idris and the Rhinogs themselves that captivate the gaze.

Note This is no place to be caught in mist when the convoluted lie of the land and paucity of clear landmarks makes navigation difficult, even for experts. In any case it would be a pity to waste a day climbing Moel Ysgyfarnogod in poor visibility when there is so much to see there. However, if you are inadvertently caught out, the best course is to make for Llyn Du and then to follow the miners' track (**RG2,1**) down to lower ground.

Unfortunately finding Llyn Du is not easy as you must first skirt round some crags. From the trig point walk on 300° for a couple of minutes, until you come to a small dip. Change to 210° downhill, again for a couple of minutes, until you cross a small sloping depression. Now walk on 150/170°, descending all the time and veering R where the rocks let you, until you pick up the faint track that leads to Llyn Du.

Craig Ddrwg route (RG1)

Start from the car park at Llyn Cwm Bychan and go through a gate across the road to pick up a track signposted to Clip. This ascends the rock-strewn, bracken-clad slopes and despite

The essence of the Rhinogs in one walk!

the rugged terrain gives easy walking, twisting steeply to a boggy plateau where it disappears for a time. There are striking views of Craig Wion's striated terraces R while the slopes of Clip gradually close in L.

Soon you pass a dilapidated wall and then a second close to the crest of the rise. Here, to atone for any earlier vagaries, there are for a time two parallel tracks. You are now at the top of Bwlch Gwylim (658329), an important crossroads for lovers of these hills, and it is time to take stock. Straight ahead the path descends, gradually veering E, eventually linking with the Cefn Clawdd track (**RG5**). Round to your R there is a superb walk via Craig Wion to the Roman steps (**RG L1**). Today's route is L, through a tumbledown wall and up a gully cleaving the shattered slopes of Craig Ddrwg.

There is a faint track at the top. However, before tackling Moel Ysgyfarnogod try to find time to backtrack to Clip, a fine top that just misses the 2000ft barrier. Its summit is a massive mosaic of rocky slabs and heathery outcrops, with heart-warming views, which is well worth exploring.

On resuming follow the E edge of Craig Ddrwg, passing rock-bound Llyn Corn-ystwc and taking in your stride a string of rocky terraces and cliffs, the last of which drops down to the beautiful and secluded Llyn Du. Follow the old mining track round its far shore and then make a final ascent up easy grass. Whenever I have been there the summit cairn has been litter-free. Let's keep it that way!

Eisingrug route (RG2)

Start where the paved road following the Afon Eisingrug splits to give two farm tracks at 629343. Be sure to take the R fork over the stream. A companion and I, when starting to walk the length of the Rhinog ridge to Barmouth (**RG H8**), once wasted precious minutes here by taking the L track. Such was our confidence (and carelessness) at the start of the day that we had not checked either map or compass. On retracing our steps we were glad to see that the car which had dropped us off had already departed and thus spared us 'tigers' the public ignominy of our retreat!

Follow the R fork up the hill where at 631339 it merges with an ancient packhorse trail coming in sharply R. This runs

from near Moel Goedog (607321) to the W of Bryn Cader Faner (647353) and beyond. It is a useful track to know about as it links a number of walks. Carry on along the packhorse trail, but be sure to spot where an old manganese mining track veers away R at 637343. This takes you across level ground just S of Llyn Eiddew-bach before starting to climb again.

Another mining track branches off R at 651348. This offers a slightly longer walk (**RG2,1**) by taking in Llyn Du before finishing as in **RG1**. The main track, meanwhile, continues to mitten-shaped Llyn Dywarchen where it peters out. You now have a spell of trackless but easy grass, striking out SE from the lake before threading NE through some minor crags.

There are two alternative starts. One (**RG2,2**) picks up the packhorse trail where it leaves the road SW of Moel Goedog at 607321. A pair of standing stones by the roadside point to a path sidling off NE. Follow this for about 90 paces until it divides. The L fork is the packhorse trail, while the other provides a cross-country route to Cwm Bychan. Pass through two fields, each with more standing stones. (The first sports a huge semi-circular cairn; the second a large collection of ancient cairn circles which you will need to drop down the slope a little to see.)

Looking across Llyn Du, and the fractured terraced pavements so typical of the N Rhinogs, to Moel Ysgyfarnogod and Moel Penolau

207

The other varient (**RG2,3**) begins with a delightful walk from Llyn Tecwyn Isaf up to the farm at Caerwych (637369). The track breaks away R just after the farm and proceeds S before veering L round the bracken and gorse-strewn slopes of Y Garn and climbing a gully beside a stream. The track fades hereabouts but can be spotted again in a SE direction where it joins the packhorse trail. Where it does you are only 300yd SW of the coronet-shaped stone circle of Bryn Cader Faner, which should not be missed. When you resume it is a trek of nearly a mile along the packhorse trail to pick up, at 637343, the mining track of **RG2**. Do not be tempted into a short cut across country as it is very marshy!

Cwm Moch route (RG3)

An exciting and lovely walk, but best not attempted on a misty day.

With a start from idyllic Llyn Tecwyn Isaf, followed by a ramble through a wooded vale to the farm at Caerwych, you might think that the best of this day comes first. Not so, this is but a foretaste of delights to come! Go through the farm and stay with the cart track that carries on E, through pretty woods above the Afon Y Glyn, to the homestead of Nant Pasgan-bach. Here you must transfer to a green path that slants over one of the Rhinog's N spurs on a bearing of 95°. To reach it simply turn R through a gap in the wall just before the dwelling, cross a field and then turn L over a stream by a ruined cottage.

The path climbs through bracken and rowan trees, passes another ruin where it becomes sketchy (just beyond this point it merges with the packhorse trail at 661364), drops down into the vast solitudes of Cwm Moch, then eases up the far slopes on a fine old drovers' road edged with gorse. Leave it near some marshy ground and a wall, where it levels off before dropping down to Llyn Trawsfynydd, then strike out S for an obvious break in Moel y Gyrafolen's N defences. (Do not confuse this with the deep menacing cleavage dividing Diffwys from Moel y Gyrafolen which you will have observed from Cwm Moch.) It is hot work scrambling up Moel y Gyrafolen's rich purple heather, but the view from the top is handsome reward.

From here to Moel Ysgyfarnogod is rousing stuff. Down into the miniature defile separating Moel y Gyrafolen from Diffwys (take the S end) and up the far side; across the flat top of Diffwys, heather everywhere with the occasional rocky pavement and lonely lakelet; across another breach in the ridge to reach Foel Penolau's E redoubt, the heather thinning now and giving way to ever larger slabs of rock; over another gap to Penolau's main top, a huge 'lost world' plateau of rock with a shapely cairn; down through Penolau's battlements (use a grassy rake near its NW tip); now over a little trough, up a final grassy slope and Moel Ysgyfarnogod is yours.

Moelfryn route (RG4)

A route similar to **RG3** may be started from Moelfryn (685358), near the shores of Llyn Trawsfynydd. Here you can pick up the other end of the track from Nant Pasgan-bach leaving it, as before, around its highest point.

Cefn Clawdd route (RG5)

Leave the road at 679338 just before the farm and take the (often waterlogged) track that alternates NW with W in driving into the fastnesses of the hills. Just after passing a spur R, and reaching a level patch by a wall where the track fizzles out (671346), strike out N over trackless heather to claim Moel y Gyrafolen. From here on follow **RG3**.

A rare approach to the Rhinogs from the E – excellent if combined with Clip and a return via Bwlch Gwylim (see **RG H2**).

Rhinog Fawr

Along with its consort, Rhinog Fach, Rhinog Fawr is the most popular peak in the range. It could scarcely be otherwise with the famous Roman steps on one side, wild Bwlch Drws Ardudwy on the other, and two lakes of such contrasting styles as Llyn Cwm Bychan and Llyn Du in close attendance (one the very epitome of lowland pastoral loveliness; the other a desolate but beautiful expanse of water, nestling high on a heathery ledge beneath Rhinog Fawr's exposed N slopes). All this without even mentioning Gloyw Lyn!

If that were not enough, the prospect from Rhinog Fawr is breathtaking. The Rhinogs themselves, with Snowdonia, completely fill the N skyline. Moel Hebog, the Nantlle ridge, the Moelwyns, Moel Pnamnen and Manod Mawr are all prominent, while the Rivals gaze attentively across the blue of Tremadog Bay.

To the E the eye is held by a colossal panorama including the Arenigs, the Hirnant hills, Dduallt, Rhobell Fawr, the Arans and the Dovey hills. The S horizon is shaped by the long, graceful profile of Cader Idris. Finally, to the W is the sea, a very tempting sight if you choose a hot day to explore these demanding yet rewarding hills.

Nearer to hand you can pick out Llyn Hywel and Llyn Perfeddau, nestling in the fold between Rhinog Fach and Y Llethr, while a stroll to the E tip of the rock-strewn summit reveals the awesome chasm of Bwlch Drws Ardudwy and Llyn Cwmhosan.

Note In mist it is a different story and an eerie atmosphere prevails; though if you are present on one of those days when the mist blows and swirls, giving fleeting glimpses of the valleys below, you will feel 10 miles high! But be careful, none of the routes off Rhinog Fawr is easy in mist as the summit is not easy to 'read' when the weather clamps down. The safest ways are then **RG6,3** and **RG9**.

Roman steps route (RG6)

Despite the debate over whether the steps are a relic of a Roman trading route or of mediaeval origin, one thing is certain: they provide the grandest way up Rhinog Fawr.

You start from Cwm Bychan in a setting that is among the prettiest in Wales. On leaving the lakeside follow the steps to the head of Bwlch Tyddiad. (There are about 500 of them in groups of 12 to 20.) As you climb, first through woods and then in an ever-narrowing defile beneath lowering crags, the sense of isolation becomes almost overpowering until, as the crest is reached, the tension is relieved with a long vista dominated by the Arans, Dduallt and Rhobell Fawr.

Continue over the top of the pass for about 250yd until a stony path branches off R, close to where a wall emerges from the rockface. The path swathes merrily between lush thickets of heather, bilberries and mosses to bring you to Llyn Du. The Rhinogs abound in lakes like this; grey, forbidding and wind-rippled one moment, sparkling and romantic the next.

Follow Llyn Du's N shore to join a track alongside a wall. This twists and turns up the N face, making lighter of the task than ever seemed likely from the lakeside. There is a minor scree slope to contend with, but no real hardship, and you are soon happily ensconced on top. A more direct route (**RG6,2**) is afforded by the gully that rises from the SE corner of the lake. This meets the main route at the foot of the scree slope. Incidentally, the wall near Llyn Du carries on down to meet Bwlch Tyddiad some distance below the top of the pass, thereby providing an easy-to-follow way down in mist (**RG6,3**). ▶

The SE face (RG7)

Start from the road-head at Maes-y-garnedd. There are two paths signposted: one slightly W of N for the W ridge (**RG9**), the other proceeding NE to the spectacular pass of Bwlch Drws Ardudwy. A path runs roughly parallel to a wall. It is boggy in places, but stepping stones cover the worst of the mire. You may notice a couple of clusters similar to the famous Roman steps in Bwlch Tyddiad. Up-valley the pass is lavishly cloaked in heather and is a memorable sight in late summer. Yet despite this there is a keen sense of wildness and isolation as Moelfre and Rhinog Fawr close in behind you, with the slopes frowning down ever more oppressively on either side.

After a while the pass temporarily widens out L, forming a sort of 'amphitheatre'. Such respite is short-lived as it quickly narrows again until, at the cairn signalling the top of the pass, the scene is enlivened by an E skyline where Arenig Fawr, Moel Llyfnant, Dduallt and Rhobell Fawr all vie for attention.

There is now a confusion of tracks so leave the cairn on a bearing of 5° to intersect the wall that crosses the top of the pass a little higher up the slope. A hole beneath this wall is just large enough to squeeze through. A climb amid twisted rocks leads to a more level interlude. While on this look for a prominent cairn on the skyline L. Climb up to it via a stone shoot and arrive on a plateau of large rocky slabs sprouting heather from their crevices.

Rock-hounds may clamber up the rock-face about 50yd beyond the top of the pass – **RG6,1**. A short walk through colourful 'bouldery' heather then brings you to Llyn Du as before.

Note Be careful not to proceed too far W or you will find yourself looking down over the pass again. Remember that the best line ascends the SE face of the mountain and so you should be looking down on the forestry plantation E of the peak.

The higher realms are a succession of miniature rocky cliffs and plateaux, reminiscent of the N ridge of Tryfan. Yet once you emerge on the summit tableland all that remains is a simple 5min stroll through springy heather and mosses to the trig point. For descent leave the trig point along a path slightly S of E, keeping L where it splits after descending a shallow ramp. The R fork leads into the S gully route (**RG8**).

Eastern approaches (RG6,4 and 7,1)

This is a convenient place to note that Rhinog Fawr (and indeed Rhinog Fach) may both be approached from the E, starting along the minor road that leaves the A470 at 713307. There is a small parking area where the road enters the woods at 684303. By forest trails marked on the map you can then reach the crest of either Bwlch Tyddiad or Bwlch Drws Ardudwy, thus leading into routes **RG6** and **RG7** for Rhinog Fawr and **RG11** for Rhinog Fach.

The approaches through the man-made woods are a bit dreary compared with the dramatic scenery of the W approaches, but to make up for it the views of the Rhinogs are uncluttered and, if anything, even more impressive (especially after a shower has lightened the air).

S gully route (RG8)

The gully provides a quick way down, but only if you have already climbed it, know how to find the start and know what to expect (see **RG7**).

This loose slither starts from the 'amphitheatre' mentioned in **RG7**. A faint track leads NE to the foot of an obvious fault line in the crags. From here on it is a relentless grind up steep, loose boulders and scree. No route-finding ability is required as the gully does it all for you; however the temperament to enjoy hard labour is necessary!

West ridge route (RG9)

The easiest, but at the same time least interesting, way up Rhinog Fawr.

From Maes-y-garnedd take the farm track to Nantcol, but just before entering the forecourt of the cottage bear L (as directed by the footpath sign) and follow the white marker stakes to a gap in the wall above the cottage. Stay on this path, guided intermittently by more white stakes, until you come to a wall at 637285. Turn R and follow the wall along until, just after crossing another wall, the one you are walking alongside makes a sharp R-angled bend at 642286 to a bearing of 345°.

Leave the bend on 72° along a narrow path across a vast prairie of heather. This rises gently for almost 1 mile until, just before the skyline, it climbs more steeply and somewhat exiguously up a bouldery slope. Here it is joined by a wall coming in L. Follow this to a ladder-stile and cross over, just beneath a large cairn, whereupon a wide stony track gives a simple walk to the summit.

It is very easy to go astray in descent near the large cairn. The correct course is to leave the summit on 230°, heading for the cairn, and then to proceed on 270° until, almost at once, you see the wall and the stile immediately below you. It sounds easy. Unfortunately a misleading line of cairns slinks away from the cairn on 200°. It gives you a path for a while but then leaves you high and dry.

There is another option after crossing the wall. In addition to the path just described, which goes off R, a more distinct track strikes off L (**RG9,1**). This provides excellent going for a time but fades at a stretch of marshy ground. You can recover it on a bearing of 220° when it leads to an old sheepfold at 645286, only to fade again. You should then either freelance on 210° or walk due W when you will soon join **RG9** at the bend in the wall at 642286.

Gloyw Lyn route (RG10)

If climbing up, the most obvious start is from Cwm Bychan although you should also consider a routing through Cwm-yr-afon as outlined in **RG L3**. Better still, combine the two in a wild scenic round-trip.

Descend on **RG9** until you come to the flat stretch of heather on the crest of the W ridge. Next head down boulder-strewn slopes to Gloyw Lyn, with only occasional traces of path to help. It is tedious going for a time! However perseverance is amply rewarded as the romantic setting of Gloyw Lyn, cupped in a lonely hollow of shaggy moorland and enclosed by hillocks and Carreg y Saeth, has few peers. Moreover, after skirting its E shore a good path (Fisherman's Path) appears in the bracken near its NE corner to give a pleasant walk back to Cwm Bychan in an increasingly sylvan setting. A delightful end to the day.

This beautiful walk is given as a descent, although it is good value either way.

Note The temptation to cut a corner by descending directly from Rhinog Fawr to Gloyw Lyn must be resisted at all costs. Seductive though it may seem, it is actually a brute with unrelieved stretches of typically 'untamed' Rhinog wilderness (deep heather concealing large, ankle-twisting boulders).

Note Since the Rhinogs chapter was written the place where the fisherman's trail to Gloyw Lyn leaves the Roman steps track has been almost totally obscured by fencing. It is still possible to find a way down from Gloyw Lyn given patience and daylight – but the reverse routing should now be avoided. However, routes to this beautiful lake via Cwm-yr Afon and Pont Crafnant (**RGL 3** and **4**) are unaffected.

Rhinog Fach

'Fach' may mean 'lesser' in relation to 'fawr', yet it can surely only be in terms of physical height that Rhinog Fach is in any way inferior to Rhinog Fawr. Both peaks are at the very heart of that untamed tract of country with which the word 'Rhinog' is so indelibly linked. As viewpoints both peaks reward the climber generously. Both peaks, too, share the wild pass of Bwlch Drws Ardudwy. True, Rhinog Fawr also enjoys the prestige of the Roman steps and the beautiful approach via Llyn Cwm Bychan, but Rhinog Fach has the epic drama of Llyn Hywel and the shattered tower of Rhinog Fach's W face.

In contrast to its wild broken flanks, the twin-topped summit of Rhinog Fach is a nearly flat plateau of stubby heather and bilberries, tilted slightly up from N to S. Both tops are prominently cairned.

Note The best ways down in mist are **RG11** from the N top, or **RG12** from the S top, down to Llyn Hywel.

Bwlch Drws Ardudwy route (RG11)
Turn R at the cairn at the top of the pass (see **RG7**) to face a peaty path struggling manfully, almost precipitously, aloft. For

once you are glad to have the deep heather to cling to! However the gradient eases over the brink, and the path then meanders more sedately until the final pull up the N top recalls the agonies of the start. Pauses for breath can be put to good use admiring the E skyline.

Another track (**RG11,1**) – which rises more gently – starts some 250 paces beyond the cairn from where it is best spotted on 105°. Ignore it if in doubt; this is no place to risk going trackless. It is little used, with such vigorous heather that at times it is almost obscured. Yet it is a gem, a real wilderness walk, especially when the heather is in bloom. The two paths discussed meet near the foot of the final rise, below a string of tight zigzags, a meeting point not easily spotted in descent. (**RG11** leaves the N top on 100°.)

Eastern approach (RG11,2)
See **RG6,4** and **7,1**.

Llyn Hywel col route (RG12)
Walk up Bwlch Drws Ardudwy as in **RG7** but leave it R near the 'amphitheatre' where there are ladder-stiles at either end. Cross the second (the more E). A stream flows directly beneath the wall and so wet feet cannot be ruled out, especially when the stream is obscured by snow. A path climbs the tangled heather and it is not until you are almost on its very shores that the delectable Llyn Cwmhosan suddenly delights the eye. Carry on to the head of this wild vale, in a landscape riddled with boulders and watched over by the shattered face of Rhinog Fach.

A ramble in such august scenery deserves a fitting climax and you will not be disappointed when, on breaching the skyline, the hollow cradling Llyn Hywel at last comes into view. This is a dramatic, awe-inspiring place. Rhinog Fach rises imposingly from a vast plethora of boulders and scree, towering to the sky as if to deny its modest height; a perfect triangle of naked rock. Nearby the huge tilted slabs of Y Llethr plunge headlong into the lake. You are fortunate indeed if you witness this scene on a windless day with the heights reflected in the lake, or in winter with a powdering of snow adding lustre to the scene.

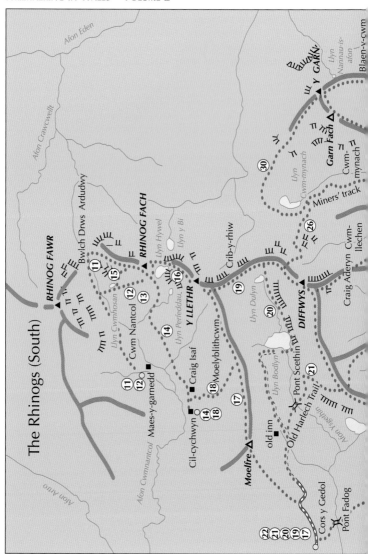

The Rhinogs (South)

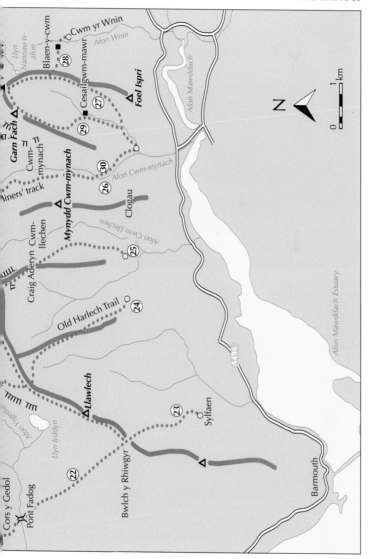

Rhinog Fawr, Rhinog Fach and Llyn Hywel

Walk round the NE shoreline until, after crossing a rockfall, a grassy rake leads up to the col midway between Rhinog Fach and Y Llethr. Here you will find a stony path running alongside a wall. This wall is a good friend to Rhinog-lovers. It starts on Rhinog Fach and carries on without a break to within sight of the lights of Barmouth – a trusty guide in thick weather. Turn L and the wall leads to Rhinog Fach; bear R and you are on course for Y Llethr.

Llyn Hywel direct route (RG13)

A route for the adventurous, not for the fainthearted, and certainly not for descent.

A scree shoot close to the NE tip of Llyn Hywel gives a 'sporting' route to the S top. Unlike many scree runs this one is actually easier than it looks, and you are soon at the foot of the splintered summit cone. The giddy breathless scramble that follows is nowhere exposed and rewards you with fine views of Llyn Hywel and Llyn Perfeddau.

The Cil-cychwyn route (RG14)

Park at Cil-cychwyn (634259) and follow a farm track, first to Craig Isaf Farm and then, above woods, to the now-derelict

Craig Uchaf. Be careful not to lose the track further on where it turns sharply R before ascending a bluff near some old mine workings. The track fades there and it is best to hug a wall beneath the shoulder of Y Llethr. It eventually reappears to guide you over a ramp to Llyn Perfeddau whence a profusion of joyful little paths cleave prolific heather to Llyn Hywel and **RG12**.

Llyn Perfeddau beneath Y Llethr

West face direct (RG15)

Follow **RG12** towards Llyn Hywel. Shortly before the lake comes into view, across a little hollow, you will spy a track snaking up a heathery break in Rhinog Fach's defences. A much rougher path (**RG15,1**) breaks away just S of Llyn Cwmhosan and also leads to the N top, but only after much boulder-hopping and scree work. In descent you should follow the well-trodden track that leaves the N top on 310°. There are several variants, and all that is certain is that you will emerge somewhere to the S of Llyn Cwmhosan.

Y Llethr

Despite being the highest top in the Rhinogs, Y Llethr is less popular than its illustrious neighbours, Rhinog Fawr and Rhinog Fach. No doubt this is partly due to the absence of the magic word 'Rhinog' in its title, although its flat grassy top – large enough for a cricket pitch – and the absence of rock must also weigh. While rarely a prime objective, as a viewpoint it is well up to Rhinog standards with the highlights being the magnificent prospects of Rhinog Fach and Llyn Hywel, and the blue of Llyn y Bi shimmering beneath its rugged E escarpment. The summit plateau is crossed by a wall running almost due N–S.

Note No other approaches are feasible except along this wall, which provides a safe escape in mist.

Llyn Hywel col route (RG16)
Climb to the Llyn Hywel col by either **RG12** or **RG14** and turn R along the bouldery path beside the wall. This soon divides. The main track branches R to wind steadily up a green rock-strewn slope. The less frequented L fork hugs the wall and gives a quicker, more sheltered, but steeper ascent over boulders. The two paths rejoin near the top by a small cairn and a stake; a key landmark in descent.

A short stroll W from the stake opens up one of the most striking prospects in the range: Rhinog Fach, like Excalibur, soars from the silver sheen of Llyn Hywel with Rhinog Fawr peeping benignly over its shoulder. A few paces E from the stake reveals Y Llethr's scarped E face, with Llyn y Bi cupped in the heather below and countless ranges beyond. When you have feasted to the full on these glorious views, continue over windswept grassland to the cairn.

Moelyblithcwm route from Cors y Gedol (RG17)
Park near the farm of Cors y Gedol and set off due E through a gate at 602231 that leads into a walled lane. A second gate

R gives access to a farm road leading to Pont Fadog and other grand walks. The views are inspiring, even this early in the day. Giant sand-dunes and the sea lie behind you; Snowdonia and the Lleyn Peninsula fill the N skyline; nearer to hand the crags guarding Llyn Irddyn and Llyn Bodlyn gradually unfold and Moelfre, too, grows in stature as you stride along with the long Moelyblithcwm ridge gradually taking shape behind it.

Leave the road at 614233 where it makes a sharp R turn and break away for Moelfre's W ridge. The slope is cruel, the rewards abundant. Moelfre, an isolated hill, is among the best vantage points in the Rhinogs. The entire Ysgethin Valley is spread out below. The path snaking down the hillside across the valley is part of the old coach route from London to Harlech. It starts its journey across the hills at 657202 and crosses the main Rhinog ridge at 637224 before dropping down to Pont Scethin in mid-valley. It then crosses Moelfre to meet the road in Cwm Nantcol at 629259.

However this view of Ysgethin, memorable as it is, is completely eclipsed when you cross the summit wall to face Cwm Nantcol. For now you have Rhinog Fawr, Bwlch Drws Ardudwy, Rhinog Fach and Y Llethr arrayed in one majestic arc – a scene of heroic proportions!

Moelfre boasts a sizeable cairn and when you resume you will notice that it also hosts, just below the top, a curious circular stone wall enclosing nothing more, it would seem, than an isolated rocky outcrop. Down-slope you come to a gate where the old Harlech trail crosses your path. Just after this (637247), where the wall makes a sharp turn NW, strike out to meet another wall straddling the Moelyblithcwm ridge. As you plod up the long slope note the curved rock strata on Diffwys and try to catch a glimpse of shy Llyn Dulyn. At the top of the rise a stile L leads into a short, sharp climb from which you emerge triumphant over the Rhinogs.

For a shortcut (**RG17,1**) – at the price of missing out Moelfre – stay with the farm road from Cors y Gedol until you pass a small plantation L. Next aim directly for the col between Moelfre and the Moelyblithcwm ridge. The ruins just beyond the woods are all that remains of an old coaching inn that used to serve travellers on the Harlech trail.

Moelyblithcwm route from Cil-cychwyn (RG18)

The quickest way up Y Llethr but lacking in interest; keep in reserve as a safe and easy way down for tired legs, or in mist.

Leave Cil-cychwyn along the lane for Craig Isaf as in **RG14**, but just before the dwelling go through a gate R to join a farm track that zigzags up the hillside. This takes you to about 645250 from where you can join the Moelyblithcwm ridge and **RG17**.

Diffwys

Diffwys is an underrated mountain. It is remote from the main Rhinog highways and can come across as little more than a dull grassy hump. But first impressions are not always right, and doubts begin the moment Diffwys is viewed from the Ysgethin Valley or Moelyblithcwm when it displays a cragginess that is unsuspected by its N neighbours. Should you also observe it from Cwm-llechen, or the heights of Clogau above Cwm-mynach, the transformation is complete. That lofty pyramid of rearing rock, exercising complete sovereignty over the surrounding lowlands, is none other than our old friend Diffwys. Like all the Rhinogs, Diffwys is a superb vantage point, the sea view over the Mawddach Estuary contrasting strongly with the wooded foothills of Cader Idris, Y Garn and the distant Arenigs.

Moelyblithcwm route from Cors y Gedol (RG19)

Follow **RG17** up Moelyblithcwm and then turn R beside the wall. This traverses Diffwys before continuing virtually all the way to Barmouth. Almost at once you pass a teardrop tarn, tucked beneath the far side of the wall, while 1 mile further on are half-a-dozen more. The one nearest the track had nine separate islands, each about 3ft square, the last time I passed by! A slight diversion R will, however, reveal the real thing – a glimpse of Llyn Dulyn, one of the most reticent of Rhinog lakes.

At the minor top of Crib-y-rhiw (667239) the ridge swings W. Just before it does so the track temporarily deserts it to cut the corner. If you forgo this and stay with the wall you will come upon a stile. This heralds the miners' track (**RG26**). A short rise over piles of boulders then leads into Diffwys's grassy dome and the solitary trig point.

Llyn Dulyn route (RG20)

Follow the walled lane from Cors y Gedol to Llyn Bodlyn, a longish trek enlivened only by the Harlech trail and the ruined inn nearby (see **RG17**). Cwm Ysgethin, though more open than either Cwm Bychan or Cwm Nantcol as it is enclosed only by the lesser Rhinog heights, nevertheless always manages to convey a bleaker appearance.

Llyn Bodlyn's appearance is not enhanced by the reservoir buildings, but they are relatively unobtrusive and it could be worse! When the road ends follow a wispy path along the S shoreline beneath the lowering crags. Tread warily when this peters out as the boulders are very slippery. Set in one of them is a plaque commemorating a climber who was killed here many years ago 'amid the wildness and grandeur of God's creation which he loved so well'.

The trackless rise ahead is not as squelchy as it looks, and 30min should see you on Llyn Dulyn's shores with Moelfre now looking a veritable giant down-valley. A pull up to the ridge puts you on **RG19** near the little lakelets beneath Crib-y-rhiw.

Choose a bright day for this walk with the wind racing the clouds or, perhaps, when a powdering of snow dusts the tops.

Harlech trail N route (RG21)

Stay with the lane until you are level with the middle of the plantation at 627239. Just before a pair of rusty gateposts without a gate, and after a slight rise, look out for a green track branching off R by a small cairn. This leads to Pont Scethin, now alone in the middle of nowhere, but once the crossing place for the trail to Harlech (which you are now joining).

Once over the bridge and a splash of bog the trail winds up the slope, true and firm, passing en route a memorial to Janet Haigh, a previous lover of these hills. Turn L on the ridge and follow the wall to the top, on easy grass all the way. Provided you can find it, this is also a good way down. On leaving Diffwys keep the ridge wall L and follow it for about 2 miles. Cross a tumbledown wall then continue on for about 100yd until you come to a wooden gate in the wall L with a white marker stake nearby. This is where the Harlech trail crosses the ridge.

For an alternative start (**RG21,1**) take the minor road that leaves Cors y Gedol S for Pont Fadog (with a burial

Another start from Cors y Gedol.

chamber R after about 0.25 mile.) Turn L after the bridge along a lane above the noisy Ysgethin until, after a R bend, the track divides at 610225. The R fork leads to Bwlch y Rhiwgyr and **RG22**. Keep L along the track that skirts Llyn Irddyn from where you can link up with the Harlech trail S of Pont Scethin on **RG21**.

Bwlch y Rhiwgyr N route (RG22)

Start with **RG21,1** but this time take the R fork after Pont Fadog. This carries on SE for nearly 2 miles to a conspicuous 'notch' in the ridge ahead – Bwlch y Rhiwgyr. An iron gate in the ridge wall marks the spot. Turn L for a long plod of some 4 miles to the top. En route you cross the old trail to Harlech but, that apart, there is little to disturb a spell of quiet contemplation.

Bwlch y Rhiwgyr S route (RG23)

This route is included solely for completeness as it is difficult to work into a round trip. Drive up to Sylfaen (633185) where it is only just possible to park, then follow an obvious trail up to the bwlch.

Harlech trail S route (RG24)

Leave the road at 657202 where a stile gives access to a green lane which soon divides by an ancient marker stone. The L fork offers a pleasant ramble up to Bwlch y Rhiwgyr (**RG H7**), while the R fork is the Harlech trail. This is walled for a time and fringed with gorse and bracken before emerging on the bare hillside.

Apart from the views, the main interest here lies in occasional white marker posts and marvelling at how a trail so narrow ever sufficed as a coach road!

In descent this is a fellwalker's dream, firm turf and satisfying gradients giving the illusion of almost gliding along. And then there are the views: deep green valleys either side, Craig Aderyn and Diffwys' splintered S face, Y Garn and the Arans, the fertile Vale of Mawddach backed by wooded foothills, and the watchful presence of Cader Idris. Beauty and serenity in close alliance.

Craig Aderyn route (RG25)

Go through a gate at 667203 and proceed up-valley on a farm road with Diffwys growing in stature with every step, and views R over Clogau and Mynydd Cwm-mynach to Y Garn. Craig Aderyn is the gradually swelling rise to your L and, just before the road ends, you must cut across the tussocky moor to the wall that straddles its crest. The ridge is steep and narrow but never exposed. The grandstand view of Diffwys' broken SE face is an unforgettable sight when the heather is out.

Miners' track (RG26)

Most routes on Diffwys are grassy, with scarcely a trace of rock or heather. However Craig Aderyn and the miners' track show a different side to Diffwys' character, and if taken together give an excellent day in a strange and remote tract of country on the Rhinogs' E flanks.

Park by the bridge at 689200 and walk up Cwm-mynach, lulled by charming woods and the burble of the brook. Where the paved road ends at 684218 branch L along a forest trail until you come to a gap in a dilapidated stone wall (680233). Follow a narrow path that sidles away L into the forest. This re-emerges over a stile at 676234 where the miners' track proper begins. **Note** It is vital to locate this path. Any other approach to the miners' track involves near impenetrable forest, boulder-strewn tussocky bogland, or both. I speak from experience!

On leaving the woods an excellently engineered path twists and turns up wild bilberry- and heather-clad slopes in a landscape reminiscent of Pen yr Ole Wen. The path fades at the old mine workings so look out for a faint, shaly track straight ahead and stay with this as it later swings L to avoid crags. A short spell of steep grass brings you to the vicinity of Crib-y-rhiw and a stile over the wall straddling the ridge. Turn L and in minutes the peak is yours.

This attractive climb is centred on Cwm-llechen, a little-known valley that rarely sees a hillwalker.

Y Garn

Y Garn is the odd man out in the Rhinogs, lying nearly 3 miles E of the main massif, and as a result is rarely climbed. This is a pity because it is in some ways a hybrid between the rough rock-strewn tops of the N Rhinogs and the grassy hills of the S. Moreover the approaches through Cwm-mynach and Cwm Wnin have a sylvan softness unique in the Rhinogs.Y Garn's relative isolation also ensures superlative views. The entire Rhinog ridge forms a thrilling line from the minor Diffwys in the N, beyond Moel Ysgyfarnogod, to the major Diffwys in the far S whose foothills sweep down so gracefully to the Mawddach Estuary. The yawning gap of Bwlch Drws Ardudwy, the Llyn Hywel col, and the precipitous E slopes of Y Llethr all contribute to a scene of awesome grandeur. The vast tract of moorland N impresses by its sheer desolation though, if you are lucky, it may be transformed by the glint of sunlight on Llyn y Fran. Across the estuary Cader Idris reigns supreme while E are the Arenigs and Arans, pre-eminent in a sea of hills stretching away in countless blue-green waves.

S ridge (RG27)

Start at the junction at 689200 in Cwm-mynach and follow the R fork steeply uphill. Pleasant woodlands, with a deep gorge R, give a bright start with lovely views of the Mawddach Estuary as you glance back.

After a long 0.5 mile turn R on to a dirt track. This crosses a bridge and then passes through a gate. After a further 100 paces a stony lane breaks away L. Follow this, past a disused barn R (at which point Y Garn comes into view), until it bears R and ends in an unsightly turning circle.

From here scramble up grassy slopes NE to gain the wall astride the S ridge. Follow this, keeping on its W side to min-imise wall crossings, but on no account miss at least one detour E to admire the rich pastures of Cwm Wnin. Near the top is Nannau-is-afon, one of the wildest of Rhinog lakes, its surface all too often ravaged by the wind. A few minutes short of the top the wall makes a sharp L turn and deserts you. If it is murky set a bearing of 315° as the cairn can be hard to find in the broken undulating terrain.

Otherwise, instead of diverting L after the bridge and the gate at 696204, stay with the dirt track as it veers round to the vicinity of Foel Ispiri, then clamber onto the S ridge from there (**RG27,1**).

Cwm yr Wnin route (RG28)

The route begins at the head of sylvan Cwm Wnin. Go through the gate where the road ends and follow the cart track round as it bears W into open farmland. After 300 paces you meet another trail running N–S. This is just S of the farmstead of Blaen-y-cwm, by a lone tree at 711218. From here it is (simply!) a matter of zigzagging up the hillside to join the S ridge and **RG27**.

The shortest way up Y Garn, but it starts from an outlying valley and so does not lend itself to round trips.

SW ridge (RG29)

Walk up the farm road from 689200 as if bound for the S ridge but, instead of taking the dirt track off to the R after the long 0.5 mile as in **RG27**, press on to the farmstead of Cesailgwm-mawr. The road ends there, but a rough cart track swings round W of the farm. Follow this to the SW corner of a forestry plantation at 693217, then climb steeply up the side of the woods through lush heather and bilberries. A cairn marks the minor top of Garn Fach, with excellent views of the main Rhinog ridge. The way on to Y Garn is trackless, threading between scattered rocky outcrops.

NW ridge (RG30)

Leave the trig point on a bearing of 300°, generally aiming for the corner of the woods at 689240 but dodging a succession of minor rocky outcrops. The going is rough, becoming tussocky as you reach the edge of the woods en route to another corner at 681244. However, by then you will have a faint path to relieve the worst of the pain. At 681244 turn L and follow the forest track down through Cwm-mynach.

Combined with the S ridge this descent gives a fine round in clear weather, in a nook of the Rhinogs as lonely as it is wild.

Strong walkers might even think of going one better and combining Y Garn's S and NW ridges with the miners' route up Diffwys, returning over Craig Aderyn and Clogau as in **RG H7**.

High-level Walks

Moel Ysgyfarnogod circular (RG H1)

This has a bit of everything: views of Snowdonia and the sea, the fascinating ridge between Moel y Gyrafolen and Moel Ysgyfarnogod, and the coronet-shaped stone circle of Bryn Cader Faner to inspire you in the evening sun. Start from

This route merely combines two routes on the same peak – but is too good to miss!

Caerwych and take the Cwm Moch route to Moel Ysgyfarnogod (**RG3**). Return on the Caerwych variation of the Eisingrug route (**RG2,2**).

Cefn Clawdd Circular (RG H2)

This round is unusual in being based on the Rhinogs' E flank.

The route pairs **RG5** to Moel Ysgyfarnogod with **RG1** back to Bwlch Gwylim. Make the short diversion to Clip if you can; it is worth every minute! The way home is easy, all downhill following a track, marshy in places, that veers steadily E on its way to the derelict homestead of Wern Fach (682332). A bridge over the stream then leads into a cart track that crosses the moors back to the road leading to Cefn Clawdd.

The two Rhinogs (RG H3)

A classic, and either Cil-cychwyn or Maes-y-garnedd provides a base.

Climb Rhinog Fawr's W ridge (**RG9**). Scramble down to Bwlch Drws Ardudwy (**RG7**) and then up the steep slopes of Rhinog Fach opposite (**RG11**). Now make for the col between Rhinog Fach and Y Llethr before dropping down to Llyn Hywel for the Cil-cychwyn route home (**RG14**). It doesn't look far on the map, but the splendour of the scene is matched in full by the ruggedness of the terrain. Your legs will be feeling the effects by the end of the day!

You can also tackle this magnificent walk from the E, parking at the entrance to the forestry plantation at 684303. My preferred routing would be as follows. Go through the woods and up to the head of Bwlch Tyddiad to join **RG6**, with short diversions to see the Roman steps and Llyn Morwynion. Head down Rhinog Fawr's SE face on **RG7** to Bwlch Drws Ardudwy. Continue on to Rhinog Fach via Llyn Cwmhosan and Llyn Hywel (**RG12**), then return to the bwlch on **RG11**. Finally make your way through the woods back to your car.

Rhinog Fach/Y Llethr (RG H4)

Another classic, which hardier souls can combine with the previous walk.

Again your starting point is either Cil-cychwyn or Maes-y-garnedd, but this time the walk begins with Bwlch Drws Ardudwy and Rhinog Fach on **RG11**. Next you drop down to the Llyn Hywel col before pulling up to Y Llethr's grassy top. The hard work is over then and you have a relatively easy homeward path, down the Moelyblithcwm ridge (**RG18**).

Cil-cychwyn/Diffwys circular (RG H5)

Start with the Llyn Hywel route (**RG16**) and then continue along the main Rhinog ridge to Diffwys – good striding country all the way. Follow the Harlech trail down to Pont Scethin.

Y Llethr is the first objective on this superb but long round.

The way home is over Moelfre straight ahead. Picking your way through the rocks is nothing like as tedious as it looks, though it is advisable to aim for the crest at about 634246 so as to find a gate in a formidable stone wall that could otherwise pose a problem. The descent to Cil-cychwyn is obvious but wet.

Moelfre horseshoe (RG H6)

The outward half is **RG19** from Cors y Gedol to Diffwys, taking in Moelfre with its stupendous views. There are three choices for the return:

Arguably the best walk in the S Rhinogs.

- Via the Harlech trail and Pont Scethin (**RG21**)
- Via the Harlech trail and Llyn Irddyn to Pont Fadog (**RG21,1**), or
- Via Bwlch y Rhiwgyr and Pont Fadog (**RG22**).

Diffwys S circular walks (RG H7)

Four routes have been described for attacking Diffwys from the S. As these can all be linked – not only on the ridge but also lower down above the Mawddach Valley (see below) – you can construct a whole host of pleasant rounds according to taste, with splendid views throughout. One of the best is a circuit of Diffwys combining the miners' track with Craig Aderyn. Another pairs Craig Aderyn with the Harlech trail; or you could climb the Harlech trail before descending from Bwlch y Rhiwgyr.

The link route in the valley is now described W–E. The first section joins **RG23** and **RG24** and starts at Sylfaen where you take the cart track that swings round to the N of Golodd. Where it meets a green path descending from Bwlch y Rhiwgyr, at 637201 near a wall (more options!), turn R across the N perimeter of a forestry plantation. You then join the road at Banc y Fran just after the Harlech trail filters in from the L by a marker stone (see **RG24**).

The second section, joining **RG24** and **RG25**, is along a quiet stretch of country road to a phone box at 667198. For the last link, joining **RG25** and **RG26**, go through a gate at 667198 (across the road from the phone box) and follow the farm road to Ty'n-y-cornell. Pass this to your L and carry on to cross some rails leading into an old mine near a cottage. Bear round L of the cottage and climb up the hillside beyond, aiming for a notch in the skyline. You emerge onto a small plateau where a wall with a gate in it runs roughly N–S. Go through the gate and a farm road leads down via Garth-gell to Pont Garth-gell in Cwm-mynach.

Rhinog ridge complete (RG H8)

A very long walk.

What more is there to say about this? Not much, because unless you already know your Rhinogs well you shouldn't be attempting it. There is little enough time for ordinary route-finding, none at all for getting lost! Yet this is still the best walk in the Rhinogs, taking in a host of highlights. These include the 'badlands' around Moel Ysgyfarnogog; Craig Wion and Llyn Pryfed; the crests of Bwlch Tydiadd and Bwlch Drws Ardudwy; Llyn Hywel; the striding edge from Diffwys down to the sea; and, of course, five of the six Rhinog tops.

Luckily the hardest work comes in the morning, and it gets progressively easier as the day wears on. But do not be misled, it is a surprisingly long way from Diffwys to Barmouth and there is a tendency for Barmouth always to be 'just over the next hillock!' As to the route, the first task is to climb Moel Ysgyfarnogod either from Eisingrug or from Moelfryn (**RG2** or **RG4**). Thereafter the route comprises parts of the following: **RG1** down to Bwlch Gwylim; **RG L1** to the top of the Roman steps; **RG6** up Rhinog Fawr; **RG7** down to Bwlch Drws Ardudwy; **RG11** up Rhinog Fach; **RG12/16** to the top of the Moelyblithcwm ridge; **RG19** to Diffwys; **RG22** to Bwlch y Rhiwgyr and so on to Barmouth.

Lower-level Walks/Easier Days

Whatever problems the Rhinogs may set for the serious hillwalker, there is no denying their generosity to the humble pedestrian seeking to sample their charms in a more leisurely way. Roads give easy access to the valleys and passes without possessing them and, as a result, the Rhinogs are richly endowed with short and uncomplicated walks where you can enjoy the rugged beauty in total peace.

Cwm Bychan/Craig Wion/Roman steps (RG L1)

In only 6 miles this magnificent walk captures the spirit of the Rhinogs, offering a taste of all their charms – fissured pavements of rock, rock-engirdled tarns, seas of heather, miniature cliffs and canyons, and long views of peaks, moors and sea. Yet no 2000ft peak is scaled nor, despite the Rhinogs' harsh reputation, is the walking other than pleasant.

Most of this walk has already been described, and it only remains to put the pieces together and supply the missing link. Start at Cwm Bychan and climb to Bwlch Gwylim on **RG1**. Then, instead of scrambling up Craig Ddrwg, begin by walking SE (parallel to the wall) but gradually trend L to Llyn Twrglas. There are only intermittent tracks but no matter as short, crisp heather gives the feel of walking on air.

A more distinct track appears along the W shore of Llyn Twr-glas and leads through a glen to Llyn Pryfed. Nestling in a rocky cradle this is a pearl reminiscent of the tarns of Haystacks in Cumbria. A peaty scramble up Pryfed's NW corner leads to the cairn on Craig Wion. The way is SE now, gradually veering SW. The roughest part of the day is to hand! So far you have been walking with the 'grain' of the land, now all that changes. A little ravine is crossed, then a narrow defile brings you to another rift crossing at R-angles with cliffs 60ft high. Next comes a huge plateau of slab rock, then a deep canyon to cross followed by another smaller canyon, and so on. To compensate there are the views: rolling moors E, Rhinog Fawr S, Llyn Cwm Bychan and the sea W. Eventually you are led into a small hollow (the 'grain' with you again now) where you can either bear L for the highest ground and spot height 518m, or trend R to Llyn Morwynion, one of the Rhinogs' brightest jewels snug in its deep rocky hollow. Return down the Roman steps.

Round Rhinog Fawr (RG L2)

Start from Llyn Cwm Bychan and walk up the Roman steps. However, instead of bearing R for Llyn Du as in **RG6**, follow the path downhill until it meets the Coed y Brenin Forest perimeter fence. Now turn R along a damp oozy track. After about 1 mile, where the fence swings from SW to just E of S, look for a track that veers away for the head of Bwlch Drws Ardudwy.

Follow the pass down to Maes-y-garnedd (**RG7**) and then transfer to the Rhinog Fawr W ridge route (**RG9**). Leave this where it levels out, before swinging E for Rhinog Fawr, and hold a N course direct for Gloyw Lyn, suffering rough trackless going for a time. However there is nothing a rest by Gloyw Lyn's heathery banks will not cure, and when you resume follow the Fisherman's Path from its NE shore back to Cwm Bychan.

Cwm-yr-afon (RG L3)

A short walk through typical Rhinog country to the enchanting Gloyw Lyn where, if it is sunny, you will find the temptation to linger well nigh irresistible.

Cross the bridge by the car park at 619296 and turn L to the farm of Cwm-yr-afon. Turn R across fields in a parkland setting to the ruin of Pandy with Rhinog Fawr rearing fiercely ahead and Clip presenting its precipitous E flank. At Pandy bear R through an old gate in a wall and aim S over marshy broken terrain, keeping another wall 100yd or so to your L, until you meet a well-defined mining track, backed by small cliffs, wending E.

Follow the mining track until you spot the ruin of Hafotty in the valley and then press on for another 0.25 mile. Next strike out L (keeping a watchful eye for wild primroses) towards a gritty track on the far side, leading beneath the crags of Carreg y Saeth to Gloyw Lyn. Having got this far it would be a pity not to summon up the energy for the 5min climb that is all Carreg y Saeth demands, for it is a pocket peak in the best Rhinogs' tradition and richly clothed in colourful waist-high heather.

Pont Crafnant to Gloyw Lyn (RG L4)

Combine this with **RG L3** for an excellent half-day out.

Park about 0.25 mile up the road from Pont Crafnant and then return to cross the bridge. Over the brook the path veers R, momentarily, before turning L to climb through woods bounded by the remains of an old wall and moss-encrusted boulders. Before long you reach open country with glorious views of the sea and a string of zigzags leading to a small 'pass' skirting the S slopes of Carreg Fawr directly ahead.

Over the 'pass' the path becomes erratic, so either drop down to join the Cwm-yr-afon route near Hafotty (634296), or contour along parallel to the valley, using a variety of little trails through the heather, eventually meeting the Cwm-yr-afon route higher up. Combined with **RG L3** this gives an easy but unforgettable half-day if you savour solitude and the wilds. Even the short walk back along the road to regain the car is a joy with the Artro tumbling merrily along beside you.

Harlech trail/Bwlch y Rhiwgyr circular (RG L5)

Leave Cors y Gedol and follow **RG21** over Pont Scethin and up the Harlech trail to the Rhinog ridge. Next make your way down-ridge to Bwlch y Rhiwgyr and home via Pont Fadog on **RG22**.

A simple half-day jaunt to blow the cobwebs away.

Diffwys S circular walks (RG L6)

See **RG H7**.

Llyn Y Bi (RG L7)

A sketchy, airy path leaves the crest of the Moelyblithcwm ridge at 661255 to traverse Y Llethr's E face on a bearing of 50°. It meanders through a wall and then drops quite steeply down to a second one where it peters out. By now grass has given way to prolific heather that fills the air with its sweetness. Most unusual Rhinog heather it is too, since it offers an easy walk down to the lake with none of the normal bouldery hazards.

This is given as an addition to a walk along the main Rhinog ridge.

Sheltered by two of the Rhinog giants, the hollow containing Llyn Y Bi is a cosy, warm place. For once Y Llethr comes off best, overshadowing Rhinog Fach and revealing as rugged a face as anything in the area. To regain the ridge look for a well-trodden trail through the heather to the N of the lake. This gives an easy walk up to the Llyn Hywel col, joining it where the haul up Y Llethr begins.

NW Lakes (RG L8)

This walk takes in Llynnau y Fedw, Llyn Caerwych, Llyn Eiddew-mawr and Llyn Eiddew-bach. The key is the Moel

An easy, but not spectacular day.

Goedog packhorse track, which can be picked up at several points as described in **RG2**. It is then a matter of local improvisation. Diversions to Y Fedw and Caerwych present no problems, being merely short strolls over easy grass. Eiddewmawr and Eiddew-bach, on the other hand, are surrounded by marsh and best approached from the manganese mine track described in **RG2**. This branches off the Moel Goedog path at 637343. An extension to Bryn Cader Faner when in the area of Llyn Caerwych should be obligatory.

Roman steps (RG L9)

Stroll up the Roman steps from Llyn Cwm Bychan. It is under 2 miles to the top of the pass and every ounce of effort is repaid, not just by the atmosphere of this desolate place, but also because this walk brings you to within 300 paces (to your L on a faint track) of lonely Llyn Morwynion, one of the most romantically sited lakes in Wales.

Gloyw Lyn (RG L10)

The latter part of this route is now almost totally obscured by fencing and not recommended.

This walk also starts from Llyn Cwm Bychan on the Roman steps route but this time, just after emerging from the woods that precede the steps, you branch out R on to a fisherman's track.

Bwlch Drws Ardudwy (RG L11)

You have only to walk up this wild and awesome pass from Maes-y-garnedd to experience something of the grimmer aspect of the Rhinogs. Yet it is grimness mixed with awe and drama, as the atmosphere gradually takes hold and the pass closes in. Find time, if you can, to extend the walk to Llyn Cwmhosan or even to Llyn Hywel as in **RG12**.

Bwlch Gwylim (RG L12)

Only Llyn Morwynion can rival Llyn Pryfed as the most enchanting lake hereabouts, so this is a good place for lunch.

This walk uses the track to Clip that starts just across the road from the car park at Llyn Cwm Bychan as in **RG1**. Even if you only get as far as the bwlch you will have traversed one of the finest miles in Wales. But it would be a pity, having got that far, not to sample just a little bit more. So turn R (SE) over easy heather, with tracks here and there, to visit Llyn Twr-glas and Llyn Pryfed.

The Roman steps

Rhinog Fawr above Bwlch Drws Ardudwy with Llyn Cwmhosan (RG L11)

More than most this is a walk that needs a little help from the elements to brighten it up.

Ysgethin Valley (RG L13)

The Ysgethin Valley offers a variety of easy walks, starting from either Cors y Gedol or Pont Fadog. One of the best is a circular tour taking the Harlech trail N route (**RG21**) to just beyond Pont Scethin, then returning via Llyn Irddyn and Pont Fadog on **RG21,1**.

Diffwys S circular walks (RG L14)

See **RG H7**.

Bryn Cader Faner (RG L15)

The easiest way of visiting this ancient stone circle is along the Caerwych route to Moel Ysgyfarnogod (**RG2,2**). It is idyllically set on a crest overlooking the sea with views over Snowdonia.

OS maps
1:25,000 – Sheet 17, 1:50,000 – Sheet 115

Peaks (by height)	Height (ft)	Map Ref	Page
Snowdon	3560	609544	245
Crib y Ddysgl	3493	611552	261
Crib Goch	3026	624552	257
Y Lliwedd	2947	622533	262
Yr Aran	2451	604515	266
Moel Eilio	2382	556577	269
Moel Cynghorion	2211	586564	273
Foel Gron	2063	560568	269
Gallt y Wenallt	2032	642532	264
Foel Goch	1985	571563	272

Mountain Lakes (alphabetically)		
Bach	2400	615555
Coch	1735	598545
Du'r Arddu	1900	601558
Ffynnon-y-gwas	1400	591554
Glas	1735	600547
Glas	2200	619557
Glaslyn	1980	617546
Llydaw	1420	630544
Nadroedd	1700	595543
Nameless (Bwlch Cwm Llan)	1640	603521
Teyrn	1240	641548

THE SNOWDON RANGE

No other peak in England or Wales approaches Snowdon in scale or nobility. Architecturally it is on its own, a vast conception, a titanic symphony of crags and lakes. Its six spiralling ridges give it the impelling majesty of some distant nebula. Few sights are more inviting than the famous view of Snowdon and its satellites from Llynnau Mymbyr. Snowdon offers walkers everything from exhilarating scrambles on Crib Goch and the Gribin, to the easy, steady plod from Llanberis; from fresh rock-girdled tarns to the delicately wooded slopes above Nantgwynant.

Snowdon is the highest, most famous, most popular mountain in Wales. So great is its acclaim that it is all too easy to become blasé, to take it for granted, even to tire from over exposure. I speak as one converted. Having climbed Snowdon many times, it was only after temporarily deserting it to explore the rest of Wales that I really began to appreciate its true stature as the most compelling and rewarding mountain in the land.

Only three ridges directly emanate from Snowdon. The others flow from Crib y Ddysgl (0.5 mile N) which, though it is the second-highest peak in Wales, may be regarded for this purpose almost as a subsidiary top. Curling round to the E two of the ridges enclose the most spectacular of all Snowdon's cwms, Dyli (Hollow of the Flood). Bounded in turn by the massive black cliffs of Y Lliwedd, Snowdon's own shattered W face, and the craggy ramparts of Crib Goch and Crib y Ddysgl, it cradles three lakes: the modest, unassuming Llyn Teyrn, Llyn Llydaw, and, huddled in a cold windy hollow nearly 2000ft up, Llyn Glaslyn. The passage of these two E arms constitutes the greatest ridge walk in the country, the Snowdon horseshoe, an exhilarating tramp of unrelenting challenge and appeal. En route it takes in all four peaks of the central massif – Crib Goch, Crib y Ddysgl, Snowdon and Y Lliwedd – as well as the minor top of Gallt y Wenallt.

The S ridge that Snowdon sends down to Bwlch Cwm Llan is not to be outshone. A short distance below the top, at over 3000ft, it crosses Bwlch Main, a narrow arête with breathtaking views and a heady sense of airiness although it is quite safe. Beyond Bwlch Cwm Llan the land surges again in one final fling to Yr Aran, a shapely wedge-shaped peak and a fine viewpoint that can sometimes be mistaken for Snowdon itself if the sovereign is shrouded in cloud.

The higher cwm to the E, Tregalan, is grassy and empty. Down-valley, where it narrows to Cwm Llan, it reflects the pastoral charm of Nantgwynant in one of Snowdon's prettiest nooks. Cwm Garegog to the W is more of a sprawling stony hollow than a cwm. It offers little of interest and is rarely visited. The Llechog ridge that bounds it N is strictly a spur of the S ridge but it is convenient to give it a status of its own, particularly as on its far side it falls precipitously into Cwm Clogwyn, the aptly named 'Hollow of the Precipice'. Cwm Clogwyn is almost as deserted as Cwm Garegog, yet it is laden with atmosphere. Host to four sparkling lakes, it is hemmed in on three sides by unscalable cliffs, and guarded on the fourth side by a bouldery ramp that shields the upper cwm and its trio of tarns from all but the most intimate gaze.

Cwm Clogwyn's N arm carries the Snowdon Ranger, one of the oldest routes up the mountain. It is breached at Bwlch Cwm Brwynog where the terrain changes abruptly. The inhospitable stone-studded slopes of Snowdon now relent, and from here on W

Snowdon across Llyn Llydaw (SN 3)

Astride the Crib Goch knife-edge (SN H1)

Sunset over Snowdon and Llynnau Mymbyr

you can tread grass along a playful little edge that crosses Moel Cynghorion, Foel Goch (not quite a 2000-footer) and Foel Gron before reaching its climax in Moel Eilio. These are not peaks whose names grip the imagination, but their elegantly scarped E faces proclaim their mountainly status and there are few finer viewpoints.

Cwm Brwynog, like its neighbour Cwm Clogwyn, is a solitary haven of bogs and boulders with an upper cwm (again like Clogwyn) that needs a little pioneering to reveal its secret – the malicious black cliffs of Clogwyn du'r Arddu and its sombre sunless lake. Of all the climbing haunts in Wales, this is surely the most forbidding. Few of the thousands who tramp the Llanberis path, Cwm Brwynog's NW rim, ever pause to savour its chilling charm.

Across the ridge and bounded on its far side by the N arm of Cwm Dyli, thus creating a flattened V, lie a cluster of secluded cwms that attain their crowning glory in the romantic hollow of Llyn Glas. Here, and in the upper cwm cradling Llyn Bach, you are very much at one with the hills, sharing their innermost recesses, deep in the wild. The spiky comb of Crib Goch and the huge knobbly snout of Clogwyn y Person seem suspended in the air in a flawless extravaganza of pinnacle and crag. There is no finer scene in Wales.

All six ridges have well-developed tracks enabling Snowdon to be climbed from many points of the compass. Given Snowdon's popularity 'well developed' could easily be a euphemism for ugly gashes of peat and scree. Happily wiser counsels have prevailed of

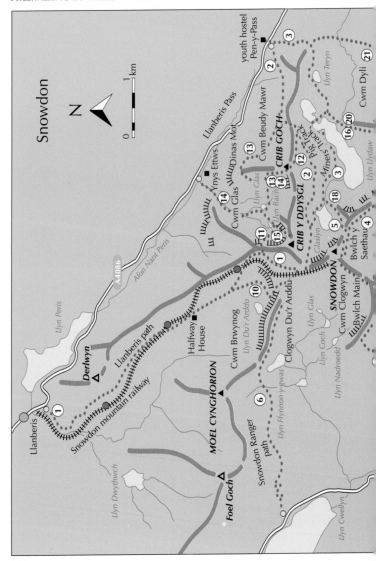

Snowdon

late, and this is a good place to pay tribute to the sterling work that has been carried out in flagging the worst areas of erosion with boulders. Thanks to this the danger has been contained, at least for the time being. No one wants artificial man-made trails in the hills but, given the alternative, one can only be grateful for the dedication and professionalism with which this difficult task of renovation has been carried out in as natural a way as possible. The zigzags at the head of the Pig Track are an excellent example.

The most exciting of the ridge routes – unequalled as a scramble – begins with Crib Goch's E ridge and continues along the N edge of Cwm Dyli. (To gild the lily you could start with Llyn Glas and pick up Crib Goch's N ridge instead.) However, all the ridges give stirring walks: the S rim of Cwm Dyli over Bwlch Saethau and Y Lliwedd; the S ridge and Bwlch Main; the Rhyd-ddu path and Llechog, especially when aglow in the setting sun; the Snowdon Ranger with its glimpses of Clogwyn du'r Arddu; even the oft-deprecated plod up the NW ridge (the Llanberis path) provided you tackle it out of season, away from crowds and the chug of the train.

As with Loch Lomond, so it is with Snowdon – you may take the high road or the low road! Amongst the lower choices a miners' track follows the shores of Llyn Llydaw and Llyn Glaslyn with scenery second to none. The Pig Track cleaves the middle ground between lake and ridge before joining the miners' track for the final zigzags to Bwlch Glas. Then there is the Watkin Path rising from Nantgwynant, revealing a gentler, more lyrical side to Snowdon's multi-faceted character.

'Multi-faceted', that is Snowdon to a 'T'. So popular that one sometimes despairs of ever avoiding the crocodiles, or weekend queues to cross the Crib Goch knife-edge. Yet, even in the height of summer, solitude is never far away: Cwm Glas, Cwm Clogwyn, the S slopes of Gallt y Wenallt and Moel Eilio all provide it. Always princely from Llynnau Mymbyr or when displaying a mighty cone to the S, yet all too often invisible inside a cold and swirling mist. Irresistible on a crisp clear day when the air is like wine and the sun imparts its warmth to even the darkest nook, yet graceless and arid in its upper realms – an inhospitable treeless waste of struggling green and grey stony slopes. Sad and melancholy on a dripping, blustery day in July when the echo of tumbling pebbles sounds a mournful note, yet magical beyond belief a moment later when the clouds part to reveal its awesome majesty.

Snowdon

Strange to relate, Snowdon is the only major Welsh peak not to have retained its original Welsh name: 'Y Wyddfa Fawr' – 'The Great Tomb'. Whose tomb it is supposed to be is lost in antiquity. Some authorities ascribe it to Rhita, a mythological giant, others to King Arthur who, according to legend, slew Rhita. We shall never know.

Weather aside, there is no such thing as a dull climb on Snowdon even though the actual summit can be sadly disappointing. Off-peak in winter, away from the queues waiting for the train and the bustle of the so-called hotel (only refreshments are available) it never fails to provide the fresh, cleansing thrill you would expect. But at other times, in spite of valiant efforts to clean it up, its appeal is tainted by a vulgar eyesore of litter and besmirched by the black smoky grime of the train and the cacophony of noise.

Above the hotel the view from the cairn is of epic proportions. If you can see it, that is, for the summit of Snowdon is one of the wettest and mistiest spots in the country. In 30-odd visits I can only recall four or five clear days, and even then haze was usually a bugbear! However, on the right day – once or twice a year maybe – the gaze carries as far as the Wicklow mountains of Ireland, to Scotland, Scafell and the Isle of Man. More usually the fare consists of the Glyders and a peep of the Carneddau, Moel Siabod and the Moelwyns, the Hebog and Nantlle ranges, over Yr Aran to the Traeth Bach Estuary at Porthmadog, Moel Eilio, Anglesey and the sea, the Rhinogs, Cader Idris… a tumbled mass of mountains without end! Yet so overpowering is its scale that Snowdon completely dwarfs these satellites and, curiously, it is its near neighbours, Crib Goch, Y Lliwedd and the spectacular Cwm Dyli, that give the biggest thrill.

Llanberis path (SN1)

Since 1896 it has shared the NW ridge with the little railway that puffs up the mountain, weather permitting, from roughly mid-March to October every year. It is gently graded throughout, stony or gravelly (no bog) and a good 6ft wide. This means it is virtually impossible to stray; ideal for non-regular walkers or family parties out for the day. The other side of the coin is that it can be dull, conveying only intermittently any sense of being on a great mountain. There are long featureless

The longest, the easiest and one of the oldest of all the regular routes up Snowdon.

Trains at Halfway Station near the Llanberis Path

stretches although strong walkers can improve matters by abandoning the path for the edge overlooking the Llanberis Pass with breathtaking views throughout.

You start from the grey slate town of Llanberis where it always seems to be drizzling. Walk down the tarmac road opposite the Royal Victoria Hotel. It rises steeply until a footpath sign sends you L, through a gate, onto the path proper. The highlight for the next mile is Moel Eilio and the elusive Llyn Dwythwch across the valley, while Moel Cynghorion's N ridge shapes up as a worthy adversary for another day.

After Halfway House (where refreshments are still available in summer – as they have been for around 100 years), excitement mounts as the dark menacing cliff of Clogwyn du'r Arddu grows in stature R with Snowdon itself beyond. 'Cloggy', as it is affectionately known, is one of the cradles of British rock climbing and a visit is as much *de rigeur* for lovers of the hills as Lords is for cricket fans.

It is easily done. About 0.5 mile beyond Halfway House, at the end of a wire fence, a collapsed cairn points to an old mining track, green with age, cavorting away on 160° (**SN1,1**). It gradually swings R, tapering to a shaly wisp suspended

The Llanberis path

between dripping, lowering crags L and the torrents of unstable scree that fall away to Llyn Du'r Arddu R. Trapped in a sunless hollow this inky-black lake is as desolate a sheet of water as you will find in many a long day. The path eventually embeds itself in the rock face high above the lake. However there is no need to go all the way to imbibe the dark drama.

The Llanberis path, meanwhile, passes under the railway close to the edge above Cwm Hetiau, Valley of the Hats, said to have acquired its name from travellers long ago whose hats were whisked away by the wind. I can quite believe it! It is worth hugging the edge round the promontory of Gryn Las. This is where **SN11** gains the crest and the prospect over the pass to the Glyders, and down into Cwm Glas, is outstanding in its savage grandeur.

The path, in contrast, is all innocence. A wicked innocence. From here in wintertime hard frozen snow or ice makes this path a death trap for all but properly equipped experts. In fair weather it is merely a grind, relieved only by successive landmarks. First is the huge straggly cairn where the path from Crib y Ddysgl comes in L; next is the Snowdon Ranger coming in R, then the 7ft obelisk indicating the top of the zigzags. After this all that remains is the final trek beside the rails. By this time most people are either striding out manfully, now the goal is in sight, or trudging, head down, in the final stages of exhaustion, quite oblivious to the views. These are especially fine if you hold the crest overlooking Cwm Dyli, L of the rails.

Pig Track (SN2)

Note the spelling. Sometimes you will see 'Pyg Track', reflecting the once-held view that the track took its name from the nearby Pen-y-Gwryd Hotel. Nowadays it is generally accepted that the name derives from Bwlch Moch (Pass of the Pigs) which you cross early on.

This path is now so well flagged for most of its length that little description is necessary.

The well-used path leaves Pen-y-pass due W through a gap in the wall bounding the higher of the two parking areas. Within minutes the hustle of Pen-y-pass seems far away as a scene of unbridled wildness unfolds, with the Llanberis lakes cupped in the V of the Glyders and the N ridge of Crib Goch.

The Pig Track wends its way across Snowdon's S Flank

Rocky steps lead round a buttress to Bwlch Moch where, for the only time until you are above Llyn Glaslyn, grassy

slopes enable you to drop down to the miners' track. The path divides here. The R fork winds aloft to Crib Goch's E ridge (**SN12**). The Pig Track continues SW, actually descending for a time, before resuming a gentle upward tilt across the S ramparts of Crib Goch. You are now poised midway between the brave souls crossing the edge above and Llyn Llydaw shimmering 600ft below, with Y Lliwedd's dark towering citadels arcing the sky beyond. Vintage Snowdonia! Even better is to come as you trend R. Snowdon's E face of shattered terraces, buttresses and gullies stands revealed in daunting splendour with Llyn Glaslyn and Gribin ridge now also in view.

It is about here that the miners' track comes in L after a crumbly 400ft climb from Llyn Glaslyn. A wary eye is needed among an unhelpful scattering of cairns as it is easy to descend L to some derelict mine workings. The advice is 'when in doubt stay high'. If you do this the main path soon reasserts itself, tiresome and slithery until the famous zigzags where clever engineering has recently constructed a neat and simple boulder-paved path to prevent further erosion. Please keep to this; it is the only way to avoid more ugly and dangerous scarring. The zigzags breast the skyline at Bwlch Glas where a 7ft standing stone provides an indispensable landmark in bad weather. All that remains is the final trudge along the railway lines.

An alternative approach as far as Bwlch Moch (**SN2,1**) is to follow the crest of the undulating ridge to the S of the Pig Track. You can pull up to it near Pen-y-pass and regain the main path at the bwlch.

Miners' Track (SN3)

The trail to the old copper mine above Llyn Glaslyn is probably more in use today than it ever was in its heyday (it closed in 1926). Starting at 1169ft along a gently graded stony track it is one of the easiest of all routes on Snowdon. You can drive a Land Rover as far as Llyn Glaslyn and for ordinary pedestrians or children, not fully bitten by the hillwalking bug but just looking for a pleasant day in the hills, this is an ideal way to enjoy some of Wales' greatest scenery.

However, there are dangers. As far as Llyn Glaslyn – provided the weather is fine – the well-paved track means you

This gives one of the easiest approaches to Snowdon, but unless you are properly equipped – and with plenty of time and energy – Llyn Glaslyn should be your limit.

can get away with stout everyday footwear. I do not recommend it, but thousands do it! Beyond Llyn Glaslyn it is a different story and you must be careful not to allow the easy going thus far to engender a false sense of security. Walking boots are now essential and the expedition becomes a slower, tougher proposition entirely.

On leaving Pen-y-pass the track rises above Nantgwynant with flowing views of Moel Siabod and the Moelwyn hills. However, in less than 1 mile the scene is transformed into something altogether more grand by the sudden emergence of Snowdon, Crib Goch and Y Lliwedd on the skyline ahead. Turning a corner reveals Llyn Teyrn (The Lake of the Monarch) where the ruined barracks in which the miners used to lodge during the week (they mostly lived in Bethesda) are a grim reminder of the so-called 'good old days'. Today this deserted lake is a haven of tranquillity, and when it is calm you may see Y Lliwedd mirrored in its clear waters. Minutes later another bend unveils Llyn Llydaw with the giants gazing down in regal splendour.

The causeway across Llyn Llydaw dates back to 1853. It has recently been raised to reduce the risk of flooding. Even so it is still submerged occasionally and you then have the choice of either wading or following a sketchy path round the SW shoreline to regain the main track near the outflow from Llyn Glaslyn. Even without floods this is well worth a try because of the matchless view of Snowdon from the far side of the lake.

Once over the causeway the gradual rise to Llyn Glaslyn scarcely raises a sweat; quite a contrast with the hardy souls clambering up the Gribin ridge L. Llyn Glaslyn has a dual nature. On sunny days it is a brilliant blue, fully justifying its ancient name of Llyn Ffynnon Las (Lake of the Blue-green Spring) and leavening most beautifully the cold austerity of Snowdon's towering battlements. All too often, however, Llyn Glaslyn is grey and forlorn, feathered in mist or whipped by a gusting wind.

The regular path ends just beyond a shingly beach and the derelict mine. From here a line of cairns, none too easy to spot in a tumble of rocky debris, scrambles up to the Pig Track at 615548. Care is needed to locate this in descent as there is a plethora of large cairns near the critical junction with the Pig Track and it is easy to end up on a crumbly slope near a clutch of old mine shafts.

Watkin Path (SN4)

It starts along a farm road off the A498 at 627506 near Bethania (car park and toilets across the road) and keeps L along a stony lane when, after 0.25 mile, the road swings away R to Hafod-y-llan Farm. Aged woods, dotted with green moss-capped boulders and fringed with rhododendrons, cast a happy spell. As the path swings first R then L, crossing and recrossing an old quarry tramway, the centre of attraction switches to the glen of the Afon Llan and its tumbling falls, to sparkling turquoise pools with tree-hung crags beyond. A radiant blend of russets, yellows and greens when seen in autumn.

Of all the ways up Snowdon this has the prettiest beginning. Not the most dramatic, nor necessarily the most beautiful, but certainly the prettiest.

After a steady rise the path levels out where the track to Bwlch Cwm Llan breaks away L at 621520 (**SN9**). The Watkin Path, meanwhile, crosses the stream and passes the ruined Plascwmllan, once the home of the local quarry manager but used in World War II as a stronghold for training commandos, as the bullet holes speckling its walls still testify! Just beyond is a slate plaque set in a rock, commemorating the spot where Mr Gladstone, then Prime Minister and aged 83, addressed a huge throng on 'Justice to Wales'. It was about the same time, in 1892, that the Watkin Path was first inaugurated as a donkey track. Mrs Gladstone is said to have been one of the early riders.

The scenery is imposing rather than pretty now, with the craggy shoulder of Craig Ddu R, Snowdon's S ridge in full view ahead, and Yr Aran's E ridge L. Soon you reach the roof-less barracks of the inevitable slate quarries. They only operated from 1840 to 1882 but the ugliness lives on. The path narrows and veers R here to begin its long steady haul across the mountainside. Despite the views across barren Cwm Tregalan, this is where you are forcibly reminded that the Watkin Path, whatever its charms, has the lowest start of all the routes up Snowdon, committing you to a good 3300ft of ascent.

The huge orange-brown cairn making Bwlch Ciliau (Pass of Retreat) comes into view at last. Y Lliwedd can be claimed by an airy scramble R (**SN17**), while for Snowdon a wide stony path rambles majestically on to Bwlch Saethau (Pass of the Arrows). This level 0.5 mile is a walk fit for the gods and not to be rushed, especially if you forsake the path for the edge. The Snowdon Horseshoe is portrayed in all its splendour, from the battlements of Crib Goch to the castellated cliffs of Y Lliwedd.

A transient dip at 616540 gives the clue to where on another day you might break away NE, near a clutch of tiny pools, for the cairns marking the crest of Gribin ridge (**SN5**). Otherwise, as is distressingly clear, loins must be girded for the most toilsome grind anywhere on Snowdon – the 900ft ascent of its SE face. There are two paths, both on shaly scree and exceedingly loose. One shadows the edge and climbs straight up the nose to the summit cairn. Marginally easier is the original Watkin Path which slants L across the shattered waste to join the S ridge by a 6ft stone finger 5min below the top.

Gribin ridge (SN5)

The Snowdon Gribin – not to be confused with Y Gribin ridge in the Glyders – is the knobbly snout that protrudes between Llyn Llydaw and Llyn Glaslyn. It joins Bwlch y Saethau at 616540 and is equally handy for tackling Snowdon or Y Lliwedd. The approach is along the miners' track before breaking away L just short of Llyn Glaslyn.

Once on the crest (and you must keep to the crest) the general line of advance is clear from polished rocks and scratch marks. The scrambling is stiff but, with care, perfectly safe for the rock is hard and scabrous and the holds plentiful. Any serious scrambling could probably be avoided altogether by careful reconnaissance, though this would not be at all easy in descent when vigilance is certainly needed at a couple of potentially exposed spots.

The view from this lofty perch, hung midway between Snowdon's E face and the cataclysmic precipice of Y Lliwedd, with Llyn Llydaw shimmering way below, is out of this world. If only Gribin were twice as long! But it is not to be, and disappointingly soon a line of cairns heralds the short undulating tongue that leads to the Watkin Path and **SN4**.

Snowdon Ranger route (SN6)

Ample parking across the road from the Youth Hostel at 564550, well signposted and graded zigzags, and beautiful views across Llyn Cwellyn to Moel Hebog and the Nantlle ridge, ensure a happy, relaxed start to the day.

After the initial climb the path levels off across a boggy depression. But any dullness is short-lived. Cwm Clogwyn (Hollow of the Precipice) comes into view R, a vast amphitheatre that can hold its own in any company, hemmed in on three sides by stupendous cliffs. The ridge furthest away R is Llechog, which carries the Rhyd-ddu path (**SN7**). The cliffs in the middle are nameless, possibly because they are too crumbly for climbing, but they fall a good 1800ft from the summit hotel (just discernible as a tiny blip) and are mightily impressive nonetheless.

The key to the Snowdon Ranger is the craggy shoulder bounding the L arm of the cwm, beyond the notch of Bwlch Cwm Brwynog ahead. (The lake nestling in the hollow just below is Llyn Ffynnon-y-gwas, 'The Spring of the Manservant'.) A stony path snakes up the shoulder, making light of the task. When the angle relents you should scramble over to the edge L to inspect Wales' most famous rock face, Clogwyn du'r Arddu (Black Cliff of the Black Hill) and the cold shy lake at its foot. You can also check out the scree rake that terminates **SN10**.

The path trends R now across a barren stony waste to meet the railway track by a standing stone. A few steps above, on the edge, is a cairn marking the conjunction of the Llanberis path with the ridge path to Crib Goch. A few paces more brings you to the 7ft standing stone marking the top of the Pig Track zigzags. There are no problems in clear weather but all these landmarks are manna from heaven in mist!

Considering this route's popularity the zigzags met early on are in prime condition with stretches of lush green turf, a far cry from those encountered on the Pig Track.

Rhyd-ddu path (SN7)

The certainty of this path never wavers, it is gently graded and strategically placed boulders now cover what used to be interminable morasses of bog. Some writers have dubbed it 'tedious'. Not me. Relaxing, sedate maybe, but certainly not tedious. There is a magnificent climax in Llechog and the famous Bwlch Main, and if you should ever use it for descent, having climbed

Despite its lowish start this is one of the easier routes.

by way of the Snowdon Ranger in the morning, the afternoon sun over Hebog and Nantlle will live in your memory.

There is ample parking on the site of the old Welsh Highland Railway station at 571526. The path itself, a quarry road at first, is signposted through an iron gate a couple of minutes walk N of the car park. It rambles between islands of rock and seas of coppery grass until, after about 1 mile and soon after crossing a stile over a wall, it bears L through a kissing-gate. This is an important crossroads. Straight ahead the quarry road carries on to Bwlch Cwm Llan and SN8. R a faint track marked by upright stones comes in from Ffridd Uchaf Farm at 576515. This is the old Beddgelert path (**SN7,1**), one of the original routes up Snowdon but largely ignored now due to the superior car parking facilities at Rhyd-ddu.

A twisty spell of broken rocky terrain makes it hard to credit that this is the same mountain that dominates Llyn Llydaw and Llyn Glaslyn so imperiously. Such doubts are soon dispelled. Llechog is in the great tradition of Snowdonia precipices and, moreover, it forms the S rim of the massive bowl of Cwm Clogwyn where four sparkling lakes lie trapped beneath the giant's crumpled W face and the serrated crest of Bwlch Main.

A gravelly path zigzags away from the brink, to avoid the eroded scar of an earlier track, before trending NE to join S ridge at 605537.

Note This junction is easily missed in descent as the cairn is miniscule and the paths merge at a very acute angle, giving the impression of two variants of the same path which will probably reunite a little later. They do not. The key is to remember that where the tracks part the L fork, headed for the S ridge, actually starts to climb while the R branch for Rhyd-ddu unmistakably declines.

You are now at Bwlch Main (Slender Gap), an exhilarating arête topping 3000ft with calamitous drops on either flank. Angular and spiky, it has a ghostly feel when mist shrouds the dank, rifted gullies below and hides the rocky spires in a blanket of grey. The crest is only 6ft wide in places but friendly

boulders hem you snuggly in and there is no exposure what-soever, except in a howling gale! (As usual I am not referring here to winter conditions when, as with so many other walks, Bwlch Main becomes a serious proposition requiring proper equipment.) Beyond the bwlch the path climbs swiftly to the top, passing a 6ft standing stone and a large cairn en route. This is about 5min from the hotel and marks the top of the Watkin Path.

Snowdon's S ridge (SN 8)

Note If you are combining the Rhyd-ddu and Snowdon Ranger paths, a good way to regain base without any road work is to follow the course of the old Welsh Highland Railway as marked on the 1:25,000 map – **SN7,1**

S ridge (W approach) (SN8)

Start along the Rhyd-ddu path, but instead of turning L through the kissing-gate as in **SN7** follow the quarry track into Cwm Garegog, the appropriately named 'Stony Hollow'. When you reach the desolate, towering slate waste of the long-since abandoned quarries, tread carefully through the old workings but cast a glance at the disused pits L. Some of these are as beautifully beflowered and vegetated now as the legendary hanging gardens of Babylon ever were! Passing a nameless tarn R brings you face-to-face with a wall. You are now at Bwlch Cwm Llan. A faint path leads along the wall R to Yr Aran. The S ridge path, horribly broken and worn, sets off L, heavily cairned.

Apart from the inspiring views – but then, which route on Snowdon does not have exceptional views? – the 2000ft plod up S ridge is a long sweaty grind. I always try to restrict it to descents! However nothing that ends in Bwlch Main can be bad, and so all is forgiven (see **SN7**).

S ridge (E approach) (SN9)

Walk up the Watkin Path until it levels out at 621520 just prior to crossing the Afon Llan. Follow the bootmarks that break away L up a banked path until you come to the old tramway that used to serve the quarries further up-valley. Three routes fan out here. On your original line you can scramble up beside a stream to gain the tip of Yr Aran's E ridge at 616516. The second option is to step ahead as before but bear L almost at once onto a soft, green path that executes a U-turn before rejoining the stream path higher up. Both routes pass some derelict mine shafts on the way and lead into **SN25**.

However for today's walk turn R and follow the tramway (if only all paths were green and firm like this) until you reach a sharp bend R after about 300yd. Once again black shades of bootmarks in the turf point the way. A vague path, gradually becoming stonier, rises L to reach Bwlch Cwm Llan by a tumbledown wall at 605522. You are now at the foot of Snowdon's S ridge (**SN8**) with a panoramic overview of the Nantlle ridge directly ahead beyond a nameless tarn.

Clogwyn du'r Arddu E terrace route (SN10)

Do not attempt this in thick weather or without a companion who already knows the lie of the land.

If you are looking for a new way up Snowdon, are not averse to a spell of stiff scrambling, and would like to savour the brooding atmosphere of Clogwyn du'r Arddu, then this could be the answer! But be warned: it is right on the borderline of practicality for walkers. The face of 'Cloggy' is like an inverted isosceles triangle with two upward sloping terraces. The W terrace is a rock climb; the E terrace a rough scramble.

Follow **SN1,1** to the rock face, staying with the little track across the screes until it splits. The lower fork continues to W terrace further along, the upper one merges into rock steps and a twisty track which veers L with more steps and zigzags on to the terrace proper. A steep scree shoot takes over higher up to land you on grass near the Snowdon Ranger (**SN6**).

Gryn Las route (SN11)

This route should not be used for descent unless you have already climbed it from below, for the spot where it joins the edge is easily missed. Either way it should definitely not be countenanced in mist.

This testing route is for experienced hillwalkers only.

Even from below it is essential to prospect the route before you are committed and this is best done from Llyn Bach (reached as in **SN13** or **SN14**). Look out W for a break in the crags of Gryn Las (Green Horn) where a sequence of rocky steps, grassy shelves and ultimately scree offers a feasible line to the skyline. You should breast the ridge about 500yd SE of Clogwyn station to finish on **SN1**.

Crib Goch

Crib Goch (The Red Crest) has a unique place in the pageant of the Welsh hills. Snowdon may be grander in scale, Tryfan more blatantly rugged, but to scramblers who eschew out-and-out climbing it is the ultimate challenge. Alone of the Welsh peaks it demands a touch of exposure before surrendering its crown, no matter how you tackle it.

Crib Goch is every inch mountain. Wholly rock, no grass, not a trace of bracken or heather and no secret nooks or niches. Pen-y-pass reveals the N and E ridges to perfection, soaring remorselessly to a small rocky platform at a pointed tip. This breezy eyrie, much frequented by seagulls, is a stirring place. The gaze is channelled through the Llanberis Pass to Anglesey and the sea, into the sunless depths of Cwm Glas, to the Glyders and Moel Siabod. Yet magnificent as they are these long views are totally eclipsed by the rim of Cwm Dyli dipping and twisting, first along a narrow arête to the Pinnacles, then up a series of rocky steps to Crib y Ddysgl and so on to Snowdon. Nearer to hand the sense of occasion is enhanced by the confluence of the three ridges that constitute the only feasible lines of attack. The N ridge is razor-sharp, the E ridge is a stony pyramid and W is the famous knife-edge leading to Snowdon and the justly famous horseshoe.

Note Purists should note that Crib Goch's highest point is not the 3023ft of the platform where the ridges meet, but a 3026ft spot halfway along the knife-edge, crowned with a small cairn high above Cwm Uchaf.

E ridge (SN12)

This classic doubles up with the Pig Track as far as Bwlch Moch. There the Pig Track descends momentarily SW from a marker cairn while the trail for Crib Goch bounds steeply aloft W until it comes to an abrupt halt at the foot of a rocky wall. This looks formidable and can be a problem in descent (though it is rare to see anyone coming down this way). However the obstacle is easily outflanked with some mild hand- and footwork by trending either L or R. Polished rocks and scratch marks galore speak louder than any words.

Above the wall an exhilarating scramble leads to the orange-brown spine of the ridge and a series of rocky steps and slabs. The angle hovers on the borderline between invigorating challenge and something more severe but never requires more than the occasional steadying hand – rather like climbing a pyramid. Keep to the crest until a path of pinkish hue sidles away R to join the N ridge just below the top.

Cwm Glas and N ridge from Pen-y-pass (SN13)

The last time I did this walk, one glowing autumn morning after a lapse of many years, I decided it was one of Snowdonia's greatest gems. Writing about it now I see no reason to change that view.

Solitude, majestic scenery and fine scrambling.

Snowdon from Crib Goch

Start along the Pig Track but at about 636554 – where it swings L to climb up to Bwlch Moch – scramble down to a lone cairn, maybe 200yd N. There a faint trail, little more than a sheep track but well cairned and dependable, becomes your friend and mentor for the next mile. The little path crosses the lonely trough of Cwm Beudy Mawr (Hollow of the Big Cowhouse) with glorious views of Glyder Fawr and the coppery-red spine of Esgair Felen, then shelves high above the battlements of Dinas Mot (the final surge of the N ridge) and drops down to a tiny trough to unite with SN14 from Blaen-y-nant.

A short climb S up a dank mossy gully brings a moment you will always remember, the sudden unpresaged emergence of Llyn Glas snuggling in an oasis of green. (Cwm Glas means 'Green Hollow'.) Cupped beneath Crib Goch's savage comb and the rearing arête of Clogwyn y Person, and sporting a heathery islet shaded by a brace of dwarf conifers, this is a place to treasure. A secluded hideaway where, even on the sunniest of days, you can repose in peace shielded from the hum of the pass, watching fellow walkers cautiously inching their way across the knife-edge 900ft above.

There are three exits:

- One is SW over a rocky lip into upper Cwm Glas and Llyn Bach followed by a laborious scramble to Crib y Ddysgl (**SN15**). Llyn Bach is a lovely rock-engirdled tarn reminiscent of the Rhinog lakes at their effervescent best, with the bonus of the soaring crags of Clogwyn y Person and Gryn Last.
- The second exit is SE up pink screes to Bwlch Coch (Red Col) which, by then tackling the Pinnacles and the knife-edge 'the wrong way round', gives you Crib Goch (**SN13,1**).
- Best of all – because it avoids any backtracking en route to Snowdon – is to work round to a point slightly S of E of the lake at 625555 where another pinkish scree run, harsh but mercifully short, gives you the N ridge.

The N ridge is sometimes talked of as the razor-edge to distinguish it from the knife-edge of the better-known crest leading to Crib y Ddysgl. However although the terrain certainly falls away sharply on both sides, cool heads should have no problem while vertigo sufferers will experience as many butterflies either way. A narrow track tiptoes below the crest, first W but later, after scaling a prominent knuckle about 2min from the top (the only tingly episode in the whole walk for nervous types), on its E side.

N ridge/Cwm Glas from Blaen-y-nant (SN14)

Tigers attempting all 14 of the 3000-footers in a single day use this route a lot as it provides a convenient link between Elidir Fawr, the last of the Glyders (if you are toiling N–S) and Crib Goch, the first peak of the Snowdon massif proper.

Drive down the Llanberis Pass, parking at one of the first two laybys after Pont y Gromlech. Continue walking, ignoring the bridge leading to the climbers' hut at Ynys Ettws, but crossing the next bridge over the Afon Nant Peris at Blaen-y-nant (623570). Climb a stile, cross a stream R over a bridge composed of railway sleepers, then follow a path parallel to the true L bank of the brook. You are soon transposed. No more than 0.5 mile brings you to a glacial hollow, laden with

Even on its own this route is a stiff test of fitness, gaining 2500ft in little over 1 mile.

the heady atmosphere of Gryn Las (Green Horn), the savage scabrous cliff facing you.

Directly ahead, past a massive boulder streaked white and capped with a small rock, a stream plunges down the black lowering rock face. A demanding scramble up its true R bank leads to the diminutive but incomparable Llyn Bach (**SN14,1**). Easier, though less exhilarating, is a gully half-L where a dithery sort of path follows the true L bank of a stream between Gryn Las and the dripping crag of Craig y Rhaeadr (Waterfall Crag). This leads to Llyn Glas, as does an easy scramble beside a third stream midway between the other two (**SN14,2**). All ways then join **SN13**.

Crib y Ddysgl

The correct name of this peak – the second highest in England and Wales – is Carnedd Ugain (Cairn of the Twenty). Crib y Ddysgl (Crest of the Dish) is strictly only the name of the ridge overlooking Cwm Glas. However 'Crib y Ddysgl' is now so well established that it would be pedantic to labour the point.

Were it not for the overpowering presence of Snowdon, a mere 20min away, Crib y Ddysgl would be a worthy objective. It lies at the end of the slender ridge leading to Crib Goch, Llyn Glaslyn glitters below, and its N flank is an intrigue of cliffs and gullies in the bosom of which rest the twin pearls of Llyn Glas and Llyn Bach. For added lustre it lies near the conjunction of three of Snowdon's six ridges. But it is near Snowdon and though not neglected (how could it be, straddling the Snowdon horseshoe?) it is certainly unsung and taken for granted.

Crib y Ddysgl is a simple 10min diversion for anyone ascending the Llanberis Path, Pig Track, miners' track, Snowdon Ranger or Gryn Las routes to Snowdon. The one direct route is given below.

Cwm Glas route (SN15)

Despite a glorious approach through Cwm Glas (**SN13** or **SN14**) I mention this little-used route with scant enthusiasm. Climbers tackling the nose of Clogwyn y Person direct have a superb day. But for walkers, denied a definite line, the scrambling is patchy and intermittent. Stretches of crumbly shattered rock and loose uneven scree are a recipe for tedium rather than pleasure. The best guidance, in an impressive but confusing tumble of boulders and crags, is to proceed half-L from Llyn Bach with the aim of gradually forging a way onto the arete. Then it is plain sailing and you join the main horse-shoe path (**SN H1**) just E of the summit.

Y Lliwedd

Y Lliwedd's twin tops straddle the most imposing cliffs in Wales. Nearly 0.5 mile wide, with a 1000ft precipice at their apogee, the plunge to Llyn Llydaw is a full 1500ft. Only the proximity of Snowdon and the odd 50ft that denies them 3000ft status prevents their becoming true celebrities. The W peak is the higher by a whisker, not that it really matters since both are exhilarating places to be. I should really say 'to stand' because spiky quivers of rock make sitting problematical!

The scramble up the NW edge is as easy as pie despite the fearsome drop. There is absolutely no exposure yet all the giddy atmosphere, to quote E.G.Rowland, 'of ascending the spire of some gigantic cathedral'. From the top of the sunless cliffs, dripping wet and darkly vegetated, the stately parade of the horseshoe is balanced by the calm of Nantgwynant and the purple heather-clad foothills of Cnicht and Moel Meirch.

It was on Y Lliwedd that I experienced, for the only time in my life, what W.A. Poucher called a 'glory'. After a morning of heavy clinging mist in the valleys I reached Y Lliwedd to find the tops above about 2700ft in brilliant sunshine. However Cwm Dyli was still a blanket of white and, as I turned to face it, I saw my shadow, moving as I moved, on the cottony mist below, framed in a tiny oval rainbow!

Llyn Llydaw route (SN16)

Follow the miners' path to Llyn Llydaw but then, instead of crossing the causeway, follow a scrappy track along the lake's S shoreline to a footbridge over a tired boggy morass at 633544. A wide stony track takes over here. It is horribly eroded and toilsome as it is the usual way home for walkers who conveniently forget about Gallt y Wenallt and think they have com-

pleted the Snowdon horseshoe with Y Lliwedd. The track breasts the ridge by a large cairn at 631535, in a sodden peaty hollow at the foot of Lliwedd Bach, before hugging the edge to give a thrilling climax as Y Lliwedd's twin tops are finally scaled.

Lliwedd (SN 17)
(photo Marion Teal)

Watkin Path (SN17)

Follow **SN4** to Bwlch Ciliau and then bear R for an exciting haul up a stairway of much scratched, golden-brown terraces sprouting the occasional tuft of heather. Keep L, overlooking Cwm Dyli, for the views. Despite the fearsome clefts and the awesome plunge to Llyn Llydaw there is no danger. The rocks are trusty and riddled with confidence-boosting footholds, scrambling at its best. Towards the top a thin shaly path meanders the final stages.

Gribin ridge (SN18)

This fine walk is a combination of **SN5** to Bwlch y Saethau, the Watkin Path along Bwlch Ciliau, and then the exhilarating scramble across y Lliwedd's NW cliff face described in **SN17**.

263

Cwm Merch route (SN19)

See **SN22**.

Gallt y Wenallt

The untrampled grass round the elegant cairn tells its own tale: a neglected peak. Why, I cannot say. Gallt y Wenallt, strictly speaking, is the last nail of the Snowdon horseshoe and it is a mystery as to why so many walkers choose instead to end the grandest of all Welsh walks with the tedious descent from Y Lliwedd to Llyn Llydaw. The jolly tramp on to 'The Slope of the Pale Height' – a rough rendering of Gallt y Wennalt – is only slightly longer. Moreover being perched at the tip of Cwm Dyli's S arm, Gallt y Wenallt is a fine viewpoint. Horseshoe, Yr Aran, Glyders, the cold splendour of Cwm Dyli one side; Moel Siabod, Cnicht and the pastoral glow of Nantgwynant the other. However it would be remiss to imply that Gallt y Wenallt rates only as an appendage to longer walks. For a quiet easy day, with pleasing restful scenery, a duo of Hafod-y-llan and Cwm Merch takes a lot of beating.

Llyn Llydaw route (SN20)

Follow **SN16** to the col at 631535 and then steer an E course along a sketchy up-and-down trail that becomes more confident with every step; a playful succession of troughs and hillocks with glorious views of Cwm Dyli and Nantgwynant. In high summer you may be lucky and see the little pool at 633536 garlanded in a flutter of bright yellow lilies.

NE ridge (SN21)

Sharp, steep, twisty, this has all the attributes of a ridge walk in miniature.

If only it were rocky this grassy arête would be a little gem. Unfortunately it is composed of soft sheeny grass but, even so, it does provide a quick enjoyable way back to Pen-y-pass for tired legs that have just survived the last nail of the horseshoe. Break away L once the angle relents and aim for a gap in the rocky bluffs E of Llyn Teyrn for the miners' track.

Note You may have a problem crossing the Afon Glaslyn. At the time of writing the pipeline that feeds the Cwm Dyli power station is being replaced and there is a bridge at 646543. Whether it remains when they clean up the mess is any-one's guess!

Cwm Merch route (SN22)

Follow the Watkin Path to a kissing-gate just above the falls at 623516. Next descend R to cross the Afon Llan over a stone slab bridge with no handrail. (This bridge also gives access to a scenic track along the N bank of the stream before rejoin-ing the main path near Plas Cwmllan.)

Pull up half-L to a gap in the wall bounding the woods above you to join an ancient miners' trail that climbs the slopes overlooking Cwm Merch. The path needs a watchful eye where it crosses another wall near the top of the woods but other-wise is sheer delight, snaking over fine sheep-cropped turf with beautiful views of Yr Aran and the knobbly skyline of the Moelwyns. Cwm Merch opens up ahead to reveal a vast panorama of humps and hollows outcropping everywhere. Though you are under 1 mile from the crowds plodding up the Watkin Path or sweating the Snowdon horseshoe, there is no better place for soaking up the spirit of the hills in peace and quiet.

The path fizzles out near some old copper mines. You may carry on NE beside a little stream until you reach a shal-low depression at 639535, where the path mentioned in **SN20** gives you either Y Lliwedd (**SN19**) or Gallt y Wenallt (**SN22**). Alternatively (**SN22,1**) you could make a beeline for the top on grass, dodging odd rocks and bog as you go. This is defi-nitely safest for a misty descent as the stream is not easy to pinpoint and any miscalculation could easily land you on craggy slopes above the yawning gash of the mines.

Hafod-y-llan/SW ridge route (SN23)

Walk down the road to Hafod-y-llan Farm (629513). Keep the farm L and cross a bridge into the woods. Follow the true L bank of the stream until a wispy path appears, weaving round bracken-clad knuckles of rock but never straying far from the vivacious brook with its grey-green pools and mini gorges garlanded with holly and rhododendrons. After a while the woods thin out and the track swings R to reveal a maze of

Tumbling falls and a wooded glen start this lovely walk.

Gallt y Wennallt, the last nail in the horse-shoe with Crib Goch, the first, peering over its shoulder

tiny dips and knolls, dotted with flaky rocky ribs and streaked white by foaming cascades.

On a sunny morning the glint of the sea beyond Porthmadog is the perfect foil to the familiar silhouettes of Hebog, Cnicht and Yr Aran. Across the Afon Merch, almost lost in Y Lliwedd's broken slopes, you can pick out the old copper mines of **SN22**. There is no path and so, when your musings allow, it is a matter of gradually wending a way between rocky stumps, twists and nascent streams until the ridge itself can be your guide.

Yr Aran

'The Height' is a wedge-shaped top running E–W, scarped on its N flank and falling away in broken rock-studded slopes to the S. Yet for all that it is a striking sight, as anyone travelling the highway from Pen-y-gwryd or Rhyd-ddu to Beddgelert will readily agree. To see it reflected on a still day in the waters of Llyn Gwynant is to enjoy one of the most charming scenes in Snowdonia.

Yr Aran is best included on the homeward leg of an ascent of Snowdon starting from Rhydd-ddu or Llyn Cwellyn. It scarcely merits a day on its own except, maybe, in thick weather. Many are the days when Snowdon stays ensconced in a thick blanket of drizzly mist while 'The Height' basks in sun, or at least is clear. On such occasions there is much to be said for forgoing the long slog up Snowdon's S ridge and settling for a lesser prize that you can at least see, especially as Yr Aran is such a superb viewpoint.

From the estuary by Porthmadog the view carries over the Hebog, Nantlle and Eilio hills, while the Rivals lead the eye to Lleyn and Bardsey Island. To the N Snowdon stands supreme, joining with Y Lliwedd in a mighty arc that cradles the featureless basin of Cwm Tregalan. Peeping over Bwlch y Saethau is Crib Goch, the Glyders and the angry knob of Tryfan. Moel Siabod stands aloof as usual while Moel Meirch rules a vast tract of heather-clad terraces that recalls the Rhinogs. SE are Cnicht and the Moelwyn hills backed by Moel Penamnen and the Arenigs. The Rhinogs themselves stretch away S with Cader Idris claiming the far horizon.

Bwlch Cwm Llan route – E approach (SN24)

Follow **SN9** to the bwlch. Turn L over a rocky knoll and in a moment a snug path materialises. 'Snug' because it runs in a shallow groove between a rocky ramp L and a wall R. It is thus sheltered from the wind and this makes it a good place for lunch or adjusting your clothing – a major feat when a gale or near-gale is blowing!

The wall turns sharp L and then R, by a secluded little shelf cradling a pencil-thin pool, before climbing again to level off at the foot of the shattered N face. It is quite feasible to wrestle with the scree in a direct frontal but it is more dignified, and decidedly less wearing, to stay with the wall as it inclines L to join the E ridge 5min from the top.

E ridge (SN25)

SN9 guides you to the ridge from the Watkin Path and it is then simply a matter of following a wall until it yields to an electrified fence. Care is needed in descent as the track from the ridge end back down to the Watkin Path is not clear at first. Follow the wall until it swings S and then look out for a couple of cairns sprouting upright poles. These indicate a vague path but you need to trend well L to avoid the inhospitable

Yr Aran over Llyn Gwynant

slopes over Clogwyn Brith, aiming instead for the pinkish screes that indicate the whereabouts of the old mine workings.

Bwlch Cwm Llan route – W approach (SN26)
This is a combination of **SN8** and **SN24**.

Hafod-y-porth route (SN27)
The entrée to this enchanting walk is an old copper-mine trail that carries on from the approach road to Hafod-y-porth Farm (no right of way; permission must be sought). Heather-clad tors, a sparkling stream and a flowing vista of hills from Ysgafell Wen to Moel Hebog are enough to enliven the most jaded soul. Where the track ends by the ruins at 611508 steer N for the E ridge. Otherwise (**SN27,1**) break away L, rather earlier, and walk up Cwm yr Hyrddod to meet SW ridge midway to Craig Wen.

Craig Wen route (SN28)

Try to fit this forgotten route into your plans.

Facing the sea, and the setting sun, the gentle SW ridge over Craig Wen provides a perfect way home from a day in the hills. You should plan to meet the Beddgelert-to-Caernarfon

road about 1.5 miles N of Beddgelert, near the entrance to the Meillionen campsite.

Yr Aran from Beddgelert (SN 25)

Moel Eilio / Foel Gron

The spur of rounded grassy hills that extends NW from Snowdon above Llyn Cwellyn – Foel Goch, Foel Gron, Moel Eilio – looks mildly pleasant rather than inviting. Nice to look at, you might think, but probably not worth wasting a day on. Not so. It is the Y Garn story all over again; smooth grassy slopes one side, cwms, ridges and crags the other. To prove it walk up the road from Llanberis towards Hafodty Newydd. Moel Eilio's pink screes, the furrowed frowning cliffs of Foel Gron, the amphitheatre of Cwm Dwythwch and the bevy of ridges feeding a sharp, undulating edge tell their own tale. In short a mini range that would be well patronised if only it could escape Snowdon's all-embracing spell, but which is still value for money on a shorter day, or when the giants are wreathed in mist. And then there is the view.

It is not simply the breadth of the view which takes your breath away – though it is extraordinarily spacious – but the dramatic quality too. Familiar faces

269

seem larger than life, more accentuated. Tryfan's knobbly crest, peeping between the shoulders of Y Garn and Glyder Fawr, appears unusually taut and angular. The Nantlle ridge lays coiled like some giant cobra, the spiky comb of Mynydd Drws-y-coed arching its back menacingly. The troughs of Brwynog and Clogwyn, and the precipices of Clogwyn du'r Arddu and Llechog, here stand revealed in all their desolate splendour.

N across the purple breast of Cefn-du the land falls away to the sea, the plains of Anglesey and Puffin Island. The Glyders are pre-eminent E. Elider Fawr's shapely cone looks inviting despite the ugly slate cliffs that ravage its W flank. Y Garn shows its dullest side while beyond the tip of Tryfan Glyder Fawr's summit tors look like twirls of icing on a cake. Beyond the Glyders are the high Carneddau and their W foothills. Snowdon dominates SE, almost overshadowing the scarped ridge of Yr Aran, while in the distance are Moel Siabod and the Moelwyn hills. The S skyline is claimed by Moel Hebog and its satellites, the Nantlle ridge and Mynydd Mawr. The circle is completed by the long curl of the Lleyn Peninsula, where the soaring cliffs of Yr Eifl rise from the sea like battlements of war.

There are a surprising number of approaches to these modest hills (Foel Goch does not even qualify as a 2000-footer) from Llanberis. However as they all join the main ridge fairly close to one another it would be laborious to describe them individually, so I give a composite outline instead. The only approach from the Llyn Cwellyn side starts along the Snowdon Ranger path. You could, in theory, drop down at other points but it is real knee-jarring stuff and best avoided.

What I do recommend is the ridge walk from Foel Goch to Moel Eilio, where short-cropped grass affords every opportunity to enjoy the views. Foel Goch is cairnless. Foel Gron boasts a small cairn on the lesser of its two humps at 564566 but the main top at 560568 is bare, only the crumbly vegetated precipice that plunges away to Cwm Dwythwch rescuing it from oblivion. The pull up to Moel Eilio is punctuated by a gap in a wall shortly before you reach the fine circular windshelter.

Llanberis approaches (SN29–35)

No less than seven routes await walkers based on Llanberis.

The key is the road-head at 573591 (no parking space). Turn R through a rusty iron gate onto a cart track. At the second stone wall pull up L to gain Moel Eilio's NE ridge, named Braich y Foel on the 1:25,000 map. A faint track follows the wall, which later becomes a wire fence, and continues to the top (**SN29**). The cart track, meanwhile, curves round the toe of Moel Eilio's N ridge to Bwlch y Groes, eventually linking up with a tarmac road from Waunfawr. At any convenient

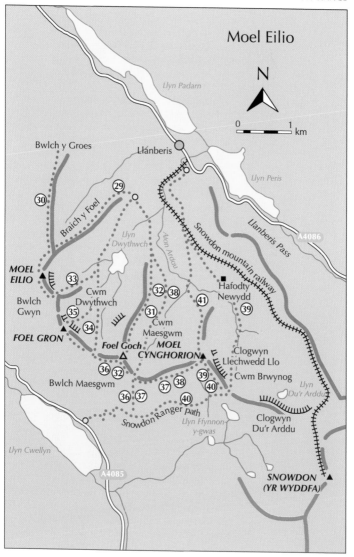

Moel Eilio

point, say 563598, you can use it to gain the N ridge where Land Rover tracks cleave the grass to join the NE ridge just below the top (**SN30**). (You could approach the N ridge from Waunfawr [**SN30,1**] but the ugly mountains of slate waste on the way are so depressing that I, for one, would go a long way to avoid them!)

Other routes are approached by turning L from the road-head. The scrappy marshes bordering the Afon Arddu make it a bit dull at first, but morale is quickly restored as the scarped cirque from Moel Eilio to Foel Goch suddenly bursts into view with Moel Cynghorion rearing fiercely ahead. Near a tumbledown dwelling at 577581 you can clamber between minor crags to join Foel Goch's N ridge (**SN31**). The original path, meanwhile, starts its long steady climb into Cwm Maesgwm, a valley of monumental loneliness enclosed by barren slopes and the immense bulk of Elidir Fawr to the rear. The path is the sort you would settle for any day – now green, now shaly, but always firm. Before long it brings you to Bwlch Maesgwm (known as Telegraph Col because of the line of telegraph poles that used to cross it) where a fence leads steeply but unerringly to Foel Goch (**SN32**).

The four routes described so far could all be classed as 'regular'. The others are in more pioneering mode, though none is difficult. They all begin from one of Snowdonia's least-visited lakes, Llyn Dwythwch, which you can reach by a little-used track that is best picked up across the road from the road-head at 573591. The track clings to drier ground beneath Moel Eilio's NE ridge but is notoriously marshy so wet feet cannot be ruled out.

From S of the lake there are three choices:

- To aim for a grassy rake that cleaves the skyline at 558574 at Bwlch Gwyn (**SN33**)
- To go for another rake at the col between Foel Gron and Foel Goch at 565564 (**SN34**), or
- Most interesting of all, perhaps, to follow the wall in the middle of the cwm until it abuts onto a sharp arête for a bull's-eye on Foel Gron at 560568 (**SN35**). The arête crumbles away in loose flaky rock L but is grassy R and, with care, quite safe.

Snowdon Ranger path (SN36)

Set out on **SN6**. After an iron gate in a wall at the end of the zigzags look out for a subsidiary path breaking away L, shortly after the main track inclines L. It is signposted 'Llanberis' (though it is uncertain how long the sign will survive) and some old telegraph pole stumps point the way. It brings you to Bwlch Maesgwm where a wire fence leads to Foel Goch as in **SN32**.

Moel Cynghorion and Moel Eilio (photo Steve Lewis)

Moel Cynghorion

The origin of the name 'Hill of the Counsellors' is lost in antiquity, but it would not be hard to imagine a meeting of dignitaries on the vast grassy dome of this pocket mountain. If their deliberations palled there would certainly be plenty of interest in the panorama which embraces Tryfan and the Glyders, the Nantlle and Hebog hills, and, of course, the towering presence of Snowdon and its most dramatic precipice, Clogwyn du'r Arddu.

In character Moel Cynghorion is part of the Foel Goch/Moel Eilio group, though it is separated from that spur by Bwlch Maesgwm just as, on its E flank, it is divided from Snowdon by Bwlch Cwm Brwynog. Its S slopes are rounded and grassy while N it displays all the cragginess that justifies my term 'pocket mountain'.

W slopes from Llyn Cwellyn (SN37)

Follow **SN36** to Bwlch Maesgwm and then bear R parallel to a wall. A path soon builds up near the edge giving an easy walk on grass, though on a hot day the cairn always seems a long time coming!

W slopes from Llanberis (SN38)

Take **SN32** to Bwlch Maesgwm, there to join **SN37**.

E slopes from Llanberis (SN39)

Walk down the road opposite the Royal Victoria Hotel as in **SN1** but ignore the sign for Snowdon and carry on to the derelict farmstead of Hafodty Newydd. Note the dark cliffs of Clogwyn du'r Arddu rearing ahead. A muddy path straggles on for a while before leaving you to the mercy of odd sheep tracks as you shadow the Afon Arddu round to Bwlch Cwm Brwynog. With Moel Cynghorion's craggy E face for company you are now well off the beaten track, making this a more atmospheric jaunt than you might have expected. A steady pull up the sheep-cropped edge above Clogwyn Llechwedd Llo completes an easy climb.

E slopes from Llyn Cwellyn (SN40)

Grass all the way.

Follow **SN6** to Bwlch Cwm Brwynog and then hold the edge above Clogwyn Llechwedd Llo.

N ridge (SN41)

Start along the road to Hafodty Newydd as in **SN39** but divert R along a farm track at 582584. A gate, a stile and a ruined barn mark the spot. Carry on to the remains of the shepherds' cottages at Helfa-fawr, over stiles and a track that almost disappears in rushes. Next work round to about 589574 to begin the rough scramble up the ridge. This soon gives way to benign grassy slopes but the low start means a tiring slog on a route better suited for descent. In that case aim NW for Helfa-fawr once you reach the broad saddle halfway down.

Note Continuing round the toe of N ridge brings you to a path that sidles up to Bwlch Cwm Brwynog, thus providing an alternative start to **SN39**.

High-level Walks

There are innumerable variations to the walks described below and the reader can have lots of fun working them out for himself. For example you might approach Crib Goch via Cwm Glas instead of the more traditional E ridge. In addition the immense scale of Snowdon means that many grand days can be had merely by combining different routes to its summit (for example, up the Pig Track, down to Rhyd-ddu); especially if you are not tied to wheels and can cross the mountain.

Snowdon horseshoe (SN H1)

This is usually tackled anti-clockwise. That way you get the hardest work over first and are faced with climbing up Crib Goch's E ridge rather than with the more awkward task of struggling down it. Also you have your R hand free to steady yourself on the knife-edge; a definite comfort provided you are R-handed!

The greatest of all Welsh ridge walks.

The day starts from Pen-y-pass and **SN12** up Crib Goch's E ridge. Most walkers use the Pig Track to Bwlch Moch, though if you can summon up just a little more energy so early in the day the knobbly ridge fringing it S gives a wilder, more atmospheric start. Safely ensconced on Crib Goch's airy belvedere with the seagulls you can inspect the way ahead; a sinuous, undulating ridge girdled with massive cliffs and unbridled

The Crib Goch knife-edge

challenge. No other top in Wales conveys such a sense of isolation and power, or urges you on quite so demandingly to still greater feats.

Now comes the highlight of the day, the knife-edge, a spiky crest with a calamitous plunge into Cwm Glas R and a gentler angle L which nonetheless demands respect. However the bark is worse than the bite. Ample footholds L, just below the edge, are ideally placed to allow you to grasp the crest with your hands. There are a couple of places (like the prominent knob of quartz) where it is momentarily easier to scramble over the crest itself, but nothing to worry a cool head properly shod! Odd traces of shaly track below the crest show where attempts have been made by vertigo sufferers to bypass the edge but, tempting as these may seem, the footing down there is actually less secure than at the top. Remember many thousands of feet have preceded you on this exhilarating jaunt, young and old, confident and fearful. They have done it, so have a go too and enjoy one of the supreme experiences of hillwalking anywhere in Britain.

As the edge abates the famous Pinnacles pick up the gauntlet. Jagged and scabrous, these huge monoliths pose yet another challenge. You can outflank them by dropping down a little L, but this is tedious and it is far better, after the rigours of the knife-edge, to keep up the good work and defeat them head on with an easy scramble straight over the top. Before you know it you are relaxing on the green saddle of Bwlch Coch (Red Col) and admiring the wondrous views. The mighty Glyders, for once, look quite innocuous against the austere grandeur of Cwm Glas and the ineffable splendour of Cwm Dyli, now irradiated by the twin jewels of Llyn Llydaw and the blue sparkling sheen of Llyn Glaslyn. **Note** Route-planners should note that **SN13,1** from Cwm Glas joins you here. You can also drop down to the Pig Track though it is rough scrappy going and not recommended.

On resuming, the track – a regular path now – romps up a rocky knuckle and then crosses another grassy saddle to confront you with a formidable-looking rock face. If you do not fancy the mild gymnastics a direct frontal requires, telltale scree drifts slightly L show a simpler line where only the easiest hand- and foot-work is necesary. **Note** Do not stray

Descending the
Pinnacles

too far L otherwise you could end up on a maverick track that eventually leaves you stranded high on the slopes overlooking the zigzags with nowhere to go.

On top a narrow arête points the way to Crib y Ddysgl, by now but a few arid humps and bumps away. Just below the trig point there is a superb panorama of Moel Eilio, and its consorts, and across Llyn Cwellyn to Mynydd Mawr and the Nantlle hills.

A stony track descends to the 7ft obelisk at the top of the zigzags and the Pig Track. Snowdon is now a simple 20min trudge, either along the railway line, or more excitingly, hugging the edge above Cwm Dyli.

The second half can be outlined more briefly, not because it is any less rewarding but because the constituent parts have already been described elsewhere. It begins inauspiciously, for I cannot pretend that the descent from Snowdon to Bwlch y Saethau is other than a horror of erosion and loose scree. You can marginally reduce the slithery agony by selecting the Watkin Path rather than dropping down directly above the cliffs of Clogwyn y Garnedd, but the gain is small. You cannot buck the ravages of time.

Along the well-cairned path to Bwlch Ciliau, and while scaling the battlements of Y Lliwedd, the magic returns. How could it be otherwise with Cwm Dyli still arrayed majestically below and the conquests of the morning now basking in the afternoon sun? From Y Lliwedd, that paragon of pinnacle and spire, it is all downhill, so a long rest in its pure air is not to be denied. An easy descent to the little col beyond Lliwedd Bach means the final decision can be delayed no longer. Do you perpetuate the untidy habit of dropping down to Llyn Llydaw or do you carry on to Gallt y Wenallt, holding the high ground and claiming the very last nail in the horseshoe? You know my view.

Little horseshoe: N half (SN H2)

For the N half follow the normal route to Bwlch y Saethau and then descend Gribin for the miners' track back to Pen-y-pass. Although most folk would be happier climbing Gribin, the problem the other way round is that you are either forced to come down off Crib Goch (awkward) or to drop down to the Pig Track at Bwlch Coch (inelegant and unpleasantly rough).

The Gribin ridge enables you to take the horseshoe in two bites.

Little horseshoe: S half (SN H3)

Climb Y Lliwedd via Gribin; return down Gallt y Wenallt's NE ridge to Pen-y-pass.

Cwm Llan horseshoe (SN H4)

Start from Bethania and ascend Gallt y Wenallt either via Cwm Merch or the SW ridge. Follow the edge round over Y Lliwedd, across Bwlch y Saethau and up Snowdon. Next carry on down Bwlch Main and the S ridge to Bwlch Cwm Llan before pulling up to Yr Aran and returning home via its E ridge.

Cwm Clogwyn/Cwm Caregog circular (SN H5)

Ascend on the Snowdon Ranger and continue down the S ridge to Bwlch Cwm Llan. Pull up to Yr Aran. Carry on towards Craig Wen but make a beeline as soon as practical to join the quarry track described in **SN8** back to Rhyd-ddu. Complete the circle either along the road or, better, by following the course of the former Welsh Highland Railway.

Cwm Brwynog horseshoe (SN H6)

A way of including the NW outliers in a Snowdon round.

Start from Llanberis and begin by ticking off Moel Eilio, perhaps by its NE ridge (**SN29**). Follow the ridge over Foel Gron and Foel Goch. A simple descent and ascent over Bwlch Maesgwm gives you Moel Cynghorion whence a quick scamper down easy grass to Bwlch Cwm Brwynog puts you on the Snowdon Ranger path. Use the Llanberis path for the homeward half.

NW foothills circulars (SN H7)

For an easier day you could do a lot worse than tackle the Eilio range and Moel Cynghorion. The views are outstanding and you are unlikely to be troubled by crowds. Though Llyn Cwellyn would provide the prettier start there is virtually only one route up or down so, to avoid backtracking, Llanberis is the better base. If you are spoilt for choice why not settle for climbing Eilio on **SN29** and descending Cynghorion's N ridge on **SN41**.

Figure of eight (SN H8)

This marathon is strictly for tigers in prime condition!

Follow the conventional horseshoe route to Snowdon; descend to Rhyd-ddu; use the old Welsh Highland Railway line to cross to the start of the Snowdon Ranger path; reclimb Snowdon; then complete the horseshoe over Y Lliwedd and Gallt y Wenallt.

Girdle of Snowdon (SN H9)

The aim is to circle the summit at a radius of about 1.5 miles. Start along the Rhyd-ddu path and stay with it as far as the wall at 593536. Next work your way through minor crags to Llyn Nadroedd. The route is then on to Llyn Coch, down by the stream to Llyn Ffynnon-y-gwas, and up to Bwlch Cwm Brwynog. Cross Cwm Clogwyn to the Llanberis path and then descend Gryn Las on **SN11** to Llyn Bach and Llyn Glas. Climb back up to Bwlch Coch and then drop down, first to the Pig Track and then to the miners' track.

Scramble up Gribin ridge, walk along Bwlch y Saethau and follow the Watkin Path until you can cut across Cwm

Snowdon from Nant Gwynant (photo Kevin Richardson)

Tregalan and pull up to cross S ridge. This could be at Bwlch Cwm Llan. Finally head W to rejoin the Rhydd-ddu path. Good luck!

Lower-level Walks/Easier Days

The best idea for an easier day is the miners' track to Llyn Glaslyn. Nothing else rewards you so handsomely for such a modicum of effort. Otherwise the scale of Snowdon makes truly independent lower-level walks hard to come by. I offer just a couple. These explore two of the main cwms which, with their attendant lakes, lie right off the beaten track.

Cwm Clogwyn and its lakes (SN L1)

Advance along the Snowdon Ranger path until you near Bwlch Cwm Brwynog. Next follow a faint path, little more than a sheep track, close to Llyn Ffynnon-y-gwas' W shore. Continue up beside the stream that tumbles down from the lip of the upper cwm. This brings you to the open waters of Llyn Coch. Follow its shoreline round, taking in first Llyn Glas and then Llyn Nadroedd (The Lake of Serpents). Llyn Nadroedd is the most scenic of Cwm Clogwyn's lakes, nestling in a trough where rocky terraces and knolls provide an abundance of sheltered hideaways.

Cwm Clogwyn (The Craggy Hollow) is best when the sun is out. On a dull day it is impressive but also grim and sombre, imprisoned on three sides by grey unyielding cliffs. A scramble from the SW tip of Llyn Nadroedd enables you to work round to the Rhyd-ddu path to complete an interesting circuit.

Cwm Brwynog and Clogwyn du'r Arddu (SN L2)

Not even the most famous climbing crags in Wales can tempt walkers into Cwm Brwynog (The Rushy Hollow). Instead they skirt its N rim along the Llanberis path, so it is virtually *terra incognita*. Yet while it does not have the all-round charisma of Cwm Clogwyn, the combination of Moel Cynghorion's intimidating E face – a vast lunar-like tumble of boulders – and 'Cloggy' itself with its black haunting lake, surely deserves better than this!

Clogwyn du'r Arddu

One track which leads to the foot of the rock face has already been described (**SN1,1**). Another possibility is to leave the Llanberis path where the slope eases, not far beyond Halfway House. A simple stroll S then brings you to a stony plateau overlooking the lake's N shore. A third choice is **SN6** to Bwlch Cwm Brwynog, then breaking away L to thread through rivers of bouldery debris. There is a track of sorts, if you can find it, contouring across to the W tip of the lake. Hard going, though magnificent in the immense sense of desolation it conveys.

THE TARRENS

OS maps
1:25,000 – Sheet 23, 1:50,000 – Sheets 124/135

Peaks (by height)	Height (ft)	Map Ref	Page
Tarren y Gesail	2186	710059	287
Tarrenhendre	2076	683042	290
Nameless	1640	699044	290
Foel y Geifr	1475	708047	288

Mountain Lakes
None

THE TARRENS

Nothing is more alluring on the road from Aberystwyth to Machynlleth than the sight of these green, lightly wooded hills that quietly flow down to the sea by Aberdovey. The compliment is returned, for few viewpoints are more enchanting than from these tops. The gaze is carried from Cader Idris to Plynlimon, coastward from Lleyn to the haze of Cardigan Bay, and along the slow twisting drift of the estuary and its peaceful pageant of woods and meadows.

The Tarrens form a small compact group, separated from Cader Idris by the Dysynni Valley and Tal-y-llyn, and from Plynlimon by the Dovey, while across the sylvan Vale of Dulas they face the equally unassuming Dovey hills. Never crowded, eschewing drama, they well repay the occasional 'away-day'. While it is true that they have little to offer in mist, they often give a sunlit day when Cader is sulking in cloud.

At only two points does the land exceed 2000ft, at Tarrenhendre and further N at Tarren y Gesail. Both tops lie on a fine striding ridge, some 7 miles long, that sends a succession of narrow, steep-sided cwms down either flank. In the S the terrain is wall-free, grassy and unencumbered in a smooth rolling landscape reminiscent of the Howgills near Sedbergh. Further N afforestation is widespread and access more restricted. Nevertheless there are still surprises, and here and there the meadows have an almost Alpine charm.

On a sunny day the hike up the SW ridge from Trum Gelli is magnificent with Cader Idris arcing N, the rolling Plynlimon hills S and the sea a shimmering blue. Couple it

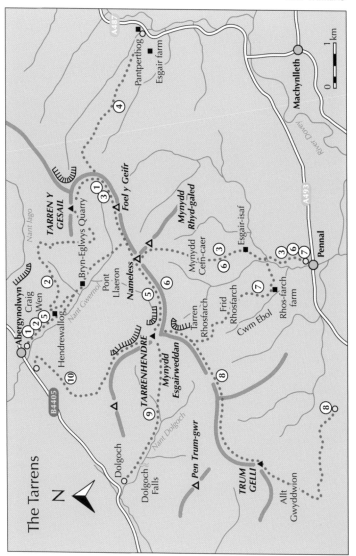

The Tarrens

N

285

Looking back to Cader Idris from TN1

with a return to Pennal over Cefn-caer or Rhosfarch and you have the finest round in the area. Other pleasant walks start from Abergynolwyn, while for a day with a difference try the forest trail from Pantperthog and be surprised by the senior Tarren's craggy E face.

> **Note** Afforestation in the Tarrens is proceeding apace so it is advisable to have the latest edition of the map. Even that may not be completely up to date. You should bear this in mind when route-finding otherwise it may sometimes be a bit confusing.

Tarren y Gesail

Tarren y Gesail's plain grassy top may earn high marks for peace and quiet, but if it's excitement you're after then you had best look elsewhere. The biggest challenge it poses is to steer a course through the forest that draws a tighter noose with each passing year. It can still be done, but for how much longer who can say? Having said that, 'plain grassy top' is not strictly accurate. You have only to abandon the beaten track and tackle it from Pantperthog for a change and you will confront a fierce towering pyramid, generously flecked with rock – the unchallenged king of all it surveys!

Abergynolwyn: E approach (TN1)

An old lane to the Bryneglwys Quarry provides an easy entrée to the Tarrens from the W. It climbs from a car park near the centre of Abergynolwyn, steeply at first, to a gate signposted to Hendrewallog Farm. Within minutes the rooftops of the village seem aeons away and, as you march along with the angle easing all the time, the scene is pregnant with greatness. Across the vivacious Afon Gwernol, its deep chasm dotted with wrinkled old trees, the thick, dark forest is cloaked in manifold shades of green that reach to the very foot of Tarrenhendre's rocky crown. Behind you lie the Cader foothills, and in front is the wavy skyline of Foel y Geifr and the nameless top to its R. Up-valley is the white plumage of distant falls and, more often than not, the characteristic glint of sunlight on wet slaty spoil heaps.

But for once the magic is not quite there. Perhaps even Nature has an off day; or maybe the scars of yesteryear are just too heavy a burden. Whatever the reason the ingredients do not quite come together; it remains a landscape of parts, scrappy rather than poetic. Pleasant enough on a bright day, it lacks the effervescent beauty of Gelli Iago or Cwm Pennant.

After 1 mile bear R where the road divides. (The L fork leads into **TN2**.) After another 0.5 mile, shortly after passing a deeply gouged quarry L at 694057, a footpath sign directs you L on to a narrow path that crosses the open moors through a plantation of trees. The path fades at times in splashes of bog but you should have no trouble if you remember it follows a wire fence most of the way, aiming for a dip on the skyline between Foel y Geifr and the nameless top at 699044 where sharp eyes can just detect a stile.

Note The reservoir shown on the map at 699049 has long since disappeared.

Suddenly Pont Llaeron appears, quite out of the blue. It is sometimes said to date back to Roman times, but whatever its origins it is still robust and elegant and just as surprising in this remote spot as Pont Scethin in the Rhinogs. Cross the bridge and aim next for the stile on the skyline (703047). Spare a moment to admire the Alpine-like pastures on the far side, then follow the fence over Foel y Geifr before veering L to a shallow col at 716053. (Do not be tempted by a couple of stiles that seem to offer shortcuts L; they fizzle out.)

At the col four fences meet and there are two more stiles. Press on W of N hugging the fence that tackles the slope directly ahead – a grind that always seems to occasion heavier breathing than it should – until you come to a sprawling cairn at a junction of fences. Turn L here to join a peaty track beside another fence and in 10min Tarren y Gesail is won. You could have followed a damp track that climbs directly to the col from Pont Llaeron (**TN1,1**) but only at the cost of missing the best of the views.

Abergynolwyn: W approach (TN2)

Stay with TN1 as far as the fork where the road divides and then zigzag L up the bare hillside to a forest gate at 698067. Before plunging into the woods try to spare a few minutes for a brief foray N to inspect the cliffs of Craig Wen and the shy green meadows of Cwm Iago. On resuming keep R at the two places in the plantation where the trail divides, and 1 mile of trail-bashing brings you to another gate at 703054. Leave the forest here and pick up a track on 40° that wends its way aloft through grass and heather to the trig point. Breezy and spacious, and with the views suddenly opening out, this is a finale that always generates a welcome sense of achievement after the confines of the woods.

Cefn-caer route (TN3)

Leave Pennal and walk down the high-hedged lane to Esgair-isaf Farm at 703019. A footpath sign off L just before the farm starts you off. Alternatively you can go up to the farm and bear L between an old stone barn and one of the shiny modern variety. Either way you soon join a gritty trail that skirts the W flank of the grassy tongue of Mynydd Cefn-caer. When it fizzles out pull up to the crest and head N to meet an extension of a forest road by a stile at 702037. Carry on N a while longer, along a road with the slopes of Mynydd Rhyd-galed R, until you reach a newish metallic sheepfold at 699042. This is a key spot where it is easy to go astray in mist. Bear R now along a little track that rises to the crest of a small 'pass' with Mynydd Rhyd-galed R and the nameless hillock at 699044 L. You are now near the stile at 703047 to finish on **TN1**.

Discerning walkers will choose this lovely walk to waft them home in the glow of eventide. A mosaic of fields, neat hedgerows, copses and woods shielding little enclaves of green, the yellow-brown sands of the estuary, the blue of the sea and a frame of rolling foothills all unite in the perfect palliative for aching limbs and burning toes. In harsher climes, when discretion is the better part of valour and shelter from the wind of prime concern, you can scamper down to a forest trail at 695030. This brings you safe and sound to the road at Rhos-farch Farm, 695013 (**TN3,1**).

Pantperthog route (TN4)

Forest walks are not to everyone's taste but this has the merit (where other routes portray it as a benign grassy mound) of revealing the raw elemental power of Tarren y Gesail's craggy E face. Leave the A487 at 749043 and follow the forest road for some 2 miles until Tarren y Gesail pierces the skyline imposingly ahead and you can see the meadows below exhibiting an almost Alpine air. Advance to the col at 716053 to finish as in **TN1**.

Tarrenhendre

Tarrenhendre is a deceiver. From the Abergynolwyn quarry road or Foel y Geifr its scarped, rocky E face gives it a touch of true class. However all you will find on top is a sodden mess of heather, peat, bog and coarse grass. It is hard to imagine anyone basking in the sun there, even on the balmiest of days. The acid test of course is the walking, and here Tarrenhendre brooks no argument. The SW ridge and the approaches from Pennal all pay handsome dividends; the one with seaward views from Aberystwyth to Lleyn, the others with a pastoral charm that would calm the most troubled mind. There is just one proviso…

Note Not in mist. The summit plateau gives no clues and there are crags along the NE rim. The best you can do if lost is to stroll SE until you meet one of the two fences leading down the SW ridge or to the Foel y Geifr col.

Abergynolwyn route (TN5)

Follow **TN1** to the stile at 703047 and then bear R. You could follow the ridge over the nameless top at 699044, but it is less tiring to skirt round its S slopes to rejoin the crest further W (passing the sheepfold mentioned in **TN3**). This is a slog that raises quite a sweat on a hot day but is enlivened by the sight of the estuary. It brings you to a fence coming in L, just short of the top. Ignore this and stay with the original fence on a NW course. When you come to another junction of fences with two stiles the cairn is a few squelchy steps N (see also **TN8**).

Cefn-caer route (TN6)

Follow **TN3** to the sheepfold at 699042. Now take the path that climbs up to the skyline L to finish as in **TN5**.

Rhosfarch route (TN7)

A route just as attractive as **TN6** starts from behind the farm of Rhos-farch at 695013. It is clearly visible from below,

swathing through the bracken carpeting the breast of Ffridd
Rosfarch before zigzagging above the lonely cwm below Tarren
Rhosfarch. It eventually meets the SW ridge about 0.5 mile
short of the top. Like the Cefn-caer route it is best in descent
and once again there is a bad weather alternative (**TN7,1**) in
the guise of a gravelly track that breaks away to the valley at
686027, then follows Cwm Ebol to the farm, passing a disused quarry en route.

Tarrenhendre

SW ridge (TN8)
Park near the kink in the road at 689998 and pass through the
gate by the dwelling onto a stony track that from time to time
doubles as a watercourse. An easy rise brings you to an appealing landscape of hillocks and hollows, outcropping everywhere and resplendent in rampant ferns. Reedy Llyn Barfog
(The Bearded Lake) beckons from across Happy Valley, Plynlimon
looms on the far horizon while the dreamy estuary and the
sea seem but a step away.

Leave the track at 647001, where it goes through a gate at the corner of a wire fence, and pick up one of several paths that sidle across the E flank of the emergent ridge (bypassing Allt Gwyddgwion) to gain the crest at 656014, beside a fence and an enormous cairn that immediately recalls Drygarn Fawr. Another large cairn signifying Trum Gelli lies just ahead. You are well and truly launched now and it is a grand tramp along the fence as it trends first W then N with glorious views of the Dovey foothills and the coast laid out like a map.

The fence lands you on the summit plateau but it does not cross the highest point. So when you top the final rise, having passed a sprawling cairn L and come to another fence crossing your path NW–SE, turn L along this new fence. After about 100yd you meet another fence with two stiles at the corner. The modest cairn of flat stones and the remains of a thick wooden post is now 25yd due N in the midst of a peaty, boggy swamp. There used to be a cairn with a protruding pole on a soft heathery bank, but on my last visit it had either been supplanted or I missed it in the thick mist.

Dolgoch route (TN9)
Leave the cairn SW and aim for the green path that runs above the Nant Dolgoch. As you approach the shady little glen that conceals the Dolgoch Falls from all but the most intimate gaze, drop down to a stile at 656042. This is the gateway to a maze of meandering paths that criss-cross the glen and which are much frequented in summer by families enjoying an outing by the falls.

Forest route (TN10)
You can also get back to Abergynolwyn by following the forest boundary NW from Tarrenhendre and joining whichever of several forest trails takes your fancy. As with all forest walks you tend to be at the mercy of any recent changes and need to decide which of the trails you meet en route are shown on the map and which are 'extras'. The only way of which I have direct experience enters the forest by a gate at 670058. It gets you down uneventfully enough, but the zigzags lower down must make the distance over double what it would be as the crow flies.

High-level Walks

SW ridge and the two Tarrens (TN H1)

Depending on when you prefer to do the road work you can either start from Pennal, or from the kink in the road at 669998. Assuming the latter the routing is **TN8** to Tarrenhendre; over Foel y Geifr to Tarren y Gesail on **TN5,1**; then backtracking slightly to descend to Pennal on **TN3**. Anyone lucky enough not to be tied to wheels could descend through the Pantperthog forest on **TN4**, another pearl of a walk.

The best walk in the area, combining both tops with the SW ridge.

Abergynolwyn circular (TN H2)

Another good way to collect both Tarren scalps is to link the Dolgoch route (**TN9**) with **TN2**, again using the Foel y Geifr ridge to bridge the gap. Once again a spell of road-bashing is unavoidable, but you can minimise it by joining the green track that penetrates Cwm Dolgoch at 655052.

Lower-level Walks/Easier Days

In a small region like the Tarrens it is hard to know where to draw the line between lower-level/easier day hillwalks and family-style outings that are really outside the scope of a book like this. Nevertheless here are four suggestions:

- **TN L1** The stony track above Happy Valley (see **TN8**).
- **TN L2** Pont Llaeron (see **TN1**).
- **TN L3** The Dolgoch Falls (see **TN6**).
- **TN L4** Llyn Barfog (The Bearded Lake) from the road-head at 643980 or the parking lot at 640986.

INDEX OF PEAKS

Peak	Group	Height (ft)	Map Ref	Page
Y Garn	NH	2077	551526	145
Y Garn	PN	2244	775851	177
Y Garn	RG	2063	702230	225
Y Llethr	RG	2475	661258	220
Y Lliwedd	SN	2947	622533	262
Yr Aran	SN	2451	604515	266
Ysgafell Wen	SM	2204	667481	112

LIST OF LAKES

Lake	Group	Height (ft)	Map Ref
Arddu	SM	1148	628466
Bach	SN	2400	615555
Barlwyd (2)	FG	1476	712486
Bochlwyd	GL	1800	655592
Bodlyn	RG	1250	648240
Bowydd	FG	1575	725468
Bugeilyn	PN	1494	822924
Caerwych	RG	1300	641351
Cerrig-y-myllt (2)	SM	1345	633472
Clogwyn-brith	SM	1575	665466
Clyd (2)	GL	2150	634597
Coch	SM	2034	669478
Coch	SN	1735	598545
Conglog	SM	2001	674474
Corn-ystwc	RG	1800	656336
Croesor	SM	1706	661457
Cwm-corsiog	SM	1772	664470
Cwmffynnon	GL	1260	649562
Cwmhosan	RG	1200	660277
Cwmorthin	SM	1082	678463
Cwm Silyn (2)	NH	1100	515506
Cwmyffynnon	NH	1300	538517
Cwm-y-foel	SM	1476	655468
Cwn (cluster)	SM	2100	662487

Lake	Group	Height (ft)	Map Ref
Cywion	GL	1970	632605
Diffwys (2)	SM	1706	659468
Diwaunedd (2)	SM	1214	684538
Du	RG	1825	657340
Du	RG	1700	656294
Du-bach	FG	1476	719461
Dulyn	RG	1750	662244
Du'r Arddu	SN	1900	601558
Dyrnogydd	SM	1300	693488
Dywarchen	RG	1700	654348
Edno	SM	1804	663497
Eiddew-bach	RG	1225	645345
Eiddew-mawr	RG	1125	646338
Ffridd-y-bwlch	SM	1080	695480
Ffynnon-y-gwas	SN	1400	591554
Glas	FG	1378	719455
Glas	SN	1735	600547
Glas	SN	2200	619557
Glaslyn	PN	1620	825941
Glaslyn	SN	1980	617546
Gloyw Lyn	RG	1275	646300
Hywel	RG	1750	664266
Idwal	GL	1223	645596
Irddyn	RG	1050	630222
Iwerddon	SM	1575	685478
Llagi	SM	1247	649483
Llydaw	SN	1420	630544
Llygad rheidol	PN	1700	792878
Marchlyn Bach	GL	1600	608625
Marchlyn Mawr	GL	2066	616619
Morwynion	RG	1400	658303
Nadroedd	SN	1700	595543
Nameless	FG	1936	727451
Nameless (2)	NH	1375	519508
Nameless (2)	PN	2150	789862
Nameless (3)	PN	1500	779879
Nameless	RG	2150	661255
Nameless (6)	RG	1975	665243

Lake	Group	Height (ft)	Map Ref
Nameless	SM	2100	665479
Nameless	SM	2098	664484
Nameless	SM	2034	669474
Nameless	SM	2034	675476
Nameless	SM	1834	654488
Nameless	SM	1300	722559
Nameless	SM	1100	637467
Nameless	SN	1640	603521
Nannau-is-afon	RG	1825	706228
Nant ddeiliog	PN	1450	861959
Newydd	FG	1575	723472
Perfeddau	RG	1500	659264
Pryfed	RG	1775	665321
Pysgod	FG	1936	728454
Stwlan	SM	1673	665445
Terfyn	SM	1902	668479
Teyrn	SN	1240	641548
Twr-glas	RG	1725	663325
Wrysgan	SM	1476	677453
Y Bi	RG	1425	670264
Y Biswail	SM	1870	649474
Y Caseg-fraith	GL	2430	670583
Y Cwn	GL	2330	637584
Y Drum-boeth	FG	1607	718464
Y Fan Fach	BM	1675	802218
Y Fan Fawr	BM	2000	831216
Y Fedw	RG	1075	625329
Y Foel	SM	1756	715548
Y Manod	FG	1378	718450
Y Mynydd	HN	1500	008252
Yr Adar	SM	1886	655480

LIST OF PEAKS FOR VOLS 1 AND 2

AG	Arenigs	FF	Fforest Fawr
AN	Arans	FG	Ffestiniog hills
BB	Brecon Beacons	GL	Glyders
BM	Mynydd Ddu (Black	HN	Hirnants
	Mountain)	NH	Nantlle/Hebog hills
BN	Berwyns	PN	Plynlimon
BS	Black Mountains	RF	Radnor Forest
CA	Carneddau	SM	Siabod/Moelwyns
CI	Cader Idris	SN	Snowdon
CR	Cwmdeuddwr hills	RG	Rhinogs
DY	Dovey hills	TN	Tarrens

2000FT PEAKS IN DESCENDING ORDER

Peak	Group	Height ft	Map Ref	Volume
Snowdon	SN	3560	609544	2
Crib y Ddysgl	SN	3493	611552	2
Carnedd Llewelyn	CA	3490	684644	1
Carnedd Dafydd	CA	3425	663631	1
Glyder Fawr	GL	3279	642579	2
Glyder Fach	GL	3262	656583	2
Pen yr Ole Wen	CA	3211	656619	1
Foel Grach	CA	3196	689659	1
Yr Elen	CA	3152	673651	1
Y Garn	GL	3104	631596	2
Foel Fras	CA	3092	696682	1
Elidir Fawr	GL	3030	612613	2
Crib Goch	SN	3026	624552	2
Tryfan	GL	3010	664594	2
Aran Fawddwy	AN	2969	863224	1
Y Lliwedd	SN	2947	622533	2
Penygadair	CI	2928	711131	1
Pen y Fan	BB	2906	012215	1
Aran Benllyn	AN	2901	867243	1
Corn Du	BB	2863	007213	1

Peak	Group	Height ft	Map Ref	Volume
Erw y Ddafad-ddu	AN	2860	865234	1
Moel Siabod	SM	2860	705546	2
Mynydd Moel	CI	2804	727137	1
Arenig Fawr	AG	2802	827369	1
Llwytmor	CA	2785	689692	1
Penyrhelgi-du	CA	2733	698630	1
Foel Goch	GL	2727	628612	2
Cadair Berwyn (S top)	BN	2723	072324	1
Moel Sych	BN	2713	066319	1
Craig Gwaun-taf	BB	2704	005206	1
Carnedd y Filiast	GL	2695	621628	2
Mynydd Perfedd	GL	2665	623619	2
Waun Fach	BS	2660	215300	1
Bera Bach	CA	2647	672678	1
Cyfrwy	CI	2646	703133	1
Nameless	GL	2636	678582	2
Bannau Brycheiniog	BM	2631	825217	1
Pen y Gadair Fawr	BS	2624	229287	1
Pen Llithrig-y-wrach	CA	2622	716623	1
Cribin	BB	2608	023213	1
Bera Mawr	CA	2604	675683	1
Craig y Cau	CI	2595	710122	1
Cadair Bronwen	BN	2572	077347	1
Moel Hebog	NH	2565	564469	2
Glasgwm	AN	2557	837195	1
Drum	CA	2529	708696	1
Moelwyn Mawr	SM	2527	658449	2
Waun-rydd	BB	2522	061208	1
Gallt yr Ogof	GL	2499	685586	2
Drosgl	CA	2484	664680	1
Y Llethr	RG	2475	661258	2
Plynlimon Fawr	PN	2467	789869	2
Moel Llyfnant	AG	2464	808352	1
Diffwys	RG	2462	661234	2
Bannau Sir Gaer	BM	2460	812218	1

Peak	Group	Height ft	Map Ref	Volume
Yr Aran	SN	2451	604515	2
Gwaen Cerrig-llwydion	BB	2450	055203	1
Tomle	BN	2431	085336	1
Plynlimon Arwystli	PN	2428	815877	2
Fan Fawr	FF	2409	970193	2
Craig Cwm Silyn	NH	2408	525502	2
Rhobell Fawr	AG	2408	787257	1
Fan Hir	BM	2400	830210	1
Craig Cwareli	BB	2393	042197	1
Craig Eigiau	CA	2390	714656	1
Moel Eilio	SN	2382	556577	2
Fan Gihirych	FF	2379	881191	2
Rhinog Fawr	RG	2362	657290	2
Pen Allt-mawr	BS	2360	207243	1
Fan y Big	BB	2358	036207	1
Pen Rhos Dirion	BS	2338	212334	1
Moelwyn Bach	SM	2334	660437	2
Rhinog Fach	RG	2333	665270	2
Trum y Ddysgl	NH	2329	544516	2
Black Mountain	BS	2306	255350	1
Twyn Tal-y-cefn	BS	2303	222324	1
Pen Cerrig-calch	BS	2300	217223	1
Garnedd Goch	NH	2296	511495	2
Mynydd Mawr	NH	2291	539547	2
Allt Fawr	SM	2287	682475	2
Mynydd Drws-y-coed	NH	2280	548518	2
Cnicht	SM	2265	645466	2
Foel Wen	BN	2263	100334	1
Twmpa	BS	2263	225350	1
Arenig Fach	AG	2260	821416	1
Foel Hafod-fynydd	AN	2260	878227	1
Gwaun y Llwyni	AN	2248	857205	1
Y Garn	PN	2244	775851	2
Mynydd Tawr	BN	2234	113324	1
Gau Craig	CI	2230	745142	1
Tomle	BN	2431	085336	1
Pen y Bryn-fforchog	AN	2230	818179	1

Peak	Group	Height ft	Map Ref	Volume
Chwarel y Fan	BS	2228	258294	1
Godor	BN	2224	095307	1
Creigiau Gleision	CA	2224	729615	1
Pen y Beacon	BS	2219	244366	1
Moel Druman	SM	2218	671477	2
Maesglasau	DY	2213	823152	1
Moel Cynghorion	SN	2211	586564	2
Ysgafell Wen	SM	2204	667481	2
Esgeiriau Gwynion	AN	2201	889236	1
Pencerrigtewion	PN	2201	798882	2
Waun-oer	DY	2197	785148	1
Carnedd y Filiast	AG	2195	871446	1
Plynlimon Fach	PN	2192	787875	2
Tarren y Gesail	TN	2186	710059	2
Cyrniau Nod	HN	2185	988279	2
Fan Nedd	FF	2176	913184	2
Mynydd Llysiau	BS	2173	207279	1
Dduallt	AG	2172	811274	1
Craig Las	CI	2168	676136	1
Manod Mawr	FG	2168	724446	2
Great Rhos	RF	2166	182639	2
Post Gwyn	BN	2165	049294	1
Nameless	FG	2159	727458	2
Pen-twyn-mawr	BS	2153	242267	1
Moel yr Ogof	NH	2149	556478	2
Mynydd Tal-y-mignedd	NH	2148	535514	2
Allt-lwyd	BB	2143	079189	1
Black Mixen	RF	2132	196644	2
Cribin	DY	2132	794153	1
Foel Cwm Sian Llwyd	HN	2125	996314	2
Moel yr Hydd	SM	2124	672454	2
Pen y Boncyn Trefeilw	HN	2119	963283	2
Pentwynglas	BS	2115	213257	1
Carnedd Llechwedd Llyfn	AG	2110	857446	1
Gyrn Wigau	CA	2109	654676	1
Drygarn Fawr	CR	2103	863584	1
Black Hill	BS	2102	275348	1
Great Creigniau	RF	2102	198636	2

Peak	Group	Height ft	Map Ref	Volume
Moel Lefn	NH	2093	553485	2
Y Garn	NH	2077	551526	2
Garreg Las	BM	2076	777202	1
Tarrenhendre	TN	2076	683042	2
Fan Llia	FF	2071	938186	2
Moel Fferna	BN	2066	116398	1
Stac Rhos	HN	2066	969278	2
Fan Frynych	FF	2063	957228	2
Foel Gron	SN	2063	560568	2
Y Garn	RG	2063	702230	2
Craig Cerrig-gleisiad	FF	2060	961218	2
Foel y Geifr	HN	2053	937275	2
Moel y Cerrig Duon	HN	2050	923241	2
Moel Penamnen	FG	2044	716483	2
Moel Ysgyfarnogod	RG	2044	658346	2
Pen y Castell	CA	2043	721688	1
Carnfachbugeilyn	PN	2041	827904	2
Craig-y-llyn	CI	2040	665120	1
Nameless	BN	2037	089369	1
Waen Camddwr	AN	2035	848207	1
Pen yr Allt-uchaf	AN	2034	871196	1
Gallt yr Wenallt	SN	2032	642532	2
Foel Boeth	AG	2031	778345	1
Cefn yr Ystrad	BB	2025	087137	1
Garreg-lwyd	BM	2020	740179	1
Cefn Gwyntog	HN	2017	976266	2
Llechwedd Du	AN	2014	894224	1
Gorllwyn	CR	2011	918591	1
Y Gyrn	BB	2010	989216	1
Trum y Gwrgedd	HN	2008	942284	2
Plynlimon Cwmbiga	PN	2008	831899	2
Bryn Garw	CR	2005	798771	1
Foel Goch	AG	2005	953423	1
Red Daren	BS	2003	281308	1
Foel Goch	HN	2001	943292	2
Bache Hill	RF	2001	214636	2
Tal-y-fan	CA	2001	729727	1

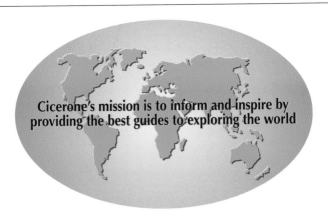

Cicerone's mission is to inform and inspire by providing the best guides to exploring the world

Since its foundation over 30 years ago, Cicerone has specialised in publishing guidebooks and has built a reputation for quality and reliability. It now publishes nearly 300 guides to the major destinations for outdoor enthusiasts, including Europe, UK and the rest of the world.

Written by leading and committed specialists, Cicerone guides are recognised as the most authoritative. They are full of information, maps and illustrations so that the user can plan and complete a successful and safe trip or expedition – be it a long face climb, a walk over Lakeland fells, an alpine traverse, a Himalayan trek or a ramble in the countryside.

With a thorough introduction to assist planning, clear diagrams, maps and colour photographs to illustrate the terrain and route, and accurate and detailed text, Cicerone guides are designed for ease of use and access to the information.

If the facts on the ground change, or there is any aspect of a guide that you think we can improve, we are always delighted to hear from you.

Cicerone Press
2 Police Square Milnthorpe Cumbria LA7 7PY
Tel:01539 562 069   Fax:01539 563 417
e-mail:info@cicerone.co.uk   web:www.cicerone.co.uk